Seed-Grains of Prayer

*A Manual for Evangelical
Christians*

By WILLIAM LŒHE
Lutheran Pastor

Translated from the Original German 36th Edition
By H. A. WELLER, A.M.
Lutheran Pastor in Orwigsburg, Pa.

With an Introduction

By Henry Eyster Jacobs, D.D., LL.D., S.T.D.
*Dean of the Faculty of the Lutheran Theological
Seminary at Philadelphia, Pa.*

Wartburg Publishing House
CHICAGO

INTRODUCTION.

THERE can be no doubt as to the great desirability of a handbook of brief and condensed prayers, in the English language, truly expressive of the faith and life of the Christian religion, as the Lutheran Church understands and confesses it. An attempt is herewith made to supply this want. The prayers are gems of devotion gathered throughout all ages of the Christian Church, which have been brought together, arranged for use, and supplemented by one of the most devout and practical pastors and theologians whom our Church has produced. His exquisite liturgical taste was not confined to the work of providing for public services; but, in various ways, to the cherishing and cultivation of the personal, religious life. These brief prayers, many of which have stood the test of ages of use, like the collects in the service, are seeds of thought, suggestive of more than they directly express, and form a great con-

trast to the tedious, diffuse and intensely sub-
jective prayers of another type of religious
and theological thought. The Rev. H. A.
Weller has done well in giving them a proper
English form. Their wide circulation in families and for individuals ought to be earnestly
promoted. The pastor will find this volume a
most important aid for his own devotion and
for leading the devotions of others.

HENRY EYSTER JACOBS.

Lutheran Theological Seminary,
Mt. Airy, Philadelphia,
January 1912.

TRANSLATOR'S PREFACE.

I N many devout hearts a desire has asserted itself that we might have in the American Church also a book of devotion, for private and family use, in the tongue in which our children are being educated. Conscious of this desire, the translator has undertaken to set into the English language this precious compilation of the prayers of many saints in the ages past.

He has recognized that, however conscientiously and faithfully his love for these long tested prayers of Christendom constrained him to reproduce the thought and expression of the sainted author, no one who has ever seriously undertaken such a work can comprehend how in every translation of devotional thought and expression, there is something elusive which needs to be fused, moulded, and worn into the daily life-language of the people; and, to translate the language of the heart of one people into the heart-language of

another so that, in its new dress, it may effect
the same crystal clearness and kindle 'the same
quickening heart-fires, is a task which few
ever hope to accomplish satisfactorily. This
seems to be especially true of these SEED-
GRAINS OF PRAYER, suggestive of more devotional thought than they directly express.

Conscious of many shortcomings, we be-
speak the forebearing generosity of the critic,
to whom all books are only material challeng-
ing the exercise of his wit, and send this
volume forth as a granary of seed grains, not
altering the title given by its author for rea-
sons set forth in the preface to his first edition. We give it into the hands of all devout
Christians with the prayer that He, Who com-
mands and desires all men everywhere to
offer up intelligent and acceptable prayers,
may deign to make this translation, as He
made the original volume, to be life-bearing
seed grains, which, planted and nurtured by
the Holy Spirit in many hearts, shall, under
His benediction, bring forth a harvest of true
prayer and consecrated devotion, so long as
men shall speak the English tongue, grateful
everywhere for the privilege of knowing the

labor of William Loehe, that devout servant of the Lord and His Church.

Grateful recognition is due to the Reverend Professor Henry Eyster Jacobs, D. D., LL. D., S. T. D., Norton Professor of Theology and Dean of the Faculty of the Lutheran Theological Seminary at Philadelphia, Pa., for his valued introduction to this volume.

THE TRANSLATOR.

Orwigsburg, Pa., Epiphany, 1912.

PREFACE TO THE FIRST EDITION.

THE prayers herein are called SEED-GRAINS, because they are little grains of seed; like seed grains they are the product of life and, in turn, bear within them the power of life. They are not a product of yesterday; but, even as man has often found long hidden grains of seed which, after centuries, served for the sowing and brought forth fruit abundantly, so these prayers have not lost the power of their nativity. May God add His blessing and prosper the same, that they may

be unto all Christian people, precious, even
as are the prayers of Avenarius.*

PREFACE TO THE SIXTH EDITION.

IN the presentation of a new edition of this
book, the author has ever kept the same
aim in view. By changes and additions he has
sought to give his book that form and com-
pleteness which might permit it to be stereo-
typed and make all further changes and additions superfluous. This was particularly
kept in view in the preparation of this sixth
edition. Would that he might have attained
his purpose. The most utilized part of the
book may well be that containing the Morning
Prayers and the Evening Prayers, yet these
alone would not suffice in every place, and a
demand for more Saturday Prayers became
evident and was duly considered. All that
was possible to do to meet this demand has
been done. The Festival Prayers, by which a

---

* Habermann.

praying soul might sink itself deeply into the import and significance of the particular festival, were especially missed in the earliei editions. Heretofore, strictly adhering to his purpose to have a booklet of short collects only, the author has yielded to a frequently expressed desire of the people, and, along with the earlier festival collects, has set some longer festival prayers together with their prefaces. By reason of this the book has been much enlarged. To the collection of Week Day Prayers very few, four, have been added.

The Introduction, or, How to Order Family Devotion, which is found at the beginning of the Week Day Prayers, is another result of many requests. The collection of hymns, and in part also of psalms, was added on motion of a man who is a very dear friend, and well worthy to be an accepted counsellor of others, especially in the matter of hymn selections. Perhaps the guide to an Order of Service, binding upon none, may be a welcome addition to many. The several other minor additions speak for themselves, as well as the greater sequences of the order and rubrics of the separate prayers which appear in many places.

May this sixth edition of the SEED-GRAINS
have the blessing of the Lord and be helpful
to His Church.   Amen.   W. L.

Neuendettelsau, July 5, 1854.

INTRODUCTION.

1.

Christian Rules of Prayer, as Laid Down by Matthesius.

To true, Christian and salutary prayer it is requisite:—

1. That a man lift up holy hands (II Tim. 2) and offer his devotions with a good conscience; for God heareth not sinners who are not repentant. (John 9).

2. That a man pray in every time of trial and need; for, the greater our need the stronger is our prayer. Therefore also God, in the 50th Psalm, says: "Call upon Me in the day of trouble." (Always and everywhere there is sufficient provocation to prayer if one will but realize it).

3. That a man pray, cry and sigh from out of the depths of his heart, without hypocrisy, anger, complaint or doubt, even as Moses prayed upon the shore of the Red Sea. Lip-service and mouth-work in which the heart participates not, is a vain service of God. (Matt. 15).

4. That a man call upon the one, true and only God as He has revealed Himself at the River Jordan, as Christ teaches in the Gospel (John 16), and in the Lord's Prayer (Matt. 6; Luke 11).

5. That a man plead the name, merit, blood, death and intercession of Christ for help, and the support of the Holy Ghost. (John 4, and 14).

6. That a man pray with all boldness as Abraham prayed, Gen. 18; with a mighty faith, as the centurion prayed; without murmuring or im-

patience, continuing instant, as did the Canaanitish woman; and with humility, as did Daniel. (Dan. 9).

7. That a man persevere, as Sirach teaches, and set no limit or goal for God, as is said in Chapter 8 of the Book of Judith.

8. He that will thus pray needs first of all to believe, that he is reconciled to God through His Son, and must base his pleas upon baptism and the blood of Christ as well as upon God's command and promise. He must embrace the promise of Christ and the example of all the saints; and remember that God has frequently helped others before us. (Ps. 22:34.)

If prayer is to be rightly offered, all these things must be well observed and kept:—1. Holy hands and a good conscience. 2. Our need.

3. From the heart, without hypocrisy. 4. Calling upon the name of the One, Only God. 5. In the name of Jesus Christ, who is the soul of all prayer. 6. Boldly. 7. Perseveringly. 8. In faith. Such prayer pervades heaven, as Sirach says; and makes our joy perfect, as Christ witnesses, John 16. It attains help, gives comfort, joy, and a sure defence against all devils and evil men.

I.

PREPARATORY PRAYERS.

The Lord is in His holy temple: let all the earth keep silence before Him. (Hab. 2: 20).

From the rising of the sun even unto the going down of the same, My name shall be great among the Gentiles; and in every place incense shall be offered unto My name, and a pure offering: for My name shall be great among the heathen, saith the Lord of hosts. (Mal. 1: 11).

Let the words of my mouth, and the meditation of my heart, be acceptable in Thy sight, O Lord, my strength and my redeemer. (Ps. 19: 15).

2.

For Grace to Pray Aright.

I thank Thee, O Lord, my God,
for Thine unspeakable favor, that
Thou hast not only commanded us to
call upon Thy saving Name, but, as
a father, hast graciously promised
certainly to hear us, and to grant in
due season all that is salutary and
profitable for our bodies and our
souls. I pray Thee, O God, pour out
upon me Thy Holy Spirit,—the
Spirit of prayer,—that I may ever
love and desire to pray; being daily
free to approach Thee, with all confidence, in the name of my Lord
Jesus Christ; to bow the knee be-

fore Thee in every time of need, as a child well beloved, O most beloved Father, Who art really a Father unto all Thy children in heaven and on earth. Grant that I may always lift up unto Thee holy hands, without fear or doubt, and in full assurance that all my prayers and sighings which come from the heart, are truly heard. Grant also, that when my help delays I shall be patient, not dictating to Thee either time or measure, but to wait and abide Thine own good time; for Thou hast pleasure in them that fear and put their trust in Thy mercy. Finally, O God, rule and remind me by Thy Holy Spirit that I may daily and frequently meditate upon the hour of my death and be momentarily prepared, while I pray sincerely for a blessed departure hence. Amen.

3.

MERCIFUL God, we do indeed not know what we should pray, neither how we should present our petitions unto Thee. We are by nature negligent and indifferent to pray, and our little earthly occupations do so easily keep us away from, or at least hinder us in our prayers. To all this come the manifold temptations of the devil, ever ready to make us err on all sides in our prayers. Therefore, I pray Thee, O Lord, my God, pour out upon me abundantly the Spirit of grace and prayer, that I may boldly surmount every hindrance and pray unto Thee diligently according to Thy will, and obtain all those things that are salutary and needful for me both in soul and body, now and evermore, through

Jesus Christ, Thy Son, my only Savior. Amen.

4.

MERCIFUL, gracious and loving Father in heaven, Thou hast commanded me to pray. Thy loving Son has taught me to pray, and by His gracious vow has promised me a hearing. Thy Holy Spirit frequently puts in my heart a reminder that I shall pray. I know that every good gift cometh from above, from the Father of light; and Thy glory, as well as my own need, demand that I shall pray. I am conscious how prayer is a blessed conversation with Thee, and Thou answerest me in the comfort of holy thoughts. Besides these I have multiplied examples of the saints and of my Lord Jesus Christ that without prayer neither help nor comfort can be attained.

Yet, I am negligent and reticent in prayer, depending more upon my own wisdom and works than upon Thy grace and support. O pardon unto me such foolishness, such self-sufficiency and disregard for Thy divine promises. Turn from me the sore punishments which Thou hast threatened unto them that despise Thy grace, when Thou sayest that Thou wilt in turn despise them, and that they who follow after another shall surely have much sorrow of heart. Grant me, instead, the spirit of grace to pray. Make me to call to remembrance Thy consoling promise:—

He that calleth upon the name of the Lord shall be saved;
before that they cry I will hear, and while they yet speak I will answer:

the Lord is nigh unto all them
that call upon Him;
whatsoever ye shall ask the Father
in My name, that will He do;
who among you will offer his son
a stone when he asketh for
bread?

By such Thy promises, Lord,
kindle my soul with a flame of
sincere and fervent devotion, and let
my prayer avail before Thee like the
sacrifice of Noah. Let it echo in
Thine ear as the bells of gold upon
Aaron's robe, and as the harp of
David.

O Lord, Searcher of hearts, Who
provest our hearts and bowels, Thou
knowest how human hearts and
minds waver, much more unstable
than are the waters moved by the
wind. Establish Thou my devotions
that I be not swayed by so many and

various thoughts. Thou, much better than I, canst quiet the ship of my
soul and establish and govern it.
Arise, O Lord, to command the winds
and waves that trouble my soul, that
they be still, and I rest in Thee, beholding Thee with open countenance
and abiding in unity with Thee. Lead
me into the solitude where I may
hear and behold naught but Thee,
that Thou mayest converse with me
and I with Thee, unheard and unseen
of men. By Thy grace remove far
from me all that hinders my devotion, be it the world, or the will of my
own flesh, or passion, or covetousness, or impatience, or unbelief, or
pride, or implacability, or impenitence. Take from me the heart of
stone that I may realize Thy Holy
Spirit's ardor, love, comfort and
most generous answer. Let the Holy

Ghost move my heart with desire; let Him cry, call, pray, praise, thank and testify, witnessing unto my soul that I am indeed a child of God. Let Him be the advocate of my soul with unspeakable sighings before Thee, and fill me, as Thy temple, with heavenly thoughts, with divine love and joy. By Thy Spirit, O God, cause me to be in unity with Thy Son, Jesus Christ, that in Him and through Him and by Him, as our head, I may pray acceptably. By Thy Holy Spirit also, cause me to be united and to abide in communion with all believing souls and Thy whole Christian church, that I, together with all Thy church, for the church and in the church, may pray as in Thy sanctuary and be heard in the name of Jesus Christ. Amen.

5.

Before the Lord's Prayer.

HEAVENLY Father, Gracious God, I am a poor, miserable sinner, unworthy to lift up mine eyes, hands or voice unto Thee in prayer. But, since Thou hast Thyself commanded us all to pray, and hast promised to hear us, giving us from Thyself both the words and manner of prayer, by Thy beloved Son, our Lord Jesus Christ; I pray, according to Thy promise, grant me the spirit of grace and of prayer, that with fervent heart I cry to Thee for mine own and the needs of all men, in true faith; that my prayer may be heard according to Thy promise. Upon Thy word and command, I come to Thee, rendering obedience to the same, and relying upon Thy gracious promises; and, together with all Thy blessed Christendom on earth, pray as Jesus Christ has taught me:—Our Father who art in heaven, etc.

(Martin Luther.)

6.

ALMIGHTY, Eternal, Heavenly Father, by Thine only Son, our Lord, Jesus Christ, Thou gavest unto the apostles a prayer, which Thou hast caused to be preserved even unto us, wherein it is revealed that Thou desirest men of prayer to pray to Thee in spirit and in truth. Therefore, we poor sinners, lost in error and lacking Thy Spirit, pray Thee, O Lord God, Heavenly Father, through Thy Son, Who is the truth, and for His sake, richly pour out and send into our hearts Thy Holy Spirit, to lead us into sonship with Thee; to aid us in our weakness and im-

potency, and teach us how and what
to pray, according to Thy holy will.
Yea, make the same Spirit to witness
within us that we are the sons of
God, to lead us unto Thee, "Abba,
beloved Father", und let our desires
and prayers be so set forth before
Thee that we may be graciously
heard, through our Lord, Jesus
Christ.   Amen.   (1536.)

To the Lord's Prayer.

7.

Our Father,

insuperable in creation,
sweet in love,
rich in every heritage!

Who art in Heaven,

a mirror of eternity,
the crown of joy,
the treasure of eternal salvation!

Hallowed be Thy name,

that it be like honey upon the tongue,
a harp unto our ears,
a devotion in our hearts!

Thy kingdom come,

joyfully, without perversion;
quietly, without sorrow;
safely, beyond possibility to lose it!

Thy will be done on earth as it is in heaven,

that we hate whatever displeases
  Thee;
love what Thou lovest;
and fulfill all things that are pleasing to Thee!

Give us this day our daily bread,

the bread of
  knowledge,
  penitence,
  pardon
  and every need of our bodies.

Forgive us our trespasses, as we forgive those who trespass against us; forgive us our trespasses against Thee, against our fellow-men and against ourselves, which we have multiplied either through the commission of wrongs or the ommission to do the good we ought to do, as we forgive all who have despised or offended us

    by word or deed,

    by giving or taking away from us,

    spiritually or temporally.

And lead us not into temptation,

    of the world,

    the flesh,

    or the devil:

    But deliver us from evil,

both temporal and spiritual, and from all sorrows in time and eternity. **Amen.**

8.

The Lord's Prayer,

in a few words, to the tune: "Erhalt uns, Herr,
bei deinem Wort."

Lord God, who art my Father yet,—
    In Jesus Christ of Thee begat,—
By His word, vow, and death I cry
    To Thee, in need and harm so nigh!

Leave us Thy word, our souls revive,
    Help us Thy will to do and live:
Give peace, protection, friends and bread,
    And save the state,—O Blessed Head!

Save us from satan, death and sin,
    From harm without, and harm within;
Grant us a time of peace and light,—
    Thine is the kingdom, laud and might.

Now, in Thy name we cry Amen!
    By grace increase our faith; and then,—
Since Thou alone art Father mine,—
    A child and heir, I shall be Thine.

II.

SPIRITUAL DAILY LIFE.

When I remember Thee upon my bed and meditate on Thee in the night watches, and when I awake my mouth shall praise Thee, because Thou hast been my help, therefore in the shadow of Thy wings will I rejoice. (Ps. 63: 6, 7).

Whatsoever ye do in word or deed, do all in the name of the Lord Jesus, giving thanks to God and the Father by Him. (Col. 3: 17).

Whether therefore ye eat, or drink, or whatsoever ye do, do all to the glory of God. (I. Cor. 10: 31).

Seven times a day do I praise Thee, because of Thy righteous judgments. (Ps. 119: 164).

A.

9.

Christian and Blessed
Daily Exercises and Memorials
of a Believing Soul.
From the Psalms.

(C. Spangenberg, 1560.)

Upon Awakening from Sleep.

1

O LORD God; lighten mine eyes, lest I sleep the sleep of death. Ps. 13:3. Open Thou mine eyes, that I may behold wondrous things in Thy law. Ps. 119:18. Make Thy face to shine upon Thy servant: save me for Thy mercy's sake. Ps. 31:16.

2

Upon Arising from Sleep.

THE Lord upholdeth all that fall, and raiseth up all those that be bowed down. Ps. 145:14. The Godless are brought down and fallen: but we are risen, and stand upright. Ps. 20:8.

3

Upon Dressing One's Self.

LET Thy priests be clothed with righteousness; and let Thy saints shout for joy. Ps. 132:9. (I Pet. 2; Rom. 13; Eph. 6; Luke 12; Isa. 59; I Thess. 5; Isa. 61; II Cor. 5; Matt. 22.)

4

While Washing.

HAVE mercy upon me, O God, according to Thy loving kindness: according unto the multitude

of Thy tender mercies blot out my
transgressions. Wash me thoroughly
from mine iniquity, and cleanse me
from my sin. Purge me with hysop,
and I shall be clean; wash me, and I
shall be whiter than snow. Ps. 51:1,
2, 7.

5

Morning Prayer.

MY VOICE shalt Thou hear in the
morning, O Lord; in the morning will I direct my prayer unto
Thee, and will look up. Ps. 5:3. Let
my mouth be filled with Thy praise
and with Thy honor all the day. Ps.
71:8. O, satisfy us early with Thy
mercy; that we may be glad and rejoice all our days. Ps. 90:14. It is a
good thing to give thanks unto the
Lord, and to sing praises unto Thy

name, O Most High. To show forth
Thy loving kindness in the morning,
and Thy faithfulness every night.
Ps. 92:1, 2.

6

Upon Leaving the Chamber.

L ORD, hold up my goings in Thy
paths, that my footsteps slip not.
Ps. 17:5. Lead me, O Lord, in Thy
righteousness, because of mine enemies; make Thy way straight before
my face. Ps. 5:9. Show me Thy
ways, O Lord; teach me Thy paths.
Lead me in Thy truth and teach me:
for Thou art the God of my salvation; on Thee do I wait all the day.
Ps. 25:4, 5. Unite my heart to fear
Thy name. Ps. 86:11.

7

On the Way to Church.

I WAS glad when they said unto me, let us go into the house of the Lord; to give thanks to the name of the Lord. Ps. 122:1, 4. My soul longeth, yea, even fainteth for the courts of the Lord: my heart and my flesh crieth out for the living God. Ps. 84:2. I will come into Thine house in the multitude of Thy mercy; and in Thy fear will I worship toward Thy holy temple. Ps. 5:7.

8

While at Work.

B LESSED is every one that feareth the Lord; that walketh in His ways, for thou shalt eat the labor of thine hands; happy shalt thou be,

and it shall be well with thee.   Ps.
128:1, 2.

9

At the Noon Hour.

I WILL say of the Lord, He is my
refuge and my fortress; in Him
will I trust.   Cover Thou me with
Thy wings, that I tremble not for the
arrow that flieth by day, nor for the
destruction that walketh at noonday.
Ps. 91:2, 4, 5, 6.   Midnight and mid-
day hast Thou created; Thou hast a
mighty arm, strong is Thy hand and
high is Thy right hand. Ps. 89:13, 14.

10

At Sunset.

REMEMBER Thy congregation
which Thou hast purchased of
old.   Thou art my king of old, work-

ing salvation in the midst of the earth. The day is Thine, the night also is Thine: Thou hast prepared the light and the sun. Ps. 74:2, 12, 16.

11

At the Lighting of the Lamps.

THOU, Lord, wilt light my candle; the Lord, my God, will enlighten my darkness. Ps. 18:28. In Thy light shall we see light. Ps. 36:9. O, send out Thy light and Thy truth: let them lead me; let them bring me to Thy holy hill, and to Thy tabernacles. Ps. 43:3.

12

Upon Retiring to Rest.

I WILL both lay me down in peace, and sleep; for Thou, Lord, only makest me to dwell in safety. **Ps.**

4:8. The darkness hideth not from Thee; but the night shineth as the day. Ps. 139:12. Therefore, O Lord, let Thy truth be my shield and defence, that I tremble not at the terrors by night, nor for the pestilence that walketh in darkness. Ps. 91:4, 5, 6. Into Thy hand I commit my spirit: Thou hast redeemed me, O Lord God of truth. Ps. 31:5.

B.

MORNING PRAYERS.

10.

As a Housefather Should Teach His Family to Pray in the Morning.

In the morning, when thou risest from the bed, thou shalt consecrate thyself with the sign of the cross, and say:

In the Name of the Father, Son, and Holy Ghost. Amen.

Thereupon, either kneeling or standing, repeat the Creed and the Lord's prayer; and, if thou wilt, thou mayest repeat the following short prayer in addition thereto:

I give thanks unto Thee, Heavenly Father, through Jesus Christ, Thy dear Son, that Thou hast protected me through the night from all danger and harm; and I beseech Thee to preserve and keep me this day also from all sin and evil; that in all my thoughts, words and deeds, I may serve and please Thee. Into Thy hands I commend my body and soul and all that is mine. Let Thy holy angel have charge concerning me, that the wicked one have no power over me. Amen.

Then, after a hymn, or the Ten Commandments, or whatever devotion may suggest, go joyfully to thy work.   (Luther's Small Catechism.)

11.

While Dressing.

LORD Jesus, Who art the second
and new Adam, clothe me with
Thyself; that I put away all evil desires and lusts, and crucify and slay
in me the dominion of the flesh. Be
Thou unto me a strong garment
against the icy coldness of this world;
that I may be preserved and warmed
by Thee. Without Thee, all things
droop, decay and die; but in Thee
we live safe, strong, and mighty. As
now I cover my body with these garments, so, O Lord, cover and clothe
me with Thyself; especially my soul;
for Thou art the garment of my salvation and the cloak of my righteousness. And unto Thee be glory
and honor and praise, together with

the Father and the Holy Ghost,
world without end.   Amen.

12.

At the Rising Of The Sun.

O LORD Jesus, Creator of all
things; Light of the glory of
the Father in heaven: I thank Thee
with my whole heart that Thou per-
mittest me again to see the joyous
sunlight.   O Bright Sun of Righteousness, arise and shine in my heart,
also; that, in Thy refulgence, I may
walk as a child of light as in the day,
and finally behold Thee blessed in
the eternal light of joy everlasting.
Amen.

C.

DAILY PRAYERS.

13.

Daily Kyrie.

LORD, have mercy upon us.
Christ, have mercy upon us.
Lord, have mercy upon us, and save Thy people, whom Thou hast redeemed by Thy precious blood; and be not eternally wroth for our sins. O Lord, remember us according to Thy mercy and the gracious purpose which Thou hast toward Thy people. Visit us with Thy salvation, that we may behold the glory of Thine elect; rejoicing in the joy of Thy people; and praising Thee in Thine inheritance. Amen.

14.

Daily Gloria.

G LORY be to God on high, and on earth peace, good will toward men!

From the rising of the sun unto the going down thereof,

Let the Name of the Lord
be praised!

Almighty and gracious God, merciful Father, let the light of Thy countenance be upon us, Thy humble servants; and increase in us true knowledge of Thy grace and mercy which Thou hast vouchsafed unto us by Thy dear Son, our Lord, Jesus Christ. Grant this, we beseech Thee, that we be moved to praise and to confess Thee, unto the salvation of Thy people everywhere, as our Lord and our God, together with Thy dear

Son and the Holy Ghost; and glorify
and praise Thee with our whole
hearts, with all the company of
heaven, in word and deed; through
the same, Thy dear Son, our Lord
and Savior, Jesus Christ. Amen.

(Strassburg, 1566.)

15.

Daily Prayer, for Grace to Keep our Baptismal Covenant.

DEAR Lord and Savior, Jesus
Christ, eternally true Son of
God, we are baptized into Thy death
and made partakers of Thy merit,
that, being redeemed from sin, we
may be truly holy and righteous before our Heavenly Father. In our
baptism we promised to die unto the
sin that remaineth in us and to walk
in newness of life. We beseech

Thee, therefore, to enlighten and to strengthen us by Thy Holy Spirit to renounce all sinful lusts and to live to please Thee; Who reignest with the Father and the Holy Ghost in all eternity. Amen.

16.

Prayer Before Daily Bible Reading.

LORD, Jesus Christ, Who hast commanded to search the Scriptures and promised that in them we have the impulse of faith, and life everlasting; Who alone art worthy to open and break the sevenfold seals of this Book; open now mine eyes to behold the wonders of Thy law. Show me the paths of righteousness, that I continue therein unto the end. From heaven above, pour out Thy Holy Spirit upon me, and from Thy throne of glory send Him to be with me; to work in me that I learn to know what is well pleasing to Thee; to do all my labor in Thy name, unto Thy glory; and to fill my heart with true faith, love, hope, humility, long-suffering, fear and blessedness in the Lord. Amen.

D.

GRACE AT MEAT.

17.

Concerning the Saying of Grace.

Deut. 8: 10.

"When thou hast eaten and art full, then thou shalt bless the Lord thy God for the good land which He hath given thee."

THERE is among many Christians
so great ingratitude and shameless indifference that they neither
bless their food before meat, nor
sanctify it with God's Word, nor offer so much as a prayer in remembrance of God's mercy; nor, indeed,
do they give thanks after meat to
the Holy Giver Who daily grants
them life and food. If they would,
they could easily convince themselves from the Holy Gospel that
Christ, our Lord, never failed to be
grateful for earthly benefits, but always and in all places rendered
thanks. When He instituted the
Holy Supper, wherein the bread and
wine are but humble vehicles of
heavenly and unspeakable gifts, the
holy evangelists tell us: "He took
bread, and, having given thanks, He
brake it:......He took the cup,

and, when He had given thanks, He gave it,".....(Matt. 26: 26, 27; Mark 14: 22, 23; Luke 21: 19). Thus He gave thanks before partaking; and, at the conclusion of the passover and the Holy Supper, we read: "And when they had sung a hymn, they went out into the Mount of Olives," (Matt. 26: 30; Mark 14: 26) demonstrating that He also worshiped and gave thanks after meat. Our Lord did likewise at other meals; and just as religiously after His passion, in His state of exaltation, as He had formerly done in His state of humiliation. According to Matt. 14: 19; Mark 8: 6; and John 6: 11; "He commanded the people to sit down on the ground, and He took the loaves and the fishes and gave thanks, and brake, and gave to His disciples to set before them."

As He did at the feeding of the five
thousand so also did He at the feeding of the four thousand. (Matt.
15: 36). As He had done in His state
of humiliation, even so also did He
after His resurrection from the dead,
when He **blessed** the food in the
presence of the two disciples at
Emmaus. Though all are familiar
with these passages, yet, how great
is the number of them that sit down
to meat and rise again like brutes
that comprehend nothing of gratitude to God. Even in this the rich,
of whom one would naturally expect
greater appreciation, because they
have every cause for such, frequently distinguish themselves from others to their lasting shame; as if they,
favored of God with greater earthly
possessions and the gift of appreciation, had less reason to thank God;

or, as though God owed them life
and food; or, as though they were
too good to be thankful and needed
God's grace no longer. Verily it
brings shame and disgrace upon the
Church of Christ, when Christians,
—Christ's servants and followers,—
neglect their duties so flagrantly and
have no more a spirit of praise and
thanksgiving in them; and, it is high
time that every one who deserves
correction shall permit himself to be
sincerely corrected through God's
Word and Spirit.

GRACE BEFORE MEAT.

18.

The Benedicite.

Let children and the whole family approach
the table reverently and with folded hands, saying:

The eyes of all wait upon Thee,

O Lord; and Thou givest them their meat in due season. Thou openest Thine hand, and satisfiest the desire of every living thing.

Then shall be said the Lord's Prayer, and after that this prayer:

O Lord God, Heavenly Father, bless us and these Thy gifts which we receive from Thy loving kindness, through Jesus Christ, our Lord. Amen.   (Luther's Smaller Catechism.)

19.

LORD God, our Heavenly Father, for Thy gracious gifts with which Thou hast again so faithfully provided us, we render praises and thanksgiving. We beseech Thee, grant us to enjoy these benefits reverently and in true gratitude, unto our strengthening, to Thy praise and the help and service of

our fellow men, through our Lord
Jesus Christ. Amen.   (1564.)

20.

GRACIOUS Father, Who feedest
and nourishest every creature,
feed and nourish our souls and bodies
that we may not abuse Thy gifts; but,
that we be rather quickened by the
same unto the glory of Thy name;
unto all honest toil and every good
work; to live and move before Thee
in righteousness and innocence.
Amen.   (1562.)

21.

BLESSED be God, Who has sustained us from earliest infancy,
and giveth meat unto all flesh. May
He fill our hearts with joy and gladness, granting what our needs
demand at all times; and, that we be
satisfied with His provision. Amen.

22.
DAILY BIBLE LESSONS.

From *Spangenberg's Spiritual Economy.*
For an entire Week. 1561.

SUNDAY.
1. Luke 11:37—42.
2. Luke 24:36—43.

MONDAY.
1. Matth. 22:1—14.
2. Luke 14:16—22.

TUESDAY.
1. John 2:1—11.
2. Mark 14:3—9.

WEDNESDAY.
1. John 21:1—14.
2. Rev. 3:19—22.

THURSDAY.
1. John 4:31—34.
2. Luke 22:14—20.

FRIDAY.
1. Mark 8:1—9.
2. Rev. 19:6—9.

SATURDAY.
1. Luke 14:1—14. (15).
2. Luke 10:38—42.

GRACE AFTER MEAT.

23.

After meat, let the children and the entire family fold their hands reverently and say:

O give thanks unto the Lord, for He is good; for His mercy endureth forever. He giveth food to all flesh:

He giveth to the beast his food; and
to the young ravens which cry. The
Lord taketh pleasure in them that
fear Him, in those that hope in His
mercy.

Then shall be said the Lord's Prayer, and the
following:

We thank Thee, Lord God, Heavenly Father, through Jesus Christ,
our Lord, for all Thy benefits; Who
livest and reignest forever and ever.
Amen.   (Luther's Small Catechism.*)

24.

LORD God, Heavenly Father, for
Thy great bounty so abundantly
shared unto us, we praise and bless

---

* Here may be added the 117th Psalm. "O
praise the Lord all ye nations: praise Him all ye
people. For His merciful kindness is great toward
us: and the truth of the Lord endureth forever."
Glory be to the Father, and to the Son, and to the
Holy Ghost; as it was in the beginning, is now, and
ever shall be, world without end. Amen.

Thee. Grant us to live and serve
Thee as faithfully as Thou hast
abundantly fed and nourished us;
through Jesus Christ, our Lord.
Amen.   (1564.)

25.

O LORD God, Heavenly Father,
for all Thy gifts and benefits
we render praise and thanksgiving;
and beseech Thee to sustain our
souls in true faith and knowledge of
Thee, even as Thou hast now nourished our bodies. Amen.   (1562.)

26.

GLORY be to Thee, O God most
Holy! Glory be to Thee, O God
most High! Glory be to Thee, O King
of Heaven and Earth, Who sustainest
us with fatherly kindness! Fill us
with joy and gladness in the Holy
Ghost, that we be found acceptable

in Thy sight, without condemnation
or shame in that day when Thou wilt
reward each according to his works.
Amen.*)

27.

WE give thanks unto Thee, O
Heavenly Father, Who hast
created all by Thine unsearchable
power; governest all by Thine unspeakable wisdom; and feedest and
prosperest all by Thine unfathomable goodness; and, we beseech
Thee, grant unto Thy children,
finally, to drink, with Thy Son in
Thy kingdom, that cup of everlasting
life which Thou hast promised and
prepared for all who love Thee:
through Jesus Christ, Amen.

---

*) Let the poor also remember his benefactor
and say:—Unto all who have shown us kindness for
Thy name's sake, O Lord, grant salvation and eternal ᾽
life through grace. Amen.

SECTION E, including Prayers Nos. 28—35, "At the Ringing of the Prayer Bells," has been omitted from this translation, since in America, the custom of ringing the· bells for Prayer does not prevail.

F.

HOURLY PRAYERS.

35.

When thou hearest the hour strike, thou shouldst pray after the following manner:

O HEAVENLY Father, my God, behold and have mercy upon me. Hasten to help me, that in this hour I begin to flee all evil and to do whatsoever is well pleasing in Thy sight. Vouchsafe unto me true faith, and love, and hope in Thee and Thine only Son Jesus Christ, that I may know Him for the heavenly gift given unto me for wisdom, righteousness, holiness and salvation, as my only Redeemer and Mediator before

Thee. Grant me to follow in the footsteps of my Lord Jesus Christ, that I may pattern my life after His life, daily dying unto and denying myself; bearing my cross in patient and humble submission to Thee; loving my neighbor and doing unto him as Christ has done for me; and safely guarding myself against everything that displeases Thee, my Lord. O Jesus, Redeemer, strengthen me unto all such labor and conflict, that I fall not, neither be wounded unto helplessness. Above all, let me neither turn from Thee, nor deny Thee; then, naught can harm me unto death. And when my last hour shall come, grant that I call upon Thy Holy Name and set my trust and hope in the merit of Thy bitter sufferings and death, which I set up between me and Thy judgment. O

Jesus, I am Thine. Save me by Thy grace. Amen.

36.

LORD Jesus Christ, unto Thee I live; unto Thee I die! Whether, therefore, I live or die, I am Thine. Jesus Christ, Thou Son of God, grant me a blessed moment when I depart from this vale of tears, that I be found pure and undefiled before Thee and hear Thy glorious voice saying unto me: "Come, beloved of my Father, inherit the kingdom which is prepared for you from the beginning of the world." Amen. Lord Jesus Christ, grant me grace, that I may daily amend my life, guard against all sin, and live and move according to Thy will. Amen. Dear Lord God, we confess our sins before Thee. Have mercy upon us

and graciously forgive us our sins.
Remember Thy great mercy which
is from everlasting to everlasting.
Amen.

_____

G.

Vesper, or Evening Prayers, for daily readiness to die.

37.

LORD Jesus Christ, Prince of Life,
humbly do I beseech Thee to
grant me the grace of Thy Holy
Spirit, that I may live this life not
unto self, but alone unto Thy glory;
that I may consider every moment,
what it is to die, and what comes
afterward for both the wicked and
the good; that ere mine hour cometh
I may have learned how to die, and
always practice what I have so
learned; that I may finally depart

from this world's pilgrimage unto
the fatherland in heaven. Amen.
Lord Jesus, in life and death lead
me. Thy merit let me inherit.
Amen.

38.

DEAR God and Lord, I live and
know not when I must die. I
must die and know not the hour.
Thou, Heavenly Father, knowest.
If this hour, or day, or night should
be my last, O Lord, Thy will be done.
Thy will alone is good. As Thy will
ordains, even so, in true faith in
Christ, my Redeemer, I am ready
to live or to die. But, Dear Lord,
grant me this prayer: — That I
die not suddenly in my sins and
be lost. Grant me true knowledge,
penitence and sorrow for the sins
I have committed, and set them

before mine eyes to realize while
yet I dwell here, that they be
not set out before me in the last day,
and I be disgraced before angels and
men. Grant me so much time and
place for repentance that I may with
all my heart realize my transgressions, and, confessing the same, attain the comfort of assured pardon
from Thy saving word. O Merciful
Father, leave me not. Take not Thy
Holy Spirit from me. Thou, O
Searcher of Hearts, knowest how my
heart and hope is in Thee. In that
assurance keep me unto everlasting
life. Whensoever it pleases Thee, let
me die, but grant me a conscious
and blessed end. Amen. Lord
Jesus receive my soul into Thy
hands, and let it be Thy charge.
Amen.

H.

EVENING PRAYERS.

At the Going Down of the Sun.

39.

L ORD Jesus, Glorious Sun of
Righteousness, depart not from
me, nor take away the glory of Thy
grace and mighty comfort. Shine
upon mine eyes that I sleep not the
sleep of death, and, after this life,
let me awake joyfully unto everlasting life, for Thy precious Name's
sake. Amen.

40.

O God, the Holy Ghost, the sun in
the heavens is now sinking. Let
not the Sun of my Righteousness,
Jesus Christ, ever become darkened
in my heart. Declare Him unto
me that I may consider Him

without ceasing. Keep me ever in remembrance, that in Him I assuredly have the forgiveness of all my sins and the hope of the resurrection of the body unto life everlasting. So rule and govern my life, that I may end my days in holiness and righteousness, as 'it is well pleasing before Thee. Amen.

41.

Psalm 51.

H AVE mercy upon me, O God, according to Thy loving-kindness: according unto the multitude of Thy tender mercies blot out my transgressions.

Wash me thoroughly from mine iniquity, and cleanse me from my sin.

For I acknowledge my transgressions: and my sin is ever before me.

Against Thee, Thee only have I
sinned, and done this evil in Thy
sight: that Thou mightest be justified when Thou speakest, and be
clear when Thou judgest.

Behold, I was shapen in iniquity;
and in sin did my mother conceive
me.

Behold, Thou desirest truth in the
inward parts: and in the hidden
part Thou shalt make me to know
wisdom.

Purge me with hyssop, and I
shall be clean: wash me, and I shall
be whiter than snow.

Make me to hear joy and gladness; that the bones which Thou
hast broken may rejoice.

Hide Thy face from my sins, and
blot out all mine iniquities.

Create in me a clean heart, O

God; and renew a right spirit within me.

Cast me not away from Thy presence; and take not Thy holy spirit from me.

Restore unto me the joy of Thy salvation; and uphold me with Thy free spirit.

Then will I teach transgressors Thy ways; and sinners shall be converted unto Thee.

Deliver me from bloodguiltiness, O God, Thou God of my salvation: and my tongue shall sing aloud of Thy righteousness.

O Lord, open Thou my lips; and my mouth shall shew forth Thy praise.

For Thou desirest not sacrifice; else would I give it: Thou delightest not in burnt offering.

The sacrifices of God are a broken spirit: a broken and a contrite heart, O God, Thou wilt not despise.

Do good in Thy good pleasure unto Zion: build Thou the walls of Jerusalem.

Then shalt Thou be pleased with the sacrifices of righteousness, with burnt offering and whole burnt offering: then shall they offer bullocks upon Thine altar.

42.

SHORT EVENING PRAYERS.

O LORD, when the darkness covers us, let Thy righteousness dawn upon our souls, that we, who now prayerfully render thanks unto Thee after the labors of another day are done, may also come before

Thy face in the morning, to pay Thee
the vows of thanksgiving; through
Jesus Christ, Our Lord. Amen.

43.

THE day is Thine, O Lord, and,
Thine is the night also. Let
the Sun of Righteousness continually
shine on our hearts to drive away
every shadow of unholy thoughts;
through Jesus Christ, Our Lord.
Amen.

44.

WE thank Thee, Lord, Who hast
kept us this day; and, as we
need Thy protection this night, we
praise and beseech Thee, O Lord,
grant that when the morning dawns,
we may be set in Thy light unharmed,
to praise Thy name at all times;
through Jesus Christ, our Lord.
Amen.

45.

ALMIGHTY and eternal God, at eventide, in the morning, and at noonday, we humbly worship Thy Majesty, and pray Thou wilt drive away from our hearts all darkness of sin, and make us to attain the One True Light, Jesus Christ; through the same, our Lord Jesus Christ. Amen.

46.

HELP, Lord, when we awake. Defend us while we sleep, that we awake with Christ, and rest in peace. **Kyrie Eleison.** Christ, have mercy upon us. **Kyrie Eleison.**
(Here repeat the Lord's Prayer and the Creed.)

47.

When two unite in prayer, the following may be said responsively:

Blessed art Thou, O Lord of our fathers:

And greatly to be praised and glorified forever.

Bless we the Father, and the Son, and the Holy Ghost:

We praise and magnify Him forever.

The Almighty and Merciful God, bless and preserve us.

Amen.

Keep us, O Lord, this night:

By Thy grace, without sin.

O Lord, have mercy upon us:

Have mercy upon us.

Let Thy mercy be upon us:

As our trust is in Thee.

Hear my prayer, O Lord:

And let my cry come unto Thee.

O Lord, visit Thy habitation and remove from us every evil design of the enemy. Let Thy holy angels

abide with us to keep us in Thy
peace; and let Thy benediction be
upon us evermore; through Jesus
Christ, our Lord.

48.

How the Head of the Family Should Teach His Family to Pray at Evening.

In the evening when thou goest to bed, thou
shalt consecrate thyself with the sign of the cross,
and say:

In the Name of the Father, and
of the Son, and of the Holy Ghost.
Amen.

Then kneeling or standing, thou shalt say the
Creed and the Lord's Prayer.

Then thou mayest add this prayer:

I give thanks unto Thee, Heavenly Father, through Jesus Christ Thy
dear Son, that Thou hast this day so
graciously protected me, and I be-

seech Thee to forgive me all my sins,
and the wrong which I have done,
and by Thy great mercy defend me
from all the perils and dangers of
this night. Into Thine hands I commend my body and soul, and all that
is mine. Let Thy holy angel have
charge concerning me, that the
wicked one have no power over me.
Amen.   (Luther's Small Catechism.)

Then lie down in peace and sleep.

49.

Upon Lying Down in Bed.

When thou liest down to sleep, consecrate thyself with the sign of the cross and say:

Now I lay me down to sleep in the
Name of our Lord Jesus Christ, Who
has redeemed me with His precious
blood. May He bless, defend and
protect me; and, after this poor life

of sorrow, lead me to life everlasting. Amen.

Keep me as the apple of the eye; hide me under the shadow of Thy wings. Ps. 17: 8. Into Thy hand I commit my spirit. Ps. 31: 5. I will both lay me down in peace and sleep: for Thou, Lord, only makest me dwell in safety. Ps. 4: 8. I lay me down and sleep: and I awake, for the Lord sustaineth me.

With these words sleep in peace, in the Name of the Lord.

Short Prayers to Repeat Upon Lying Down or Upon Waking at Night.

50.

O GOD, who lightest the darkness and makest light to follow the night, grant that we pass this night without hindrance of the devil, and in the morning repair to Thine altars

to give Thee thanks; through Jesus
Christ, our Lord. Amen.

51.

L ET Thy peace descend from
heaven, O Lord, and rest in our
hearts, O Christ. Make us to sleep
in peace and awake in Thee, that we
fear no terrors of the night; Who
livest and reignest with the Father
and the Holy Ghost, ever one God,
world without end. Amen.

52.

E VERLASTING Redeemer, watch
over us lest the ever resourceful
tempter overtake us; for Thou art
our helper unto all eternity. Amen.

53.

L ORD Jesus Christ, Redeemer of
mankind, Who hast purchased
us by Thy precious blood, grant us

rest in our bodies, that we be ever
awake in Thee, Who with the Father
and the Holy Ghost, one true God,
art glorified forever. Amen.

54.

O Thou, Beloved Shepherd of our
souls, Who slumberest not,
spread Thy holy protection over us
as wings to cover us, that no terrors
of the night may weary us, and let
Thy divine Majesty watch in our
minds while we sleep; through Jesus
Christ. Amen.

55.

G RANT, Lord, we beseech Thee, a
peaceful night, that a blessed
day of praise and song may follow
the darkness of the night; through
Jesus Christ, our Lord. Amen.

56.

L ORD Jesus Christ, Who bearest
the lost sheep back into the fold
in Thine arms, and deignest to hear
the confession of the Publican, graciously remit all my guilt and sin.
Lord, Who hearest the penitent thief;
Who hast set an heritage of mercy
for Thy saints; and, hast not withheld pardon from the sinner; hear
the prayers of Thy servants according to Thy mercy. Amen. May the
Almighty Lord grant us a peaceful
night and a blessed end. Amen.

57.

Upon Awaking in the Night, or During a Sleepless Night.

O GREAT God, my Light and my
Salvation, my Shield and
Buckler, the Power of my Life
against every enemy of body and

soul, my soul's Comforter against all
that troubles me for my sin's sake:
my heart is awake unto Thee, and I
give hearty thanks unto Thee that
Thy dear Son, by his bitter night of
anguish, has redeemed me from the
terrors of the eternal night of hell.
O support me and all who can not
rest for sorrow or pain of mind, soul,
or body. Defend us from all harm.
Graciously vouchsafe unto us our
nightly rest until we reach the true
rest in Thy home of love in heaven,
and behold Thee blessed, without
rest or weariness; through Jesus
Christ, our Pillar of Grace. Amen.

58.

(I Pet. 5: 8, 9.)

BE sober, be vigilant; because your
adversary the devil, as a roaring
lion, walketh about, seeking whom

he may devour: whom resist steadfast in the faith, knowing that the
same afflictions are accomplished in
your brethren that are in the world.''
Almighty and Most Merciful God,
the Father, Son, and Holy Ghost
bless and keep us. Amen.

III.
THE CHRISTIAN WEEK:

Let us come boldly to the throne of grace, that we may obtain mercy, and find grace to help in time of need. (Heb. 4: 16).

The Lord our God be with us, as He was with our fathers: let Him not leave us, nor forsake us: that He may incline our hearts unto Him, to walk in all His ways, and to keep His commandments, and His statutes, and His judgments, which He commanded our fathers. (I Kings 8: 57, 58).

59.

CONCERNING THE REGULATION OF FAMILY WORSHIP.

A.

In General.

This order may be patterned after the example of the daily matin and vesper services of the Church, or after other acceptable rubrics. In the former case the separate parts follow in regular sequence as here indicated:

I. For Morning or Matin Services.

1. The Hymn. (A morning hymn.)
2. The Psalmody. (One or more Psalms).
3. The Scripture Lesson.
4. The Prayer. Which shall embrace the Lord's Prayer, a morning prayer, and a prayerful benediction.

II. For Evening or Vesper Services.

1. The Psalmody.
2. The Lesson.
3. The Hymn. (An evening hymn.)
4. The Prayer. Embracing the Lord's Prayer, an evening prayer, and a prayerful benediction.

In case another than the churchly rubric is desired, a rubric may be established somewhat after the following manner:

I. For the Morning Service.

1. Begin with a morning hymn, or several stanzas thereof.
2. Then, one of the morning prayers indicated for the day. On festival days let it be the festival prayer.
3. Follow this by repeating the Lord's Prayer in unison; and, on Sundays at least add the Apostle's Creed.
4. A Psalm should be read, followed by the Gloria Patri.
5. A hymn, or, at least, some stanzas of a hymn.

6. A prayer for blessing:—The Lord bless
us and keep us, etc.

After the morning prayer it would be very
proper for the entire household to repeat the *Amen,*
and add another of the prayers indicated for the
day; and, following this second prayer, the Lord's
Prayer and the Creed.

II. For the Evening Service.

1. An evening hymn, or, several stanzas
thereof.

2. A prayer, as indicated in the prayers
for that day.

3. The Lord's Prayer: adding also the
Creed, at pleasure.

4. One of the Evening Psalms, with the
Gloria Patri.   (See page 82.)

5. A hymn or several stanzas thereof.   It
may be from the opening hymn or from
another.

6. A prayer for blessing.

In the evening service the Psalm may be read
responsively, immediately after the opening hymn;
and the evening prayer with the Lord's Prayer and
the Creed be offered just before the last hymn.

As in the morning service, one loves to set the
prayer most prominently at the beginning, so, at the

evening service it may seem best to have it near
the close. If it be not desirable to set apart a
special hour for Bible reading, but to unite this
with the morning and evening services, the Scripture
lesson may take the place of the Psalm, or follow
immediately after it. Where but few minutes can
be devoted to the morning service, then retain the
prayer, the Lord's Prayer, and the Creed as most
necessary. The Psalm and one or both hymns may
be omitted.

B.

· In Particular.

1. THE HYMN.

The following list of hymns is submitted, not
that one be confined thereto, but as a guide. The
last indicated hymn in the list of week-days is desirable as a closing hymn for the evening service,
while the others indicated will serve· better for the
beginning of such service. — The numbers given
refer to the Church Book.

FOR SUNDAY.

1. O Holy Spirit, enter in.   No. 249.
2. O Light, O Trinity most Blest!   No.
642.*

3. All Glory be to God on high. **No. 9.**
4. A mighty Fortress is our God. No. 274.
5. How shall we show our **Love to Thee?** No. 478.*

FOR MONDAY.

1. Now that the sun is beaming bright. No. 512.
2. My God, I leave to Thee my ways. No. 431.
3. Awake my soul. No. 510.*
4. My Jesus, as Thou wilt! No. 421.
5. Sunk is the sun's last beam of light. No. 521.·

FOR TUESDAY.

1. Lord, for the mercies of the night. No. 514.
2. My Hope, my All, my Savior Thou! No. 437.*
3. Who puts his trust in God most just. No. 422.
4. O Jesus, Lord of heavenly grace. No. 21.*
5. The day is past and over. No. 520.*

FOR WEDNESDAY.

1. Songs of immortal praise belong. No. 70.
2. Thy way, not mine, O Lord. No. 645.*
3. Abide with us, our Saviour. No. 59.
4. Now thank we all our God. No. 11.
5. Hail! holy, holy, holy Lord. No. 259.

FOR THURSDAY.

1. Commit thou all thy griefs. No. 433.
2. God of my life, to Thee I call! No. 480.
3. Author of good! To Thee we turn. No. 414.*
4. Thine forever! God of love. No. 326.
5. All praise to Thee, my God, this night. No. 522.

FOR FRIDAY.

1. All praise, Lord Jesus Christ, to Thee. No. 597.
2. Jesus, Refuge of the weary. No. 161.*

3. Lord Jesus, Who, our souls to save. No. 188.*

4. When sorrow and remorse. No. 488.

5. O that I had an angel's tongue. No. 103.*

FOR SATURDAY.

1. When, streaming from the eastern skies. No. 507.*

2. O Thou Who all things canst control. No. 398.*

3. When my last hour is close at hand. No. 547.

4. Lord Jesus Christ, true Man and God. No. 549.

5. The day, O Lord, is spent. No. 516.

FOR THE ADVENT SEASON.

1. Once He came in blessing. No. 121.

2. Hail to the Lord's Anointed. No. 122.

3. O how shall I receive Thee. No. 114.

4. Come, Thou Savior of our race. No. 118.

FOR THE CHRISTMAS SEASON.

1. Hark! the herald-angels sing. No. 128.*

2. Rejoice, rejoice, ye Christians. No. 132.

3. All praise, Lord Jesus Christ, to Thee. No. 597.

4. Emmanuel! we sing Thy praise. No. 133.

FOR THE PASSION SEASON.

Sunday: Awake, my soul! stretch every nerve. No. 458.*

Friday: Lamb of God, Who once was slain. No. 339.

For the other week days the hymns recommended for the day of the week may be used; not omitting the hymn: "Now to the Lamb that once was slain." No. 165.

FOR THE EASTER SEASON.

1. Christ the Lord is risen again. No. 612.

2. Jesus Christ, my sure defence. No. 195.

FOR ASCENSION DAY.

1. A hymn of glory let us sing. No. 201.*

FOR WHITSUNTIDE.

1. Come, Holy Spirit, God and Lord. No. 248.

2. O Holy Spirit, enter in. No. 249.

---

* The translator has permitted himself the liberty to note the hymns suggested in the original and translated in the Church Book, by reference to the numbers of such hymns in the Church Book of the General Council; and, where the particular hymn indicated by the author was not found translated, he substituted from the Church Book related hymns, and marked these with an *.

2. THE PSALMS.

At morning prayer the Psalms are to be read in sequence. The Evening Psalms are here indicated:

SUNDAY.

Ps. 110, 111, 112, 113, 114, 115.

MONDAY.

Ps. 116, 117, 120, 121.

TUESDAY.

Ps. 122, 123, 124, 125, 126.

WEDNESDAY.

Ps. 127, 128, 129, 130, 131.

THURSDAY.

Ps. 132, 133, 135, 136, 137.

FRIDAY.

Ps. 138, 139, 140, 141, 142.

SATURDAY.

Ps. 144, 145, 146, 147.

For the morning one may select a particular series of Psalms, even as one need not at evening prayer restrict himself to the old order of the Evening Psalms. (See list of Psalms for the weekday morning and evening prayers.)

We append here a free selection of Psalms for each day, one for morning and the other for evening prayer.

FOR SUNDAY.

Read the Gospel and Epistle Lessons for the day, (Pericopes), instead of the Psalms.

FOR MONDAY.

Ps. 91 and 127; 63:1—8; and 108, 121, and 119:1—16; 33:1—12; 33:13 ff.

FOR TUESDAY.

Ps. 92 and 119:33—48; 139, and 145:1—12; 62 and 67; 30 and 40.

FOR WEDNESDAY.

Ps. 47 and 98; 31:1—8, and 119:73—80; 103:1—12 and 119:105—112; 19 and 119:137—144.

FOR THURSDAY.

Ps. 34:1—10 and 119:169—176; 146 and 42; 86:1—13 and 20; 27 and 46.

FOR FRIDAY.

Ps. 6 and 13; 51:1—11 and 116; 51:12 ff. and 31:1—8; 116 and 130.

FOR SATURDAY.

Ps. 90 and 107:1—9; 49 and 73:24 ff.; 84 and 17; 107:1—9 and 126.

For the Festival Days, from Advent to Whit-suntide, excepting during the season of Lent, the following order of a two weeks' selection may be followed:

I.

SUNDAY.
The Pericopes. (Gospel and Epistle Lesson.)

MONDAY.
Ps. 119 and 45:13 ff.; 20 and 24.

TUESDAY.
Ps. 37:1—11 and 111; 118:14 ff. and 113.

WEDNESDAY.
Ps. 147 and 99; 29 and 8.

THURSDAY.
Ps. 97 and 103:13 ff.; 30 and 40.

FRIDAY.
Ps. 32 and 102:12 ff.; 107:1—9 and 62.

SATURDAY.
Ps. 84 and 36; 64:5 ff. and 111.

During the Passion Season the following may be used:

II.

SUNDAY.
The Pericopes. (Gospel and Epistle Lesson.)

MONDAY.

Ps. 34:12 ff. and 49; 23 and 63.

TUESDAY.

Ps. 31:1—8 and 37:34 ff.; 113 and 61.

WEDNESDAY.

Ps. 66 and 57; 25 and 107:1—9.

THURSDAY.

Ps. 5 and 32; 85 and 43.

FRIDAY.

Ps. 143 and 51:1—11; 51:12 ff. and 130.

SATURDAY.

Ps. 13 and 39; 126 and 16.

For the Festival Days, the following order, as it was observed in the ancient church, may be used:

FOR ADVENT.

Ps. 19, 25, 80, 85.

FOR CHRISTMAS.

Ps. 2, 19, 45, 48, 72, 85, 88, 96, 98, 109, 110, 111, 129, 131.

FOR THE FESTIVAL OF THE CIRCUMCI-
SION. (New Year.)

Ps. 2, 19, 24, 45, 87, 96, 97, 98, 99.

FOR EPIPHANY.

Ps. 29, 46, 47, 66, 72, 86, 87, 96, 97.

FOR HOLY THURSDAY.

Ps. 69, 70, 71, 72, 73, 74, 75, 76, 77.—51, 90, 63, 67, 148, 149, 150, Exodus 15, Ps. 116, 10 ff., 120, 140, 141, 142.

FOR GOOD FRIDAY.

Ps. 2, 22, 27, 38, 40, 54, 59, 88, 94.—51, 143, 63, 67, 148, 149, 150, and Habak. 3.

FOR THE GREAT SABBATH.

Ps. 4, 15, 16, 24, 27, 30, 54, 76, 88.—51, 43, 63, 67, 148, 149, 150, and Isa. 38, Ps. 117.

FOR EASTER.

Ps. 1, 2, 3,—8,—16,—139.—Te Deum.

FOR ASCENSION DAY.

Ps. 8, 11, 19, 21, 30, 47, 97, 99, 103.

FOR WHITSUNDAY.

Ps. 48, 68, 104. Te Deum.

FOR TRINITY SUNDAY.

Ps. 8, 19, 24, 47, 48, 72, 96, 97, 98.

3. SCRIPTURE LESSONS.

For daily Scripture lessons one may follow many orders according to the object in view, the purpose, or the pleasure of the reader; but, one may well order his lessons from the Old and the New Testaments according to the following ancient order of the Church:

a) From December 1st to Christmas, the lessons are from the prophecy of Isaiah.
b) From Christmas to Septuagesima: from the Epistles of St. Paul.
c) From Septuagesima to the fifteenth day preceding Easter: from the Heptateuch i. e. from the Seven Books:—Gen., Ex., Num., Deut., Josh., and the Judges, (also the Book of Ruth).
d) From the fifteenth day before until Easter: from the prophecy and Lamentations of Jeremiah.

During the Holy Week the Passion History according to the four Evangelists is read. (See Church Book, pp. 321—344. Trans.)

e) From Easter to Whitsunday, choose lessons from the Acts of the Apostles, the so-called catholic epistles, and the Book of Revelation.

f) From Trinity Sunday to August: from 1st and 2nd Samuel, 1st and 2nd Kings, and 1st and 2nd Chronicles.

g) From August 1st to September 1st: from the Book of Proverbs, Ecclesiastes, and the Song of Solomon. (To which may be added the Book of Wisdom and Sirach from the Apocrypha).

h) From September 1st to October 1st: from the Book of Job, Esther, and Ezra, (to which may be added the Books of Tobias and of Judith from the Apocrypha).

i) From October 1st to November: from the Maccabees.

j) From November 1st to December: from the prophecies of Ezekiel, Daniel, and the twelve minor prophets.

This order of Scripture Lessons conforms most closely with the church-year. It furnishes food for thought and presents texts for short discourses. It leaves latitude to free choice and yet points out a beautiful and established order. Besides these one has the regular Gospel and Epistle Lessons for his Sunday devotions as well as for the festival days.

1.

THE LORD'S DAY.

I have hated the congregation of evil-doers; and will not sit with the wicked.

I will wash mine hands in innocency: so will I compass Thine altar, O Lord: that I may publish with the voice of thanksgiving, and tell of all Thy wondrous works.

Lord, I have loved the habitation of Thy house, and the place where Thy honor dwelleth. (Ps. 26: 5—8).

A day in Thy courts is better than a thousand. I had rather be a doorkeeper in the house of my God, than to dwell in the tents of wickedness. For the Lord God is a sun and shield: and the Lord will give grace and glory: no good thing will He withold from them that walk uprightly. (Ps. 84: 10, 11).

The sum of all true Christian doctrine concerning our
eternal salvation and glory is:

God grants.
Christ merits.
Faith apprehends.
Works do testify it.
The Sacraments seal it.
Believers have it,
Here, through hope, temporally;
But there, in possession, eternally.
Therefore, here, be patient,
In faith firm, consistent,
And thou shalt live, blessed forever.

60.

The Song of Zacharia. Benedictus.

Blessed be the Lord God of Israel:
  For He hath visited and redeemed
  His people,
And hath raised up an horn of salvation for us:
  In the house of His servant David;
As He spake by the mouth of His
holy prophets:
  Which have been since the world
  began;
That we should be saved from our
enemies:
  And from the hand of all that hate
  us;
To perform the mercy promised to
our fathers:
  And to remember His holy covenant;

The oath which He sware to our father Abraham:

That He would grant unto us,
That we, being delivered out of the hand of our enemies:

Might serve Him without fear,
In holiness and righteousness before Him:

All the days of our life.
And thou, child, shalt be called the prophet of the Highest:

For thou shalt go before the face of the Lord to prepare His ways;
To give knowledge of salvation unto His people:

By the remission of their sins,
Through the tender mercy of our God:

Whereby the dayspring from on high hath visited us,

To **give** light to them that sit in darkness and in the shadow of death:
    To guide our feet into the way of peace.
Glory be to the Father and to the Son:
    And to the Holy Ghost;
As it was in the beginning, is now, and ever shall be:
    World without end.   Amen.

61.

The Ambrosian Hymn of Praise.*)

Lord God, our praise to Thee!
    Lord God, our thanks we bring
To Thee, Eternal Father; Thou
    Art praised in all the wide, wide world.

---

* No metrical translation can do justice to this noble hymn. Trans.)

All angels and the hosts above,
  And all that else before Thee bow;
Yea, cherubim and seraphim
  Raise ever high the holy hymn:—

    Holy, holy is our God!
    Holy, holy is the Lord!
    Holy, holy is our God!
    The Lord, our God of Sabaoth!

Thy might divine and glory shine
  Far o'er the earth and heavens
  Thine.
The sacred, called apostles twelve
  And prophets all,—now dead so
  long—
The martyr host, all join the song
  Of praise to Thy most glorious
  Self.
Adoring comes the Christian band;
  They praise Thy Name on every
  hand,—

Thou, Father on the highest throne!
  Thou, only true, eternal Son!—
And loves to laud and serve with fear
  The Holy Ghost, with comfort near.
O King of Glory, Jesus Christ,
  The Father's own, eternal Son,
Thou spurnest not the virgin's womb;
  Nor from mankind to avert its
  doom.
Of death Thou rob'st his power and
might,
  And lead'st Thy Christians home
  to light:
Co-equal with the Father reign'st
  At His right hand, from whence
  Thou camest,—
And comest again to judge at last,
  The dead and living of the past.
O help us, Lord, Thy servants blest
  Whom with Thy blood Thou pur-
  chasest.

Make us in heaven to have our part
  With all the saints, by Thy blest
  heart.
Help all Thy people, Christ, our
Lord,
  And bless Thine heritage abroad.
Defend, preserve us everywhere
  Until Thy peace in heaven we
  share.
Lord God, we praise Thee daily here;
  And serve Thy name with holy
  fear.
Defend us now, most precious God,
  Against all sin and evil thought.
Have mercy on us, in our need,
  Thy mercy-hand reveal indeed:—
E'en as our trust on Thee is stayed,
  Our confidence is undismayed:—
Thou wilt not let us come to shame—
  We trust; we rest in Thy dear
  Name! Amen.
(Martin Luther,—after the Te Deum Laudamus.)

62.

Sunday Morning Prayer.

BEHOLD, He that keepeth Israel shall neither slumber nor sleep. The Lord preserve me from all evil: the Lord preserve my soul. The Lord preserve my going out and coming in forevermore. The Lord bless me and keep me: the Lord make His face to shine upon me and be gracious unto me: the Lord lift up His countenance upon me and grant me peace. Amen.

O, ever blessed Trinity, unto Thy grace I commend my all this day,— this Sunday,—my body and soul, my walks and ways, and all my deeds and undertakings; and beseech Thee to open my heart and my lips rightly to praise Thy name,—holy above every other name. Since Thou hast created me unto the glory of Thy holy name, let me so live that I may honor and serve Thee in love and fear. Amen.

63.

ETERNAL, Omnipotent God and Father, I give Thee hearty thanks that throughout the night now past, as throughout all my days, Thou hast, through Thy holy angels, so graciously preserved me from all evil to body and soul; and hast caused me to live on in health and peace to see this blessed sabbath day, in which not only Thou didst create the light, but didst raise up my Savior for my righteousness sake. I beseech Thee, most heartily, pardon all my sins by which I have merited Thy wrath, and kindle my heart with Thy Holy Spirit so that

I may daily increase before Thee in knowledge and in grace. Vouchsafe unto me Thy grace, that throughout this happy day I may fall into no sin or shame; but keep the day reverently, according to Thy will; and so to walk, that I, together with the loved ones whom Thou hast given me, may be defended from every evil of body and soul, ever remembering Thee in heart and mind. When at last my hour shall come, that I must depart hence, grant me to fall asleep blessed in the true knowledge of Thy Son unto eternal life. Amen.

(J. Gottfried Olearius' Handbook, 1669.)

64.

UNTO Thee, O Gracious Father, I render thanks for Thy paternal and gracious preservation and defence during the night now past,

and for Thy mercy which permits
me to see this day, when I shall again
receive Thine eternal gifts. O Holy
Father, cleanse my heart through
faith, and kindle it with a flame of
Thy love, that I may yield unto Thee
my body and my soul, an acceptable
sacrifice. Thou wilt perform in me
Thine holy will, that I may know Thy
beloved Son, so as to leave this world
and its pleasures behind me; to complete the day in Thy service; growing in holiness of life, strong in the
spirit; and, let Thy grace abide
with me. Amen.

Lord Jesus, open Thou mine ears
that I may hear Thee calling me
unto Thyself. Touch my heart and
mind that I may truly rejoice in
Thy grace and goodness unto me.
Incline my will that, as to a tower of
refuge, I may go into Thy temple,

reared unto the glory of Thy name and appointed as the place where Thy blessing and true unity with Thee is attained. O gentle Jesus, without Thee I may not rise; therefore, go Thou with me. Clothe, adorn, and sanctify me for Thine habitation. Amen.

Lord God, the Holy Ghost, by the enlightenment of my mind, open Thou to me the gates of everlasting life, and let me find the true pasture of Thy divine doctrine and comfort, that I may hear the voice of my great Shepherd Jesus, to come to Him in faith, obey and follow Him in love, and so to go unto all my fellow-men, proving my faith; to the end that I may abide in Thy kingdom of grace here unto the end, and finally be received in the kingdom of everlasting glory; through Jesus Christ our Lord. Amen.

65.

LORD Jesus Christ, eternal, true Light, Who banishest the darkness of the night and the shadow of death, I will praise Thy name and render thanks unto Thee for Thy protection during the past night and for bringing me unto the light of this day. Thou hast preserved my body, Thou hast surrounded my soul like a shield, and like a shepherd Thou hast defended me and all that is mine. For all this let Thy mighty and beneficent Name be magnified. I will sing aloud of Thy mercy in the morning: for Thou hast been my defence and my refuge, my help and my God in whom I put my trust. Thou gladdenest my heart and makest my countenance to rejoice. I beseech Thee, let Thy mercy arise and go forth this day like the morning light, and descend upon me like the spring rains. Enlighten my blinded nature—my dark heart— with Thy glory, and arise upon my soul, O Thou true Light that lightest man unto eternal life. Have mercy upon me, O God, for upon Thee do I wait. My soul waiteth for Thee more than they that watch for the morning. Be Thou my strong arm early and my salvation in the hour of tribulation. Shield my body and my soul that no evil come nigh unto me and no pestilence unto my habitation. Banish all evil spirits from me, sustain me against the godless, be nigh unto me against all evildoers, and save me that the hand of the enemy may not touch me. O Lord

God, establish Thou the works of our
hands upon us; yea, the work of our
hands establish Thou. Strengthen
our hands, defend our souls that we
sin not against Thee. All this, we
beseech Thee, grant us for the sake
of Thy mercy which abideth forever.

(Lord's Prayer, the Creed, Psalm 121, and the
Gloria Patri.)

66.

A Prayer of Thanksgiving for Creation.

ALMIGHTY God, Heavenly
Father, Who art neither created nor born, but hast existed from
the beginning and from all eternity,
I pray unto Thee, I worship Thee,
I praise Thee, and I give most
hearty thanks to Thee for all Thy
glorious works, especially that Thou
hast created heaven and earth, the

sun, moon, and every other creature
by Thine almighty and divine Word;
and, by Thy wisdom governest and
preservest all. O Lord, how lovely,
how glorious are all Thy works! All
continue and abide as Thou hast
made them; and all do Thy will in
whatsoever Thou hast need of them.
The rising sun proclaims the day, it
is a miracle of the Lord! He must
be a great God Who created the sun
and set its swift course! The twink-
ling stars illumine the night, they
retain their order by God's Word,
and they tire not. I thank Thee, O
God, that Thou hast created the
earth for man's sake, and hast made
it, together with all its creatures,
subject to man's pleasure by Thy
grace and mercy. But above all will
I praise Thee, my Maker and my
Lord, that Thou hast created me, a

creature endowed with intelligence, and after Thine own image; and that Thou hast given and still preservest unto me my body and soul and all my members; together with my mind and all my senses. Great and mighty is Thy goodness unto me whom Thou hast preserved and nourished in my mother's womb, and didst cause me to be born thence, neither blind, deaf, dumb, lame nor infirm. Who can tell all the mighty acts of the Lord, or who can sufficiently praise Him for all His beautiful works! Although I, a poor sinner, can not render unto Thee the praises Thy greatness and worthiness deserve, and which I justly owe unto Thee, I will not therefore keep silent, but will praise Thy holy name without ceasing. Long as I live will I be praising Thy righteousness, Thy grace, and Thy mercy; and so long as I have breath I will not forget all Thy benefits unto me. My tongue, which Thou hast created, shall be full of Thy praise, continually saying:—Praise God in His sanctuary; praise Him in the firmament of His power; praise Him for His mighty acts; praise Him according to His excellent greatness. Let everything that has breath praise the Lord. Hallelujah!

67.

Prayer for the Indwelling of Christ.

O LORD Jesus, Gentle Jesus, my only Salvation, my only Joy and my Glory, very God of very God, uphold Thy servant. I call upon Thee, with my whole heart, I cry unto Thee, come into my heart and my soul and make these an agreeable habitation, that Thou mayest dwell therein as in a holy temple, for it is meet that my pure and holy Lord shall have a holy and pure dwelling place. Therefore, O Lord, cleanse unto Thyself the vessel which Thou hast created. Cleanse me from all evil and fill me with Thy grace, that here, in time, and yonder, to all eternity, I may be a worthy temple wherein Thou canst delight to dwell. Amen.

68.

Prayer to the Holy Ghost for His Indwelling.

O HOLY Ghost, Comforter of the sorrowing, come to my heart with all the train of Thy gifts. Banish from me all darkness and impurity, and enlighten my soul with Thy bright beams. Kindle in me

Thy love, that I may henceforth no more cling unto transitory things. Teach me to do Thy will, for Thou art my God; and I am assured that where Thou dwellest Thou makest also a sanctuary, holy and acceptable unto God the Father and the Son. Come then, O gracious Comforter of my troubled soul: come Holy Spirit, Who healest every wound and every transgression, Who art the strength of the feeble, the life of the helpless, Who carest for the lowly and resistest the proud, Who art a father to the widow and the orphan, the hope of all them that are poor. Have mercy upon me and make me acceptable unto Thee for Thy habitation; through Jesus Christ my Savior. Amen.

69.

Concerning the Indiscretions of Reason and the Flesh in Divine Things.

LORD Jesus Christ, we realize not only from Thy Word, but our own experience in the world frequently in very deed teaches us, how the presumptive knowledge and selfish wisdom of our flesh, the puffed up exaltation of our human understanding, the discoveries of reason and its powers, are not satisfied to exercise their limited functions in that which is visible and created, but, behold, these presume even upon spiritual and heavenly things whose source and ruler Thou only, Lord Jesus Christ, art evermore. Reason aspires to be God's counsellor and to usurp the Holy Spirit in the councils of heaven. With exceeding pride it lauds its presumed knowledge. It counts its lies for truth, and its imaginings for knowledge. It counts its darkness for heavenly illumination, and, with it, life itself is death and destruction. After its own thought and imagination it judgeth all things, and refuseth all correction, witholding itself from all research of Thy divine and heavenly wisdom, rejecting all exhortation, judgment, instruction and every research. It glories in its wit and concedes naught but that in everything it alone must be right. To this it holds itself with all obstinacy and becomes the brood-mother of jealousy, contention, strife, great calamity and much misery. It sets up its court upon things that pass and perish, and lives thus in shameful security. It persuades

itself that it is prepared to
weather every storm, especially
when it has armored itself with
its own approved selection of proverbs and quotations from holy
Scriptures. Then it deems its
imaginings to be strong walls and a
sure defence. Then follows its trust
in a self-imagined heaven, and it
has none but only sweet (though
false and unstable) rest and an
amiable peace of conscience, life and
being. Whereupon follows the glory
of a self imagined faith, the semblance of a pious life with much out-
ward shimmer, a preaching of human
traditions and an unhealthy mixture
of doctrines. All heavenly and
spiritual things must comport themselves, therefore, to the pottery of
human reason, and men accept as
true what, in fact, is nothing but

very untruth, hypocrisy, foolishness,
injury and certain destruction, error
and deception, constantly opposed
to God, meriting nothing but God's
wrath and displeasure unto eternal
condemnation. Therefore, O Lord
Jesus Christ, Who hast redeemed us
poor creatures by the death of Thy
body of the flesh, we poor, miserable
and misguided souls, pray Thee to
grant us divine wisdom instead. We
bring unto Thee this natural man of
flesh with his many shortcomings
and weaknesses, together with all
that foolish indiscretion of thought
and self-elected, unwise wisdom, and
do humbly beseech Thee, by Thy
Holy Spirit, to convince us that our
flesh is nothing, but as the grass of
the field which withereth, and has no
power over things divine.

Renew, O Lord, this body of

sin, and, by Thy grace, change the old man in us. Sprinkle our unworthy flesh with Thy precious blood that we be wholly clean. Season us with the salt of Thy divine wisdom. By Thy bright beams kindle and enlighten us unto a true, vital understanding of heavenly things, so that, by Thy Holy Spirit, under Thy guidance, we may strive after heavenly truth to show us the way to walk in the spirit. O lead us away from this indiscreet prying tendency of our reason. Let us not rest in our own vain imaginations, but by Thy divine light make us to grow strong. Let us not always err, but train our footsteps in the paths of Thy truth. Make us to abide therein, though our own flesh and all the world account us for unwise and foolish in so doing. Make us to render all glory to Thy wisdom alone, that we confess our foolishness before Thee, be ashamed thereof, and in all divine things flee our own imaginings. Turn all our weakness and nothingness into divine strength, our helplessness into divine power, and our body into a habitation of Thy Spirit. Grant, therefore, that we put off the old man of sin and begin now to bear Thine image, as new men conceived after the mind of God, to follow Thee in all humility, and constantly to grow in Thy similitude; so that, in the day when Thou comest again, we may be found blameless and without blemish in body and soul, unto the glory of God, Thy Father, with whom Thou livest and reignest, in unity with the Holy Ghost, world without end. Amen.

70.

For Singleness of Mind and Understanding in Divine Things.

ETERNAL, Merciful God, Thou art a God of peace and of love and unity, and not a God of divisions and schisms with which, in Thy righteous judgment, Thou now afflictest this world because it has departed from Thee, Who alone canst re-establish unity, and has followed after its own wisdom. Thou hast permitted it to be divided and scattered, especially in those things which pertain to Thy divine truth and the salvation of human souls, that it may come to shame in its assumed wisdom and turn it again unto Thee, Thou eternal Friend of Unity. We poor sinners, to whom Thou hast mercifully granted to realize these things, beseech Thee and invoke Thee, by Thy Holy Spirit, to gather again all that is now scattered, to unite and make whole all that is now divided. Grant also that we may return into unity with Thee, to seek Thine eternal truth and turn away from all schisms, so that all may be of the one heart and mind, will, knowledge, thought and understanding which is patterned after Jesus Christ our Lord, and may with one heart and voice praise and glorify Thee, heavenly Father of our Lord Jesus Christ, through the same, our Lord Jesus Christ, in the Holy Ghost. Amen.

71.
Prayer Before Going to Church.

ALMIGHTY God, Heavenly Father, by Thy great goodness I am about to go into Thy house, and in Thy fear to pray towards Thy holy temple. Lord, lead me by Thy righteousness. Prepare Thou Thy way before me. Lead me in the paths of Thy commandments, for Thou art my God and the Lord of my salvation. I desire Thy habitation and am glad in the congregation of the saints who praise and confess Thee. How amiable are Thy tabernacles, O Lord of hosts! My soul longeth, yea, even fainteth for the courts of the Lord. O come, let us worship and bow down: let us kneel before the Lord our Maker, for He is our God, and we are the people of the pasture, and the sheep of His hand. O magnify the Lord, our God. Worship at His footstool, for He is holy. I call upon Thee in an acceptable time. By Thy great mercy, O God, hear me, and grant me Thy true help. Amen.

72.

Prayer Upon Entering the Church.

O COME let us sing unto the Lord, let us make a joyful noise unto the Rock of our Salvation. Let us come before His presence with thanksgiving, and make a joyful noise unto Him with psalms. O come let us worship and bow down: let us kneel before the Lord our Maker, for He is our God; and we are the people of His pasture and the sheep of His hand. Today, if we hear His voice, let us not harden our hearts. How amiable are Thy tabernacles, O Lord of hosts! My soul longeth, yea, even fainteth for the courts of the Lord. My heart and my flesh crieth out for the living God. Yea, the sparrow hath found an house, and the swallow a nest for herself,

even Thine altars, O Lord of hosts,
my King and my God. Blessed are
they that dwell in Thine house, they
will praise Thee forever more. Sela.

(George Zeaman's Vademecum. 1634.)

73.

Prayer for Fruit of the Lips that Confess the Name of the Lord.

A LMIGHTY, merciful God and
Father of our Lord Jesus
Christ, Who hast earnestly commanded us to pray for laborers in
Thy vineyard, that is, for upright
preachers of Thy Word, we beseech
Thine unsearchable mercy to send us
faithful preachers and servants of
Thy divine Word, and, to give unto
them Thy saving Word in their
hearts and upon their lips, that they
many faithfully fulfill Thy command-

ment and preach nothing contrary to Thine holy Word; that we may ever be exhorted, instructed, fed, comforted and strengthened by the same, and do whatsoever is acceptable to Thee and profitable for ourselves.

Grant unto Thy congregation, Lord, Thy spirit and divine wisdom, that Thy Word may have free course and increase among us, being preached with all joy as it should be, and that Thy holy congregation may be made better thereby, so that we serve Thee in constant faith and abide steadfast in the confession of Thy name unto the end; through our Lord Jesus Christ, Thy Son, Who liveth and reigneth with Thee, and the Holy Ghost, one true God, world without end. Amen.

74.

Further Worship at the Beginning of the Services in Church.

a) Thanksgiving.

LORD, Triune God, the place wherein I stand is holy. This is none other than the house of God, and the gateway of heaven. But Thou, Father, Son, and Holy Ghost, art the great invisible God Who here revealest Thyself, and we praise and worship Thy name. How amiable are Thy tabernacles, O Lord of hosts! My soul longeth, yea, even fainteth for the courts of the Lord, and my heart rejoiceth to hear Thy Word. Therefore, thanks be unto Thy great goodness and mercy that in this place also Thou hast gathered Thy church, hast caused this house to be built among us unto Thy name, and grantest rest and peace to them that dwell in this congregation, that they may behold the beautiful services of Thy house, and visit in Thy temple. Lord, Thou hast received me also into the fellowship of the saints. I owe it all to Thy goodness that I am a member of the household of God, and to Thy mercy that I this day have leisure and opportunity to come into the house of the Lord, my God.

Now, Lord, my God, behold me as I come before Thy face with thanksgiving. I laud Thy holy name in the place where Thy honor dwelleth, and am come to hear what Thou sayest to me in Thy Word, to present to Thee my prayer for my needs, and to publish Thy praises in the congregation. Praise the Lord in His holiness! His praise shall be on my lips evermore.

b) Petition.

L ORD, Thou provest man's heart
and bowels. Of myself I am
totally unapt for all that is good,
untractable in Thy Word, disinclined
to Thy service, and continually
tempted by strange conceits which
disturb my devotions. Therefore,
dear Father, make me free, here in
Thine house, from all fleshly
thoughts and worldly cares. Keep
me from unnecessary distractions
and gaping about, from useless
tattle and every such unbecoming
attitude, which is not meet for this
holy place. Banish from me all
sleepiness and inattention, lack of
devotion and indifference, unbelief
and resistance to Thy Word, and
whatever else may hinder me in the
exercise of my devotions. Help that
I give no offence in this assembly,

that I may be attentive to what is needful for me to hear, and that I do not abuse that which I do hear, nor count worthless what does not please my senses. Let me not play at speculation upon Thy mysteries, nor doubt and become unbelieving at anything, which my understanding can not comprehend. Guard me against all loathing and weariness of Thy Word, that I may not become an impatient hearer, nor the time spent in Thy house hang heavy upon me. When the service is over and I depart hence, grant that I go not profitless and unhelped down to my house.

c) Prayer.

O GOD, my Redeemer, Thou hast commanded not to despise Thine assemblies. Behold me here

in Thy house and in Thy congregation. Help that I may be reverent
in Thy sight as in the presence of
God and all holy angels. Here, in
Thy church, make my heart to be
Thy temple; increase in me the gifts
of Thine Holy Spirit; send down
Thy wisdom from above and prepare
me to serve Thy name in true fear
and devotion. Though I hear but a
human being preach, even as I am
human, yet do Thou so rule and
govern my mind that I may regard
him as the servant of Christ, and
hear him as a messenger in God's
stead, for by him Thou instructest
me. Therefore, make me to have
desire to the word which falls from
his lips, and though all that he says
may not please me, let me be mindful of other hearers beside me, who
may find which I least regard, as

most necessary and beneficial · to
themselves. Meanwhile do Thou
Thyself speak within my soul when
he speaks to my ears. Cause my
heart to burn within me like the
hearts of the two disciples on their
way to Emmaus. Open my heart as
Thou once didst open the heart of
Lydia, the seller of purple, that I
may give heed to what is said unto
me. Grant me such measure of
grace that I may rightly judge · and
divide all that Thy servant says: the
words of the text which he explains,
the doctrine which he draws therefrom, the truth which he thereby
shows forth, the errors which he
therewith opposes, my own self-examination which he may provoke
therein, the sins which he con-
demns, the good which he com-
mends, the instruction unto godli-

ness which he gives, and the comfort which we may receive against every care of this miserable life. Grant, O God, that I may hear all this with diligence, receive it with joy, understand it rightly, consider it carefully, know Thy will therefrom, feel the power of Thy Word within me, and so, become ever more perfect and ready unto all good works. Finally, let Thy house be unto me a house of prayer. Open Thou my lips, and my mouth shall show forth Thy praise; and govern me by Thy Holy Spirit that I may always have desire to join with the congregation to sing and pray, and, in my prayer, not to omit others who for their misery's sake desire to be remembered in our prayers. Hear, therefore, what I pray; for Thy Name's sake. Amen.

d) Intercession.

O GREAT and mighty God, let Thine eyes be open this day upon this house and this people who are called by Thy name. Fill us all with holy contemplations, sincere devotion, and brotherly love, that all things be done decently and in order, none giving offence to another, but all in unity to sing and pray and the hearts of many, yea, of all, be enlightened by that which shall here be preached unto us, and be won and converted unto Thee. Lo, Lord, we are here assembled before Thee and before Thy servant to hear all that Thou hast commanded him. I know Thou art the Lord also of the office of preaching, for Thou hast instituted and established it. It is not Thy servants that speak, but the Spirit of the Father speaketh by

them. At Thy command they keep
watch over our souls and must render account of their stewardship of
the same. Whosoever heareth them,
heareth Thee, and whosoever despiseth them, despiseth Thee. Now,
therefore, Lord, since it pleaseth
Thee to save us by the preaching of
the Word, bless unto us in this hour
what Thou hast Thyself ordained.
Grant such strength unto Thy servant that he may joyfully speak Thy
Word when he openeth his lips, and
so govern his tongue unto the truth
of Thy word and the needs of all
them that are gathered here, that he
may present naught than what may
serve unto the strengthening of their
faith, the improvement of their lives,
and the certain advancement of their
souls' salvation. When he so exer-
cises the office according to the gifts

which God has proffered, rule Thou
and govern the ears of all of us who
hear him, that we may be satisfied
with the gift which Thou hast granted unto him, and receive what he
says, not as the word of man, but for
what it really is,—the Word of God.
Let not this assembly be like unto
an uncultivated field, lest the power
of Thy word be lost to any. Wherefore, give unto all who are present
attentive ears, enlightened minds,
and obedient hearts, that all may
know Thee Who alone art true God,
and Him, Whom thou hast sent,—
Jesus Christ, and be abundantly
profited in all their walks, and
finally, all meet together again in
the church triumphant, in eternal
life; through Jesus Christ, Thy dear
Son, our Lord. Amen.

75.
The Kyrie. Et in Terra.*
(To be prayed at the opening of the service, by minister and people.)

Kyrie — Eleison.
Christe — Eleison.
Kyrie — Eleison.

GLORY be to God on high, and on earth peace, good will toward men. We praise Thee, we bless Thee, we worship Thee, we glorify Thee, we give thanks to Thee for Thy great glory, O Lord God, heavenly King, God the Father Almighty.

O Lord, the Only-begotten Son, Jesus Christ; O Lord God, Lamb of God, Son of the Father, that takest away the sin of the world, have mercy upon us. Thou that takest away the sin of the world, receive

---

* Et in Terra = "and on earth" (peace).

our prayer. Thou that sittest at the right hand of God the Father, have mercy upon us.

For Thou only art holy; Thou only art the Lord; Thou only, O Christ, with the Holy Ghost, art most high in the glory of God the Father. Amen.

76.

The Credo, or Confession of Faith.

(As it was confessed by the fathers in the Councils of Nice and Constantinople, [325 and 381, A. D.].)

(This is to be sung or said by the minister and congregation, after the reading of the gospel.)

I BELIEVE in one God, the Father Almighty, Maker of heaven and earth, And of all things visible and invisible.

And in one Lord Jesus Christ, the Only-begotten Son of God, begotten of His Father before all worlds, God of God, Light of Light,

Very God of very God, Begotten, not made, Being of one substance with the Father, by Whom all things are made; Who for us men, and for our salvation, came down from heaven, and was incarnate by the Holy Ghost of the Virgin Mary, and was made man; And was crucified also for us under Pontius Pilate. He suffered and was buried; And the third day He rose again, according to the Scriptures; And ascended into heaven, And sitteth on the right hand of the Father; And He shall come again with glory to judge both the quick and the dead; Whose kingdom shall have no end.

And I believe in the Holy Ghost, the Lord and Giver of Life, Who proceedeth from the Father and the Son, Who, with the Father and the Son together is worshipped and glorified, Who spake by the Prophets.

And I believe one holy Christian and Apostolic church. I acknowledge one Baptism for the remission of sins; And I look for the Resurrection of the dead; And the Life of the world to come. Amen.

77.

Silent Prayer Before the Sermon.

COME Holy Spirit, fill the hearts of Thy believers and kindle in them the flame of Thy divine love, Who hast through manifold tongues gathered all the nations of the earth into the unity of the faith. Hallelujah! Hallelujah!

78.

Since the American Church has provided practically the same form of public Confession and Absolution as was laid down by Loehe under No. 78, the translation of Loehe's No. 78 in the original has been omitted, and the reader is referred to the Church Book, page 372.

79.

The General Prayer.

ALMIGHTY and most merciful God, the Father of our Lord Jesus Christ: We thank Thee for all Thy goodness and tender mercies, especially for the gift of Thy dear Son, and for the revelation of Thy will and grace, and we beseech Thee so to implant Thy Word in us, that, in good and honest hearts, we may keep it, and bring forth fruit by patient continuance in well doing.

Most heartily we beseech Thee so to rule and govern Thy Church universal, with all its pastors and ministers, that it may be preserved in the pure doctrine of Thy saving Word, whereby faith toward Thee may be strengthened, and charity increased in us toward all mankind.

Grant also health and prosperity to all in authority, especially to the President (and Congress) of the United States, the Governor (and Legislature) of this Commonwealth, and to all our Judges and Magistrates; and endue them with grace to rule after Thy good pleasure, to the maintenance of righteousness, and to the hinderance and punishment of wickedness, that we may lead a quiet and peaceable life, in all godliness and honesty.

May it please Thee also to turn the hearts of our enemies and adversaries, that they may cease their enmity, and be inclined to walk with us in meekness and in peace.

All who are in trouble, want, sickness, anguish of labor, peril of death, or any other adversity, especially those who are in suffering for Thy name and for Thy truth's sake, comfort, O God, with Thy Holy Spirit, that they may receive and acknowledge their afflictions as the manifestation of Thy fatherly will.

And although we have deserved Thy righteous wrath and manifold punishments, yet, we entreat Thee, O most merciful Father, remember not the sins of our youth, nor our many transgressions; but out of Thine unspeakable goodness, grace, and mercy, defend us from all harm and danger of body and soul. Preserve us from false and pernicious doctrine, from war and bloodshed, from plague and pestilence, from all calamity by fire and water, from hail and tempest, from failure of harvest and from famine, from anguish of heart and despair of Thy mercy, and from an evil death. And in every time of trouble, show Thyself a very present Help, the Savior of all men, and especially of them that believe.

Cause also the needful fruits of the earth to prosper, that we may enjoy them in due season. Give success to the Christian training of the young, to all lawful occupations on land and sea, and to all pure arts and useful knowledge: and crown them with Thy blessing.

These, and whatsoever other things Thou wouldst have us ask of Thee, O God, vouchsafe unto us for the sake of the bitter sufferings and death of Jesus Christ, Thine only Son, our Lord and Savior, Who liveth and reigneth with Thee and the Holy Ghost, ever one God, world without end. Amen.

80.

After the Sermon and the General Prayer.

a) Thanksgiving.

PRAISE be unto Thee, Heavenly Father, for the proclamation of Thy holy word which we have just heard, and for all the good we have before known but are again put in remembrance of therein. Lord, we acknowledge Thy truth. We submit ourselves under Thy commandments. We believe Thy promises. We fear Thy wrath. We feel wherein Thy word has become personal unto us. We desire to amend our lives wherever necessary. We will follow as Thou teachest us. We will go forth with Thy comfort and serve Thee according to Thy word so long as we live.

b) Petition.

DEAR God, we have again heard what is good and what Thou desirest of us. If we have not heard so devoutly as we ought, nor remembered so much as we might have embraced, pardon, dear Father, all inattention that has overtaken us, each strange thought that has come into our minds, every idle word that we spake, and all other negligence and weariness which has overmastered or caused any indifference within us. Let not Satan rob our hearts of the word which we have heard. Let not the cares of this life stifle its power, nor let that which we have heard unto our salvation become unto us, in any manner, a word of condemnation.

c) Prayer.

LORD Jesus, Thou hast said: Blessed are they who hear the Word of God to keep it. As Thou hast now granted us to hear, so grant us also to keep it; and help that in pure and honest hearts we may retain all we have heard and bring forth fruit with patience.

Grant that we may ourselves consider it diligently, repeat it at home, and speak of it in our families; that we may govern our whole lives in accordance with it, and, finally, in the last hour, die in peace by that word.

d) Intercession.

DEAR Father, Thou hast now instructed Thy children in doctrine and in the truth that they may

always know what is right. Grant
unto all both to will and to do according to Thy good pleasure, that
all may walk worthy of Thy gospel
in all godliness and honesty.

Unto all who this day were hearers, but waited not unto the end,
or heard with indifferent ears, or
have mocked and despised what they
have heard, or yet have already forgotten, graciously vouchsafe Thy
pardon, and so rule and govern their
hearts by Thy Holy Spirit that
they may confess their fault and
come again, better knowing and
considering what serves their peace.

In our general prayer, we have
brought before Thee the needs of all
Christendom. May the same be
faithfully commended to Thee, and
watch Thou over the prosperity of
Thy church, the maintenance of all

in authority, and the needs of all men
in their several callings, that Thy
kingdom may everywhere increase,
our common well-being be promoted,
and home, living, and calling be
everywhere richly blessed unto all
men.

Have mercy especially upon the
sick and the afflicted, and upon all
manner of sufferers who have already been included in our church
prayer. And since Thou hast Thyself said: Where two shall agree on
earth as to anything they would ask,
it shall be done unto them of my
Father in heaven, therefore, hear
now their prayers and our own, and
grant unto everyone what may be
good and salutary, according to Thy
wisdom.

And, finally, fulfill what Thou
hast promised upon all who were

here assembled this day and love
Thee and keep Thy word. Let all
of us bear great comfort from Thy
house, and grant that all may at
last appear together in the congregation of Thy holy angels and the
elect, to serve Thee forevermore.
Amen.

81.

To be Sung Prior to the Beginning of the Service of Holy Communion.

Psalm 51: 10—12, 2.

CREATE in me a clean heart, O
God; and renew a right spirit
within me. Cast me not away from
Thy presence and take not Thy
Holy Spirit from me. Restore unto
me the joy of Thy salvation; and
uphold me with Thy free spirit.
Wash me thoroughly from mine

iniquity, and cleanse me from my
sin.

82.

Exhortation Before the Holy Communion.

DEARLY Beloved! Forasmuch
as we purpose to come to the
Holy Supper of our Lord Jesus
Christ, wherein He hath given us
His Body to eat and His Blood to
drink, it becometh us diligently to
examine ourselves as Saint Paul
exhorteth. For this Holy Sacrament
hath been instituted for the special
comfort and strengthening of those
who humbly confess their sins, and
who hunger and thirst after righteousness. But if we thus examine
ourselves, we shall find in us nothing
but sin and death, from which we

can in no wise set ourselves free.
Therefore, our Lord Jesus Christ
hath had mercy upon us, becoming
incarnate for our sins' sake, that so
He might fulfill for us the holy will
and law of God, and for us and our
deliverance suffer death and all
that we by our sins have deserved.
And to that end that we should the
more confidently believe this, and be
strengthened by our faith in cheerful
obedience to His will, He took bread,
and when He had given thanks He
brake it, saying, "Take and eat,
this is My Body which is given for
you," that is to say, I have taken
upon Myself human nature, and all
which I do and suffer, I do and suffer for you. It is all for you, and
unto your certain knowledge and
testimony of this, I give you My
Body to eat. After the same man-

ner, also, He took the cup, and when
He had given thanks, He gave it to
them, saying, "Drink ye all of it;
This cup is the New Testament in
My Blood, which is shed for you,
and for many, for the remission of
sins; this do, as oft as ye drink it,
in remembrance of Me," that is to
say, since I have interested Myself
in you, and have taken your sins
upon Me, I shall offer Myself for sin
unto death, shed My Blood, work out
for you all grace and the pardon of
your sin, and so set up a new testament wherein your sin is forgiven
you and will be no more remembered
eternally. Unto your certain knowledge and testimony of this, I give
you My Blood to drink.

Therefore, who eateth of this
bread, and drinketh of this cup, firmly believing the words of Christ, and

the evidences which he receives of
Christ, dwelleth in Christ, and Christ
in Him, and hath eternal life.

We should also do this in remembrance of Him, showing His death,
that He was delivered for our offences, and raised again for our
justification, and rendering unto
Him most hearty thanks for the
same, take up our cross and follow
Him; and, according to His commandment, love one another even
as He hath loved us. For we are all
one bread and **one** body, even as we
are all partakers of this **one** bread
and drink of this **one** cup. For, as
from many berries all crushed together, **one** wine and **one** drink comes
forth; and from many grains **one**
flour is ground and **one** bread or loaf
is baked, so also all who are members of Christ through faith shall in

brotherly love, for Christ our Redeemer's sake, be **one** body and meat and drink in deed, not in words alone, but in very deed and truth, as St. John teacheth (1. John 3). Showing forth faithfully this relation one to another without shadow of deception. To all this may the Almighty and merciful God and Father of our Lord Jesus Christ help us by His Holy Spirit. Amen.

83.

The General Preface, or the Prayer of Thanksgiving Before the Holy Sacrament.

The Lord be with you.
　　And with thy spirit.
Lift up your hearts.
　　We lift them up unto the Lord.

Let us give thanks unto the Lord our God.

It is meet and right so to do.

It is truly meet, right, and salutary that we should at all times, and in all places, give thanks unto Thee, O Lord, Holy Father, Almighty and Everlasting God, through Jesus Christ Our Lord, through Whom the angels praise Thy majesty, kingdoms worship, powers fear, and Whom the heavens and all the heavenly hosts, together with the seraphim, laud and magnify with one voice. With these we join our voices, evermore praising Thee and saying:

(Here follows the Sanctus.)

(The festival prefaces will be found with the festival prayers.)

84.

Sanctus.

Holy, holy, holy, Lord God of
    Sabaoth;
Heaven and earth are full of Thy
    glory;
Hosanna in the highest.
Blessed is He that cometh in the
    Name of the Lord.
Hosanna in the highest.

85.

The German Sanctus of Martin Luther.

Unto Isaiah, the prophet of old, it
    came
To see the Spirit of the Living God
On a great throne, in glittering flame,
His garment filled the temple all
    about.

Two Seraphim were standing by,—
Six wings had each, and evermore
With two their countenance they
    hide,
And two their feet they covered o'er,
And with the other two they train,
Calling, each to each, with great ac-
    claim:

> Holy is God, the Lord of
>   Sabaoth!
> Holy is God, the Lord of
>   Sabaoth!
> Holy is God, the Lord of
>   Sabaoth!
> His glory filleth all the
>   world!

Lintel and roof did tremble at the
    song,
While smoke and mist filled all the
    house along.

86.

The Words of Institution.

OUR Lord Jesus Christ, in the night in which He was betrayed, took bread; and when He had given thanks, He brake it and gave it to His disciples, saying, Take, eat; **this is My Body,** which is given for you; this do in remembrance of Me.

After the same manner, also, when He had supped, He took the cup, and when He had given thanks, He gave it to them, saying, Drink ye all of it; this cup is the New Testament in **My Blood,** which is shed for you, and for many, for the remission of sins; this do ye, as oft as ye drink it, in remembrance of Me.

87.

The Agnus Dei, or Hymn of the Christian Church to the Lamb of God.

O Christ, Thou Lamb of God, that
takest away the sin of the world,
have mercy upon us.
O Christ, Thou Lamb of God, that
takest away the sin of the world,
have mercy upon us.
O Christ, Thou Lamb of God, that
takest away the sin of the world,
grant us Thy peace.　Amen.

Prayers Before Receiving the Sacrament.

88.

LORD Jesus Christ, our only comfort, our hope, our righteousness, our strength and sure defence,

we beseech Thee, kindle in our breasts a fervent desire, hunger, and thirst for that eternal food of the soul,—Thy true body and blood,— that we may gladly and frequently receive the glorious Sacrament in true realization of our sins and strong reliance upon Thee, unto the strengthening and assurance of our souls, until at last life's pilgrimage ended, we come to Thee in the true Fatherland, to see Thee face to face, and abide with Thee through all eternity. Amen.

89.

LORD Jesus Christ, I am not worthy that Thou shouldst enter my sinful heart; yet, Thou deignest to recognize my great poverty and need. Therefore, I fervently desire Thy presence, to nour-

ish, comfort, and strengthen my poor
soul. Speak Thy word to my soul
and it shall be well with me. Amen.

90.

LORD, though I am unworthy that
Thou shouldst enter my heart,
yet, am I needy for Thy help and
desire Thy grace, unto the end
that I may be saved. I come with
no plea, but relying upon Thy
promise because Thou hast invited
me to Thy table, and assured me,
an unworthy sinner, that by Thy
body and blood, which I eat and
drink in this Sacrament, I shall receive forgiveness of my sins. O Dear
Lord, I know that Thy divine word
and promises are true, and holding
not a doubt, I eat and drink. Be it
unto me according to Thy word.
Lord Jesus, come unto me. Abide

in me and I in Thee, that I remain
unseparated from Thee both in time
and eternity. May Thy Holy Body
feed me, Thy Holy Blood be drink
unto me, and Thy bitter suffering
and death strengthen me. Lord
Jesus Christ, hear me, in Thy Holy
Wounds hide me, and let me nevermore depart from Thee. Save me
from evil and keep me in the true
faith; so will I be ever praising
Thee, in the company of all the elect,
now and evermore. Amen.

Thanksgiving After Receiving the Sacrament.

91.

LORD Jesus Christ, let Thy body,
given unto death for us, and
Thy blood, shed for many, not serve
unto our condemnation, nor yet unto

judgment; , but, according to Thy tender mercy, let it be a bulwark unto our bodies and souls, and a life-giving cordial unto eternal life. Amen.

92.

WE do heartily beseech Thee, O Lord, that with pure minds we may accept what we have received in our mouths; and that this temporal gift may increase into a heavenly cordial, through Jesus Christ our Lord. Amen.

93.

WE thank Thee, Heavenly Father, that Thou hast refreshed us with this Thy salutary gift; and we beseech Thee, of Thy mercy, to grant that it may serve to strengthen us in faith toward Thee and in fer-

vent love toward all men; through
Jesus Christ, our Lord.   Amen.

94.

A LMIGHTY and Everlasting God,
we praise and magnify Thy
divine goodness, that Thou hast fed
us with the salutary Body and Blood
of Thine only Son, Jesus Christ; and
we humbly beseech Thee so to move
us, by Thy Holy Spirit, that as we
have with our mouths received the
Holy Sacrament, we may also by
faith apprehend and eternally enjoy Thy divine grace, the forgiveness
of sin, unity with Christ, and life
eternal, which are therein offered
and vouchsafed unto us; through
Jesus Christ, our Lord.   Amen.

95.

The American custom of singing a hymn during the dispensation of the Sacrament, has made
Loehe's No. 95 superfluous. It is therefore omitted.

96.

Sacrifice and Consecration Unto God.

(Prayer during Communion, and at other times.)

O GOD, Heavenly Father, I beseech Thee in the Name of Thine Only-begotten Son, our dear Lord Jesus Christ, that Thou wouldst embrace me with Thy grace and help, that I may know and have power to offer myself a living sacrifice, holy and acceptable before Thee. Without Thy help I am and continue but a blemished sacrifice through my guilt. I desire greatly to supplant every lack in my sinful, imperfect sacrifice, through the merit of the holy sacrifice of Thine Only-begotten Son, our Lord Jesus Christ, which, as our high priest, He offered upon the altar of the cross. In Him and through Him I offer and consecrate unto Thee this day and all my time, my soul with all its powers, memory, understanding, the will to love, my faith, my hope, and my heart with all its motives and desires, my body and life with all its spiritual and temporal powers, my health, power, strength, fortune, honor, and possessions, together with my parents, my spouse, my children, friends and relations, and all over which or about which I may have any consent to give, with the humble confession that it is all Thine own; for, I have received all of Thy great mercy without any worthiness or merit in me. O Lord, make all these, as I do repeatedly beseech Thee, to be a holy and acceptable offering before Thee, and grant me always to use all these gifts, which I have from Thy hand, justly and rightly according to Thy word, that I may never esteem myself other than as a steward of the same, who must finally render account of my stewardship unto Thee. Grant me to enjoy the same with gratitude, with a calm mind, and without vanity, that I yield myself in self-denial as a burnt-offering, repressing my own will, meekly taking up my cross and sincerely and faithfully following Jesus.

O Lord, do unto me as Thou wilt, and as Thou deemest best for Thy honor and the salvation of my soul. And lest I be tempted to murmur or be unwilling in the flesh at what Thou sendest me or my friends to bear, I beseech Thee, O God, let not Thy mercy be turned from me, for, I do now yield myself with all my heart and will unto Thee, a sacrifice

unto Thy divine will, and will even
now heartily regret if, out of the
impotency of my heart, I should at
any time to come be tempted to
think or desire otherwise. Therefore, Dear Lord, as with Thine own,
do unto me according to Thy good
pleasure. The spirit is willing and
ready to suffer whatsoever Thou desirest to lay upon me for my sin's
sake, and all I ask is grace and help
to bear all with patience, accepting
all with a truly penitent heart, unto
Thy glory. Unto Thee I yield also
a spirit ready and joyful to praise
and serve Thee, and acknowledge my
debt to remain earnestly and zealously faithful in all things, until
death overtake me. I will renew my
baptismal covenant also and the
vows I have made therein. I have
hitherto, indeed, been an unworthy

servant. I pray Thee now for knowledge, power, strength and wisdom to know and henceforth to serve Thee according to Thy good pleasure. Condescend unto me and to all creatures, and make me wholly Thine own. O Lord, remove from me every hindrance toward Thee, and make of me a being according to Thy works in me. Protect me this day from all harm and danger in body and soul. Grant me Thy blessing, O Triune God. The Lord bless me and keep me. The Lord make His face shine upon me and be gracious unto me. The Lord lift up His countenance upon me, and give me peace. Amen.

97.

The Nunc Dimittis, or Simeon's Song of Praise.

(Luke 2:29—32.)

Lord, now lettest Thou Thy servant depart in peace: according to Thy word;

For mine eyes have seen Thy salvation: which Thou hast prepared before the face of all people;

A light to lighten the Gentiles: and the glory of Thy people Israel.

Glory be to the Father, and to the Son: and to the Holy Ghost;

As it was in the beginning, is now, and ever shall be: world without end. Amen.

98.

The Magnificat, or Song of Mary the Mother of Jesus.

(Luke 1 : 46—55.)

MY soul doth magnify the Lord: and my spirit hath rejoiced in God my Savior.

For He hath regarded: the low estate of His handmaiden.

For behold, from henceforth: all generations shall call me blessed.

For He that is mighty hath done to me great things: and holy is His Name.

And His mercy is on them that fear Him: from generation to generation.

He hath showed strength with His arm: He hath scattered the proud in the imagination of their hearts.

He hath put down the mighty

from their seats: and exalted them of low degree.

He hath filled the hungry with good things: and the rich He hath sent empty away.

He hath holpen His servant Israel, in remembrance of His mercy: as He spake to our fathers, to Abraham, and to his seed, forever.

Glory be to the Father, and to the Son: and to the Holy Ghost;

As it was in the beginning, is now, and ever shall be: world without end. Amen.

99.

For Chastity.

(At a remembrance of the desecration of Sunday evenings.)

LORD Jesus Christ, Son of God, Who wast crucified for us and raised again from the dead, Who of a truth lovest purity and chastity,

both within and without the holy
bonds of wedlock, unto Thee we
pray, incline unto chastity the hearts
and thoughts of all who call upon
Thee. Defend and uphold all the
laws and bonds of matrimony.
Hinder and repress the devil, who,
from hatred and jealousy of God,
seeks to lead humanity into manifold uncleanness, to overthrow us
thereby. Thou knowest how in
these days our nature groweth
ever weaker, while the assault and
folly of our enemies waxes daily
greater; for they know that judgment must soon come, when their
sin and shame shall be revealed before the eyes of men and angels.
Therefore, Lord Jesus Christ, Only
Son of the Father, Who wast crucified and didst rise again from the
dead for our sake, we beseech Thee

so to rule and govern us, our youth, our homes, and our children, and to move and incline our hearts unto chastity, and unto sincere prayer, by the Holy Spirit, unto the Everlasting Father. Amen.   (Philip Melanchthon.)

Evening Prayers.

100.

NOW thank we all our God, Who, from our mother's womb, has kept us alive and showered His benefits upon us. May He grant us joyful hearts and great peace in this our day, that His grace abide, and redeem us while we live. The grace of our Lord Jesus Christ, the love of God, and the communion of the Holy Ghost be with us evermore. Amen.

O Lord, Almighty God, Heavenly

Father, I bless Thee for all the goodness and mercy which Thou hast this day so graciously bestowed upon me, and hast preserved me in joy and health from all evil. As Thy beloved, I pray Thee graciously to preserve me in Thy word, which alone is able to save, until my latest breath, and enlighten my soul with Thy Holy Spirit, that I may know what is good and what is evil. By Thy mercy blot out every transgression that I have committed this day, whether consciously or ignorantly, and every secret fault, and grant me this night the precious rest of Thy Christian people, that I may rise again refreshed and strong unto Thy praise. Grant also, Dear Father, that by Thy grace I begin a new life, acceptable unto Thee, unto the salvation of my soul;

through Jesus Christ, Thy dear Son,
our only help. Amen.

101.

LORD Jesus, I confess my guilt,
that I have not lived this whole
day unto Thy praise and glory. I
have lacked in gratitude toward
Thee, and have not taken to heart
Thy bitter sufferings and death as
I should. O Lord, so many sins *
have I this day committed against
Thy law. I have neglected so much †
and have not improved myself.
Gracious Redeemer, forgive me for
the sake of Thy blood which Thou
didst shed for me. Defend me this
night against all harm and sin. Let

---

* Here think what sins and omissions you have
especially to lament and confess.

† Think upon the things which you have
especially neglected to do.

my heart find rest and awake again
in Thee, unto Thy praise. This day
and at all times I commit and commend unto Thee my body, soul,
spirit, honor, possessions, and living,
to do with me according to Thy good
pleasure. When matters go contrary to my pleasure, grant me grace
and patience. Let me realize how
this life is a vale of sorrow, and have
desire only for the blessed fatherland, that I may joyfully contem-
plate death and praise Thee at last,
with all the elect in everlasting life,
world without end. Amen.

102.

ALMIGHTY God, our Lord, according to Thine ordinance,
darkness and night are now falling,
and we retire to rest and sleep. We
call upon Thee and beseech Thee,

graciously grant us Thy care and
protection, nor let night and darkness, nor enemies, nor death, nor
powers, nor hell itself harm us; and,
while our weak flesh lies down in
slumber, cause our hearts and minds
to be awake unto Thee. Be Thou a
pillar of fire unto our hearts and
minds always, that these may follow
Thee even in the darkness; and
grant that we be ever found before
Thee as the children of the light of
eternal day, and not as the children of the darkness of night;
through Jesus Christ, our Lord.
Amen.

103.

I RENDER thanks unto Thee, O
true and everlasting Light, that
Thou hast this day protected me by
Thy light and spirit against every

grievous sin. And now, during the
night which Thou hast ordained for
the rest of my poor body, O Lord,
grant unto my weary soul to find
rest and peace in Thee against all
the wiles and onslaughts of the evil
one. Cause my mind and my
thoughts, together with my hands
and my feet, to glorify Thee and be
silent before Thee, Who art present
and mindful of Thine own, when
deep slumbers embrace them. O,
let not this wicked flesh overmaster
my poor soul, lest I forget Thee in the
night watches. Into Thy hands I commit my spirit, O Gentle Shepherd,
into Thy faithful hands. Thou hast
redeemed my soul, O Lord God, Most
Faithful, permit me not to fall away
from Thee. Watch by me and cover
me with the protection of Thy
wings. When the night is past,

awaken me and grant me the light
by which I may walk and dwell
safely with Thee in yonder eternity.
Hear my prayer and answer me, O
Thou Who slumberest not nor sleepest; through Jesus Christ. Amen.

The Lord's Prayer.

The Creed.

Psalm 103,

and the Gloria.

2.

MONDAY.

Let Thy work appear unto Thy servants, and Thy glory unto their children. And let the beauty of the Lord our God be upon us: and establish Thou the work of our hands upon us; yea, the work of our hands establish Thou it. (Ps. 90: 16—17).

Pursue thy way,
Go not astray:
Though hate thou bear,
Of hate beware!
In perils sore
God's help implore;
Be calm in need,—
If thou take heed,
Great things thine eyes shall witness.

104.

Upon Entering the Week of Labor.

R ULE Thou, O God the Father,
Who hast created us, together
with all creatures, not unto idleness
but unto labor, and bless each now in
his appropriate calling. May He
Who ruleth and governeth all the
world, also guide those in authority
over us, and graciously support them
with His power and wisdom.

Rule Thou, The Son, Who hast
redeemed us and paid the price of
sin in our stead. May He remove
from us the burden of sin which we
committed during the past week,
and grant us His peace. May the
Great Bishop and Chief Shepherd of
our souls help all servants of His
Word who labor in this and every

other community on earth, to bring forth fruit unto everlasting life.

Rule Thou, O God the Holy Ghost, Who hast sanctified us and regenerated us in Holy Baptism. May He create in us a clean heart, and renew a right spirit within us, that we carry none of the evils of the past week over into the new, but slay every purpose and inclination of the old Adam within us. May He govern our hearts mightily; and should this week mark for any the end of the days, may the Holy Spirit help such in all bitterness of the hour of death, fill his heart with grace which is better than life, teach his hands to do battle and conquer the last enemy, and, for Christ's sake, grant unto him the rest and glory of an eternal sabbath.

May the Triune, Eternal God, be

and abide with us and the Church forever. Unto Him be glory, laud, and honor, forever more. Amen.

Morning Prayers.

105.

GOD, be merciful unto us and bless us. Make Thy countenance to shine upon us that we may acknowledge Thy ways in all the earth. The Lord, our God, bless us. The Lord bless us and grant us peace. Amen.

O Holy and Ever Faithful God, Heavenly Father, most heartily do I praise, laud, and magnify Thee, that Thou hast granted me to rest and sleep in safety during the night now past, and hast caused me to awake refreshed and in good health, through Thy Fatherly love.

Most heartily do I beseech Thee,
graciously to defend me and all believing Christians, this day and
through all the days, against all harm
and danger in body and soul, that I
may always yield unto Thy will. Into
Thy care and guidance I commend
myself, body, soul, heart, mind, will,
and thought, and all my purposes,
my walks and ways, my rising up
and my lying down, my coming in
and my going out, my life and death,
and all that I am or have. Let Thy
holy angel have charge concerning
me, to defend me from all harm
in body and soul. I ask it for
Jesus Christ, Thy dear Son's sake.
Amen.

106.

I N Thy Name, O crucified Lord
Jesus Christ, Who hast so pre-
ciously redeemed me with Thy blood,

I do now arise. I beseech Thee,
bless me and mine this day. Protect
us, and grant that our course may be
holy, and we live our lives unto Thy
glory. Amen.

107.

LORD Jesus Christ, be Thou this
day and at all times the beginning of all my labors and deeds. Be
Thou my comforter, my blessing, my
support; and protect me and mine
from all evil, that the devil and evil
men may have no power over us.
Amen.

108.

LORD Jesus Christ, Thou, my
Lord and my God, knowest how
Thou hast taught the utter weak-
ness and hesitancy of man, that

he can accomplish naught without
Thy help and support. When he
depends and trusts in himself alone
he falls into a thousand errors.
Have mercy, Great God, upon Thy
child in this distress. Grant me Thy
gracious support that, by Thine enlightenment, I may ever see that
which is truly good, desire the same
by Thy guidance, and finally attain
the same by Thy might. To this
end I yield, yea, entirely commend
myself, with body and soul, unto
Thee alone, Who art worshipped,
together with the Father and the
Holy Ghost, one true and almighty
God, unto all eternity. Amen.

The Lord's Prayer.

The Creed.

Psalm 127.

and the Gloria Patri.

Prayer for Blessing and Prosperity in One's Calling.

109.

D EAR Father, my calling is founded upon Thy word and commandment. Upon these I this day go forth to cast out my net, and to Thy care will I leave the result. Beside this, my only plea is that Thou wilt bless and prosper all. Amen. (Dr. Martin Luther.)

110.

M Y Lord, and my God, I realize that man's work does not depend upon his own powers nor is it in any man's province to ordain his walks and ways. So rule and govern me at all times, by Thy Holy Spirit, that I may keep mine eyes straight before me in my calling, and faithfully perform my duty. Guide me evermore in the right paths, that I turn neither to the right nor the left therefrom.

Direct me always by Thy good pleasure, and let Thy Spirit lead me in the true paths, for Thou art my God. I realize also that Thou hast called me to labor in Thy vineyard, and how, even in my baptism, I promised Thee that I would labor. To this end, I beseech Thee, grant me a healthy body, and strengthen me, O Lord, cheerfully to bear the heat and labor of my calling, always ready and faithful unto Thee. And since I know not the hour when my labors shall cease, teach me to be ready at all times unto a blessed departure, willingly to leave this world, and to fall asleep in peace and joy; that I may celebrate the eternal day of rest with Thee and all Thine elect.   Amen.

111.

HOLY and Gracious Father, Thou only Wise God, Who ordainest and appointest all things according to Thy divine wisdom, and entrustest his talent unto each of Thy servants, I beseech Thee, grant that I may always order the work of my calling, and all my affairs according to Thy divine Word; and so doing, ever consider, first the glory of Thy name, the increase of Thy kingdom, and the fulfilment of Thy holy will. Give me that spirit of counsel, and of wisdom, and understanding, that I err not in my purposes. For what man knoweth the counsels of God, and who has conceived the will of God? The thoughts of the mind are deceptive, and our purposes fraught with danger. Therefore, let the angel of the higher council be my teacher and counsellor, and grant me Thy Holy Spirit from on high, that all I do on earth may be right. Enlighten my understanding with Thy divine light, for Thou settest up my candlestick, and makest my eye single; Thou makest my darkness to be light. Shed upon me Thy wisdom, to be with me and labor with me. Give charge to Thine angel to go before me and order all the way of my calling, and remove every hindrance of Satan, even as Thou hast granted such grace unto all Thy faithful servants from the beginning. Fit me for the work which I undertake. Grant me holy courage, good counsel, and right

works. Make me an instrument in
Thy hands and a vessel of Thy
grace, that I may humbly and rightly
apply the gift which Thou hast entrusted to me, unto Thy glory and
the good of my fellowmen. All is in
Thy hands. Thine is the beginning,
the progress, and the end. Therefore, promote Thou all that I have
or shall have to do, and hold over me
always Thine almighty arm of grace.
Let all things prosper by me as Thou
didst prosper the things of Joseph
and Daniel. Grant me the necessary health and strength of body
and soul, and let all my members,
my understanding, memory, sight,
and hearing be committed unto
Thee, until I shall have attained
a blessed end. Defend and protect me against the wiles and
deceptions of the evil one and all his

power, and against the perversity of
his servants, that their pride, hypocrisy and unrighteousness may not
obtain over me nor bring harm upon
me. Teach me to watch and pray,
lest I enter into temptation, and
grant me to hear with mine ears and
see with mine eyes. For Thine, O
Lord, is the glory, Thou only Source
of all Grace. O Thou, Who keepest
Israel, keep watch and ward over
me, and protect my going out and
my coming in from this time forth
forevermore, that my watchword,
unto Thy glory, may ever be:
"Whatsoever God prospereth will
succeed." These things grant me,
O Lord, the Father, through Jesus
Christ, by the power of the Holy
Ghost. Amen.

112.

A Domestic Benediction for Christian Householders.

(To be used at the beginning of the week.)

GOD the Father, God the Son, God the Holy Ghost, Most Holy Trinity, unto Thee I commit, for Thine own, this house and all it shelters. This house is Thine, therefore, enter now with Thy train of blessing. Thine is the soul of the householder and of all that are his. Thine are their bodies. Our Father, Who hast created us, together with all things, preserve us in body and soul unto everlasting life. O Son of God, Who hast redeemed us, grant us to participate in the merit of Thy life and death. O Holy Ghost, Who dost gather us into the kingdom of grace by the Word and

Sacrament, preserve us in the Name
of our Lord Jesus Christ, and help
us to follow the example of His
humility unto our end. Comfort us,
Most Holy Comforter, when our sins
distress us. Spirit of Truth, preserve us against all errors that can
endanger our souls, and against
every wile of the devil and the
machinations of the world. Spirit
of Holiness, sanctify us wholly, that
we may be changed from glory to
greater glory, until we attain the perfect image of Jesus Christ. Spirit of
Joy, remove all sorrow from us,
slay the old man of sin and his
whims within us, and grant us
minds centered upon heaven, that
our hearts may cleave to that other
world where Jesus Christ, our Most
Precious Treasure is. So work in
us that we seek first the kingdom of

God and His righteousness, and be
Thine in body and soul, in life and
in death, for time and eternity.

O Lord, Thou hast promised that
all other things shall be added unto
them who seek first Thy kingdom
and its righteousness. We beseech
Thee, of Thy gracious goodness,
grant us also these other things,
so far as they may be good and needful for us. Bless our fields and
meadows, our vineyards and our
gardens. Send us the rains in due
time, and grant us fruitful seasons.
Preserve us from failure of harvest,
from hail and tempest. Fill cellar
and garner with Thy blessing, that
we may enjoy Thy gifts with gratitude and also have sufficient to share
with the needy. Preserve house
and home from danger by fire and
water, and both man and beast from

pestilence and sudden plague. All fruit and food that is in the house, bless Thou unto the nourishment of our bodies. Cover Thou all our possessions as with a shield. Build Thy walls round about us against Satan and all his host, against thieves and robbers. Let the dishonest be made known, and preserve us against any Judas among us. Make known also if there be any unrighteous possession in this house, that we may put the curse from us. Watch over the purity of our bodies, that in this house none may fall into dishonor or evil repute. If in this house some mother come unto the hour of her labor, grant her the favor of Thy countenance and turn her anguish into joy. Let Thy peace from heaven come upon all, so far as this roof-tree reaches. Let

peace and unity dwell in this house.
Let gray hairs here find a sheltering
rest as did Jacob and Joseph in the
goodly land of Goshen, and crown
the aged among us with honor.
Grant the heritage of heaven and
frankly obedient hearts to all the
children in this house. Grant us
peaceful neighbors; and, wherever
strife threatens to come, cause Thy
holy Word and the remembrance of
Jesus Christ quickly to adjust all
differences. Let no evil tongue
divide us in hatred and envy, and,
when we suffer unjustly, grant us
true humility. When Thou layest a
cross upon us, let us acknowledge it
as the greatest domestic blessing, and
render thanks to Thee for the same.
When we fall ill or grow old, make
our hearts so much the stronger, and
more youthful in faith and love unto

Thee. When things go hard and haltingly with us, let Thy grace be sufficient for us. Should any one of us die, cause us to realize that we are pilgrims and strangers on earth, but in heaven there is joy sufficient for us. Preserve us from sudden and evil death. When our day is come, may we come unto Thee, filled only with faith and the Holy Ghost, and not trusting in our own lives or works. In the last hour grant us to enjoy once again the refreshing assurance of Thy Holy Sacrament. Unto our bodies vouchsafe a safe burial in some quiet spot amidst the graves of our beloved dead, and, with all pious Christian bodies, may they rest in peace until the last of the days; then waken us unto the resurrection of the body, and clothe us mercifully in the gar-

ments of grace. Spare us in the day
of judgment, and lead us home into
the mansions eternal,—O Bishop of
our Salvation; and, in that blest
home, accept our eternal thanksgiving and everlasting praise.   Amen.

113.

Encouragement at the Beginning of Work.

G O with Jesus to thy task!
⠀⠀All on Him dependeth.
Jesus, if Thou wilt but ask,
Strength and courage lendeth.
Rise with Jesus ev'ry day,
Be with Him while sleeping,
Walk with Jesus on thy way,
Happy in His keeping.

Call on Him at break of day,
In the morning hour.
'Tis the proper time to pray
For His shielding power.

Be it morn, or even-tide,
Or when darkness reigneth,
He is ever at thy side,
And the strength sustaineth.

Having Jesus ever near,
What though foes be raging?
He is there to stay thy fear,
Thou His help engaging.
Boldly take with Him thy stand,
Who the foe can banish.
Be assured, at His command
All thy ills must vanish.

If with Jesus thou pursue
Ev'ry undertaking,
He will prove thy Helper true,
Never thee forsaking.
Show'rs of blessing shall to thee
Here on earth be given,
And at last thy soul shall see
All the joys of heaven.
Now, Lord Jesus, be to Thee

My affairs commended.
Do Thou as Thou wilt with me,
Till my life is ended.
To my task I gladly go,
While in Thee reposing.
Amen, yea, it shall be so,
Thus say I in closing.

114.
Prayer of a Servant.
(Dr. Martin Luther.)

O LORD God, I praise Thee that Thou hast ordained me to this calling, occupation, and service, wherein I know that I can please and serve Thee more than all the monks and nuns who have no command unto their kind of service. In the fourth of Thy commandments I am directed to honor father and mother, and faithfully to serve and obey lords, mistresses, and masters, to work for them, and to be of their

household; therefore, cause me joyfully and lovingly to fulfil my mis-
sion. I will rejoice to do whatsoever
I can to please my lord, my master
and my mistress; and to leave undone whatsoever shall displease them.
Though, at times, I may be abused,
what is the harm, since I know that
my station is a service and a life
that is well-pleasing unto Thee.
Therefore will I gladly both suffer
and labor unto the honor of my calling; but Thou, Lord, must grant me
grace and patience thereunto. Amen.

Upon Undertaking a Business Journey.

115.

ALMIGHTY God, in Thy Name I
undertake my way, and begin
my journey by invoking Thy Mercy.
Thou art my God, Who protectest

my going and my coming again, and
settest my feet upon the right paths,
that they stumble not. I beseech
Thee, let holy angels accompany me,
and give them charge to defend me
in all my ways, and to lead me by
sure paths to the place whither I
purpose to go; and bring me home
again refreshed and strengthened,
even as young Tobias was led unto
Rages in Midian and back again by
the angel Raphael. And now, Lord,
I commend my all into Thy hands,
through Jesus Christ. Amen.

116.

O LORD, Almighty God, Who, in
times past, didst miraculously
lead Thy people Israel through a
wilderness, guiding them with
clouds and fire, a covering by day
and a light in the night, since I must
now undertake a journey in pursuit

of my calling, I most heartily beseech Thee to accompany me and go before me, to lead me in the right way and in due time to bring me back in safety. Bear me, O merciful God, dear Father, as a man bears his little son, upon all the way which I will have to go. Protect me with Thy hand and save me from the hands of enemies. Cause Thy holy angels to go with me, and prosper all my undertaking, that I may deal wisely, succeed in my work, and return to my home joyfully. Preserve my going out and my coming in, from this time forth and forever. Amen.

Upon Undertaking a Voyage on Sea.

117.

LORD, my Creator! O Lord, my Maker! Lord, Thou hast caused it to be written what Thou hast spoken by the mouth of the Prophet Isaiah, that I shall not fear, because Thou hast redeemed me, I shall not tremble, because Thou hast called me by my name, and I shall not despair, because I am Thine. O Lord, I am Thine! O Lord, Thou hast redeemed me and purchased me with the precious blood of Christ! In my baptism Thou hast called me by my name, and hast accepted me for Thy child. Let me now know the assurance of Thy promise, "When thou passest through the waters, I will be with Thee; and through the rivers, they shall not overflow thee." Still Thou the waves before me, and, though they be moved and lift themselves with threatening noise, guide and uphold the ship with Thy right hand, and bring me safe to land again. Be

Thou with me in the ship, then will
I not despair. Thou speakest, and
the sea becomes calm. Thou shalt
speak, and my fears will depart.
Thou wilt walk before me upon the
waves of the sea, and I will fearlessly follow, and, though I sink,
Thou wilt stretch forth Thy hand
unto me, as Thou didst unto
Peter, so can I walk in safety, and
fear no more. If on my journey
Thy hand leads me, I will rejoice
evermore. If I have but Thee and
am with Thee, then am I in the ark
which can not sink, and the stormy
depths will bear me unto the blessed
end, and, though they swallow me
up, it were but a shortening of the
way unto Thee, for Thou wilt rescue
my soul and lead me into Thy haven
of eternal rest and peace. Thus
would I, at one step, have crossed

over the Red Sea to join all the
elect in the song of Moses, that man
of God. Blessed be He who is with
me to help me! My soul, body, life,
blood, and all my property I commend into Thy hands. Lord Jesus,
unto Thee I live, unto Thee will I
die, whether therefore I live or die,
I am Thine, and where Thou art,
there shall I be also. Amen.

118.

Upon Entering the Ship.

B E merciful unto us, O Lord. Hear
our cry, and with holy hand
bless this vessel and all who voyage
therein, even as Thou didst bless
the ark of Noah that sailed over the
waters of the flood. Stretch forth
Thy hand, O Lord, as Thou didst
unto the Apostle Peter when he

walked upon the sea, and send forth Thy angel from heaven, who shall defend and save this ship with all that is therein from all harm. Let every evil be kept far from Thy servants, and, by Thy grace, grant us a peaceful voyage and the attainment of the haven to which we journey, so that, having reached our journey's end, we may with joyful hearts render praise and thanksgiving unto Thee, Who livest and reignest with the Father, in unity with the Holy Ghost, One Lord, unto all eternity. Amen.

119.
During a Storm.

(Read the gospel concerning Christ's ship, Matt. 8:23—27, to consider the same during a storm.)

AND when Jesus was entered into a ship, His disciples followed Him. And, behold, there arose a great tempest in the sea, insomuch that the ship was covered with the waves: but He was asleep. And His disciples came to Him, and awoke Him, saying, "Lord, save us: we perish."

And He saith unto them, "Why are ye fearful, O ye of little faith?" Then He arose, and rebuked the winds and the sea; and there was a great calm.

But the men marveled, saying, "What manner of man is this, that even the winds and the sea obey Him!"

———

O THOU Who goest down into the ship with all Thy people that voyage upon the seas, without Whose will neither storm nor wave arise, Who knowest how great need and many dangers always surround us upon our way, Who Thyself slumberest not nor sleepest when we are troubled or weep, Who hearest them of little faith, whom Thou rebukest, as well as them that are strong in faith, when their ship is covered with waves and they cry, "Lord, save us: we perish," Lord Jesus Christ, have mercy upon us poor sinners. Speak but the word, and the storm will cease, for wind and wave are obedient unto Thee, and our hearts will be quiet as Thy creatures, praising Thee Whom wind and wave obey.

If this be not Thy will, and it befall that we be swallowed up in the waters, by Thy good pleasure, to become food for the fishes of the sea, then, Lord, surely Thou wilt stretch forth Thy hand to grant us a blessed death. If Thou be with us,

the ship of this life will soon come
to the haven, and we will be praising
Thee on the other side of the Red
Sea; because Thou leadest Thy
saints most wonderously, and bringest all to a glorious end. Let our
bodies be commended unto Thee,
Who art Lord over earth and sea,
and Who wilt summon all in the day
of the resurrection from the dead,
whether their bodies were food for
the fishes of the sea or for the earth-
worms. Thy will, O Lord, be done
Remember us in Thy Kingdom
Amen.

_____

'Mong the lilies blooming yonder
Thou shalt wander,
O my soul, and be at home.
Rise, then, as on eagle-pinions,
Thy dominions
Are above where angels roam.

Guide my ship, O First-born Brother,
To no other
Than that peaceful haven, where,
Sheltered from all storms forever,
I shall never
Know of sorrow, sin, or care.

120.

Prayer After a Sea-Voyage.

(Psalm 107.)

O GIVE thanks unto the Lord, for He is good: for His mercy endureth forever.

Let the redeemed of the Lord say so, whom He hath redeemed from the hand of the enemy;

And gathered them out of the lands, from the east, and from the west, from the north, and from the south.

They wandered in the wilderness

in a solitary way; they found no city to dwell in.

Hungry and thirsty, their soul fainted in them. Then they cried unto the Lord in their trouble, and He delivered them out of their distresses.

And He led them forth by the right way, that they might go to a city of habitation.

O that men would praise the Lord for His goodness, and for His wonderful works to the children of men!

For He satisfieth the longing soul, and filleth the hungry soul with goodness.

Such as sit in darkness and in the shadow of death, being bound in affliction and iron;

Because they rebelled against the words of God, and contemned the counsel of the Most High:

Therefore He brought down their heart with labor; they fell down, and there was none to help.

Then they cried unto the Lord in their trouble, and He saved them out of their distresses.

He brought them out of darkness and the shadow of death, and brake their bands in sunder.

O that men would praise the Lord for His goodness, and for His wonderful works to the children of men! For He hath broken the gates of brass, and cut the bars of iron in sunder.

Fools because of their transgression, and because of their iniquities, are afflicted.

Their soul abhorreth all manner of meat; and they draw near unto the gates of death.

Then they cry unto the Lord in

their trouble, and He saveth them out of their distresses.

He sent His word, and healed them, and delivered them from their destructions.

O that men would praise the Lord for His goodness, and for His wonderful works to the children of men!

And let them sacrifice the sacrifices of thanksgiving, and declare His works with rejoicing.

They that go down to the sea in ships, that do business in great waters;

These see the works of the Lord, and His wonders in the deep.

For He commandeth, and raiseth the stormy wind, which lifteth up the waves thereof.

They mount up to the heaven, they go down again to the depths:

their soul is melted because of trouble.

They reel to and fro, and stagger like a drunken man, and are at their wit's end.

Then they cry unto the Lord in their trouble, and He bringeth them out of their distresses.

He maketh the storm a calm, so that the waves thereof are still.

Then are they glad because they be quiet; so He bringeth them unto their desired haven.

O that men would praise the Lord for His goodness, and for His wonderful works to the children of men!

Let them exalt Him also in the congregation of the people, and praise Him in the assembly of the elders.

He turneth rivers into a wilderness, and the watersprings into dry ground;

A fruitful land into barrenness, for the wickedness of them that dwell therein.

He turneth the wilderness into a standing water, and dry ground into watersprings.

And there He maketh the hungry to dwell, that they may prepare a city for habitation;

And sow the fields, and plant vineyards, which may yield fruits of increase.

He blesseth them also, so that they are multiplied greatly; and suffereth not their cattle to decrease.

Again, they are minished and brought low through oppression, affliction, and sorrow.

He poureth contempt upon princes, and causeth them to wander in the wilderness, where there is no way.

Yet setteth He the poor on high from affliction, and maketh Him families like a flock.

The righteous shall see it, and rejoice: and all iniquity shall stop her mouth.

Whoso is wise, and will observe these things, even they shall understand the loving-kindness of the Lord.

Glory be to the Father, and to the Son, and to the Holy Ghost; as it was in the beginning, is now, and ever shall be, world without end. Amen.

PRAYERS FOR DIVINE PROS-PERITY TO OUR LABORS IN THE FIELDS.

121.

For Favorable Weather.

LORD, Heavenly Father, Who art gracious and merciful, and hast promised us, through Thy Son, graciously to care for us in every need, we beseech Thee, regard not our sins and transgressions, but remember our need and Thy mercy instead, and send us the blessed rain (sunshine), that by Thy grace we may have our daily bread, and acknowledge Thee, and render praises unto

Thee, the merciful God; through
Jesus Christ, Thy dear Son, our
Lord. Amen.

122.

For Sunshine.

LORD Jesus, if we but wept for
our sins the heavens had no
need to weep. Since we are so entirely hardened, however, Thou afflictest
us with this wet and destructive
weather. Have mercy, then, upon
the poor, and the little children, and
let them not suffer for our sins.
Lord, close up the windows of heav-
en, let the clouds scatter, and the
beloved sunshine again break forth.
Our hope, our comfort, and our
refuge is in Thee Who hast created
heaven and earth. Help us, O God
of our salvation. Amen.

123.

Dr. Martin Luther's Prayer for a Fruitful Rain.

HEAVENLY Father, Eternal God,
Thou hast taught us in Thy
word that if we heed not Thou wilt
make the heavens like iron and the
earth like brass, that there be no
rains and no fruits to prosper the
people. But, again, Thou hast promised that if we obey Thee, love Thee,
and serve Thee with our whole
hearts, Thou wilt give the rain in
due time unto the land. Now we
behold with sorrow that the fruits
which Thy gracious hand has set
are drying up from the summer's
heat, and are withering for lack of
the fruitful rains which are withheld.
Our manifold sins have, indeed, deserved such a rod and punishment at

Thy hands, and have merited that
the earth should refrain from ripen-
ing for us even a seed. We know no
other means whereby we may appease Thy just wrath and avert this
blighting heat than with our earnest,
believing prayer which shall pene-
trate the heavens and come before
Thee, and accomplish its petitions
before Thee. Therefore, we bow
down under Thy rod. We beseech
Thee, of Thine everlasting mercy, let
the heavens be again unbarred and
send us the fruitful rain (even as
Elijah with his prayer obtained from
Thee, that it rained), in order
that the fruits of the earth may be
refreshed and quickened, and we
may harvest them with great thankfulness, unto the preservation of our
earthly lives, and be preserved in
body and soul by Thy grace from

heaven, unto Thy glory here and unto all eternity. Amen.

124.

For the Grains of the Field.

(Dr. Martin Luther.)

O LORD, our God, graciously preserve the grains of the fields. Cleanse the air. Give blessed rain in due season that the grains may prosper, and not be poisoned, neither that we nor our cattle shall therein eat unto ourselves a pestilence or other sickness. Gracious Lord, let the grain be blessed that it may prosper us Thy blessing unto healthfulness, and we misuse it not unto the harm of our souls or the increase of sin, debauchery, and idleness, whence come unchastity, adultery, cursing, swearing, murders, wars, and every evil. Grant us grace to use Thy gifts unto the improvement of our lives, and that the grains may serve to preserve and increase in us health of body and soul; through Thy beloved Son, Jesus Christ, our Lord. Amen.

Thou makest the outgoings of the morning and the evening to rejoice. Thou visitest the earth, and waterest it: Thou greatly enrichest it with the river of God, which is full of water. Amen.

125.

For Our Daily Bread.

ALMIGHTY and Everlasting God, Father, All-merciful and of great riches, I, a poor human being, who have brought nothing into this world, but was born naked, poor, and miserable, am, nevertheless, in need of nourishment for my weak body and this transient life. Therefore, I approach the richly laden tables of Thy house, and beseech Thee, regard not the lack of merit in me, for I am not worthy to receive a crumb of bread nor a drop of water. Turn Thine eyes away from my sin, regard only my poverty and need, and have mercy upon my misery. O Lord God, the Father, it is all Thine that Thou givest me. From Thy throne do I daily receive the food I eat. Daily I drink the waters that flow from that living fountain which is with Thee. Thou art the great Householder Who feedeth all creatures, the Gracious Father Who provides for all His children. Therefore, open Thy hand and satisfy my desire. Bless my food, and give

me bread as I may have need. Let
me enjoy Thy good gifts, in health
and peace, and never squander the
same in idleness and ease. Grant me
the spirit of frugality, that I may
save the surplus for my future needs.
Awake my heart unto true thankfulness, that, as Thou dost daily nourish
me and mine, we also may daily and
without ceasing praise and magnify
Thee for Thy great mercy. Amen.

126.

In Poverty.

ALMIGHTY and Everlasting God,
Thou art the Father and Pre-
server of all that is mine. From
Thee we have our body and soul, our
honor and possessions, our mind and
understanding, yes, all that we have
we owe unto Thee alone. Though

it be little that we have, Thou canst
increase it, and though it were
much Thou couldst decrease it. All
is in Thy hand, all is Thine, O Lord.
My wife, my children, and I are now
in great poverty, and hunger oppresses us. Of bread we have little
store, and have no means to buy.
None will lend us, nor sell us on
credit, so that we are almost totally
forsaken of men. From our youth
up we have learned to put our hope
and trust in Thee, and know that
Thou hast mercy upon the poor, and
art the only true helper of them
that are in want. We have not and
command none other help in all our
needs than Thee alone. Upon Thee
we cast our every care, for Thou
satisfiest every living thing. We
heartily beseech Thee to behold us
with Thine eye of mercy, to bless

what little of bread we have, and nourish, sustain, and preserve us in body and spirit; through Jesus Christ, our Lord. Amen.

Evening Prayers.

127.

IN Thy Name, O Lord Jesus, I now lay me down to my temporal rest. Grant me finally the eternal rest, when I may lie down in peace to sleep and rise again and enter into eternal glory. Amen.

128.

ALMIGHTY and Everlasting God, I thank Thee, that Thou hast this day preserved me, Thine unworthy servant, not for any merit on my part, but out of pure, divine grace, and beseech Thee, Merciful

Lord, grant me to spend this present night with a pure heart and body, that I may rise again, refreshed in health, to serve, praise, and glorify Thee; through Thy beloved Son, Our Lord. Amen.

129.

ALL-GRACIOUS and Merciful Father, most heartily will I render thanks unto Thee, that Thou hast this day, and unto this moment so graciously protected me against every evil in body and soul, and beseech Thee, for the sake of Jesus Christ, Thy well-beloved Son, mercifully to pardon all my sins which I have this day in any manner committed against Thee, in thought, in word, or in deed, and remember them not again forevermore. As I am about to give myself unto rest, I

pray Thee, defend me this night
against every evil in body and soul;
that I may be preserved against
every wile and power of Satan and
from all evil, useless, and shameful
dreams; to sleep safely, in peace,
and to rise again refreshed in health,
unto Thy praise. Into Thy hand
alone I commit my all. Thou hast
redeemed me, O faithful God.
Amen.

<h2 style="text-align:center">130.</h2>

ALMIGHTY and Ever Faithful
God, I thank Thee that Thou
hast this day so paternally protected
me and mine, and kept from us all
evil. In Thy name let me now retire
to rest, and sleep upon my bed under
Thy protection. Pardon, dear Lord,
all my sins by which I have this day
either consciously or unconsciously

offended against and pained Thee. Grant me a quiet night and peaceful sleep, that no terrors overtake me. O Thou, Who keepest Israel, Who neither slumberest nor sleepest, watch over me. Abide with me, for the day is now far spent and evening is at hand. Charge Thy holy angels to be with me, to protect me as a wall of fire about me, that Satan, nor evil dreams, nor any phantasies may disturb me. In the darkness be Thou the light unto my soul, that, though I sleep in darkness, I may have no fear. Let my soul rest in Thee; and, though death seek to embrace me, preserve Thou me in mind and spirit, that I may awake unto Thee, to be Thine, whether living or dying. I commend unto Thee also all who are mine, my friends and neighbors, together with

all my house and home. Grant also,
O Lord, unto all who are in distress,
sickness, want, sorrow, or temptation, and unto all who without Thy
merciful hand find no sleep because
of pains in body or soul, that they
may enjoy a quiet and peaceful
night. Preserve us from all evil.
Awaken me early in Thy peace, unto
the glory of Thy Name, and teach
me to do Thy pleasure according to
Thy will. And when, at last, I close
mine eyes in death, and fall asleep
in blessed communion with Thee,
awaken me again with joy in the
day of the resurrection of all flesh,
unto eternal life. Amen.

The Lord's Prayer.

The Creed.

Psalm 123,

and the Gloria Patri.

3.

TUESDAY.

Fight the good fight of faith, lay hold on eternal life, whereunto thou art also called, and hast professed a good profession before many witnesses. (I Tim. 6: 12).

Be strong in the Lord, and in the power of His might. Put on the whole armor of God, that ye may be able to stand against the wiles of the devil—praying always with all prayer and supplication in the Spirit.

Eph. 6:10, 11, 18).

Morning Prayers for Tuesday.

131.

HEAR, O Lord, the prayers of all who call upon Thee, according to the benediction of Aaron (Num. 6), upon Thy people, that all who dwell in the earth may acknowledge that Thou, Lord, art the everlasting God. (Sir. 36.) Let the people praise Thee, O God; let all the people praise Thee. Then shall the earth yield her increase. The Lord, our God shall bless us: the Lord shall bless us, and all the earth shall fear Him. Amen. Amen.

Lord Jesus Christ, I, a poor, miserable sinner, am about to rise in Thy name. Thou wast crucified and didst die for me, and with Thy precious blood didst redeem me upon the cross. Govern, sanctify, and defend me in body and soul, and strengthen me unto all good works. Be my defence against every evil, and after this life grant me the life eternal. Amen.

132.

L ORD Jesus Christ, Who alone art the Redeemer of the world, unto Thee do I lift up my heart, my will, and all my senses, to thank Thee that of Thine inexhaustible love and mercy Thou hast this night again preserved me against the craft and power of the evil one. Lord Jesus Christ, Thou art my treasure and my heritage, my salvation is all in Thy hand. I know of none other helper in heaven or earth than Thee alone.

Therefore, of Thine unspeakable suffering and anguish, and the inexpressible bitterness of Thy death which Thou, Dear Lord, hast suffered in so great love for so miserable a sinner as I am, I beseech Thee to be gracious and merciful to me; and, do Thou, this day and throughout the days Thou grantest me, bless, prosper, defend, and preserve me from all evil; from this weary, miserable moment henceforth, until the day when Thou wilt graciously call me into eternal joy and blessedness. Grant this for the sake of Thy most Holy Name. Amen.

133.

BLESSED art Thou, O God, my Creator; blessed art Thou, O God, my Redeemer; blessed art Thou, O God, Most High Comforter,

Who art my shield, the horn of my salvation, and my defence; and hast again so graciously preserved me against every enemy of soul and body, during the night now past, I beseech Thee, most humbly, to cause Thy grace to cover me, and fill me this day with Thy mercy, that I may be graciously preserved from all sin and every evil. Surround me completely with Thy shielding presence, that Satan, the deceiver, with all his instrumentalities which threaten me on every side with their power and guile, their deceptions and temptations, both inwardly and outwardly, secretly and openly, may do me no harm. Preserve me in Thy fear, that I may commit no sin, but love Thee with all my heart, and be Thy servant forever. Grant me the needed grace to perform the duties

of my calling diligently and faithfully. Let my calling and station
prosper; bless my food and my
drink; and give guidance to all my
acts and deeds, unto Thy praise and
unto my temporal and eternal welfare. Keep far from me all grievous
diseases and whatsoever can harm
me in body and soul. Especially
save me from a sudden, evil death,
and from all misery. Let not Thy
Holy Spirit depart from me. Let
Thy holy angel ever be betwixt me
and mine enemies, that they may
not harm me. Let Thy grace and
blessing be ever upon me. Amen.

(George Zeamann, 1633.)

134.

O THOU, One, True, Almighty
God, King of kings, Father,
Son, and Holy Ghost, let the true

Morning-Star arise upon every human heart; let the true Light, which came into the world to enlighten all men, arise and shine upon every conscience; let the imperishable Word of Truth be heard by the mind to instruct it, that all men may become, and continue to be temples and sanctuaries of God; growing in love, in knowledge, and in wisdom throughout time and eternity. Amen. Amen.

The Lord's Prayer.
The Creed.
Psalm 92,
and Gloria Patri.

135.

For Strength in Daily Battles.

IN the Name of the Father, and of the Son, and of the Holy Ghost. Amen.

All praise and glory be unto Thee, Heavenly Father, Who hast again this night shown so great mercy unto me, a miserable sinner. I have no power,nor is it of my virtue that I continue to escape so manifold dangers amid so many enemies. O Lord, in how great dangers had I been this night if Thou hadst forsaken me! Yea, how would that great enemy of mankind not have spared me, hadst not Thou prevented him. For all this I thank Thee with my whole heart, and beseech Thee, O Merciful Father, cause all darkness of my heart, all restless timidity of my conscience, all fear and terror of devilish temptation to depart from me, as the night that is now past and ended. With the day at hand, grant unto me and all Christians the light of true faith, peace of conscience, and the joy of Thy divine presence. I lift up mine eyes unto Thee, O Lord, Whose throne is in heaven. As the eyes of a servant look unto the hand of his master, because there is none other succor, so do mine eyes turn unto Thee, O Lord, my God. Incline unto me this day, and have mercy upon me, for I am lonely and full of sorrow. Cares and anxieties, trials and labor multiply. Help me, O Lord, in every need. Behold, many are the enemies that hate me. Preserve my soul, and defend me. In Thee do I put my trust, let me not be ashamed, for my hope is in Thee. Hide not Thy countenance from me, lest I be like them that go down into the pit. Cause me to hear Thy loving-kindness in the morning. Let Thy way in which I shall go be made known unto me, for unto Thee do I lift up my soul. Teach me to do Thy will, for Thou art my God, Thy good spirit leadeth me in the paths of righteousness. Quicken me, O Lord, for Thy Name's sake. Of Thy mercy cut off mine enemies, and destroy them that afflict my soul, for I am Thy servant. O Lord, have mercy upon me and bless me. Lift up Thy countenance upon me and be gracious unto me. O Lord, preserve and defend me. Make Thy face to shine upon me, and grant me peace. Today and at all times I commend into Thy protecting hand my soul and body, my acts and purposes, my thoughts, and words, and deeds; my going out and my coming in, my life and my death, my wife, children, friends, kin, goods and possessions, house and home, and all that Thy

great mercy has bestowed upon me.
Lord, I know that I can not defend
myself at all times, that without
Thy help all my efforts will be in
vain, therefore be Thou this day and
at all times the house-father over me
and mine. Govern all things according to Thy will. Keep us, that we
speak and think nothing that is
contrary to Thee. Let us this day
so live that we despise not Thy
grace, but serve Thee with praise
unto Thy glory; and so be ready to
publish Thy praises evermore.
Amen.

136.

For Steadfast Faith.

LORD Jesus Christ, I know that
true Christian faith and hearty
confidence in Thy Name is the pure

and noble gift of God unto them
that are obedient to Thy word. I
thank Thee that Thou hast also
kindled this light in my soul, and
granted that even I, though yet in
great weakness, with such weak
faith, may rest all my trust in Thee
alone. Savior, maintain and increase
my faith within me. I do believe:
help Thou mine unbelief at all times.
Let not the bruised reed be broken
nor the smoking flax be quenched
so long as I live; that I may always
embrace Thee in a believing heart,
trust Thee with my whole heart's
confidence, delighting always in the
heavenly treasure of Thy grace, unto
mine own peace and comfort, and
daily find my joy in Thee, even unto
the end. Amen.

137.

Against the Kingdom of Darkness.

MOST beloved Lord and Savior,
Jesus Christ, Who, by Thy
power divine, didst all alone crush
the serpent's head, and, all alone,
hast rent asunder and broken up the
kingdom of the devil by Thy might:
we beseech Thee, graciously to defend and preserve us, poor, slow-of-
faith weaklings against the deceit
and temptations of the evil spirit,
against his great and burning zeal,
and the terrible wrath of his members; for he purposes none other than
to draw us away from Thy divine
Word, and to rob us of Thy comfort.
Help us, therefore, that in face of
the gates of hell, we abide steadfast
in the true faith by Thy divine
promise, and the true Word, even

unto the end of our days, unto Thy
glory and our salvation. Amen.

138.

Against Spiritual Enemies.

ALMIGHTY Son of God, Lord
Eternal, Who art come unto us
that Thou mightest crush the head of
the serpent with Thy heel, and
destroy the power and work of the
devil: we render thanks unto Thee
that by Thy mighty finger Thou dost
through Thy Word and Baptism
drive out from us the evil spirit, and
dost consecrate us to be holy
temples and pure sanctuaries of Thy
spirit. We beseech Thee, by Thine
almighty arm and unconquerable
power, let not satan again desecrate
Thy habitation and temple within us;
and leave him no power over us to

rob our hearts again of holiness, lest
our latter state become worse than
the first; Who dost battle and care for
us henceforth and eternally. Amen.

139.

Against the Power of the Devil.

(How weak Christians overcome the mighty devil.)
Dr. Martin Luther.

D EAR, Heavenly Father, praise
and thanksgiving be unto Thee
that I, miserable man, and though
I were a thousand such as
I am, could not withstand a single
devil, yet, by the help of Thy holy
angels I do withstand them. There
is in me not a drop of wisdom, while
the crafty evil one has a whole ocean
full, yet shall he not know how, nor
be able to harm me. My foolishness
and great weakness put even his
wisdom and power to shame. For

all this, O Gracious God and Father
of our Lord Jesus Christ, I owe
gratitude unto Thee alone; for it is
of Thy glory that Thou showest
forth Thy wisdom and power in mine
unworthiness, foolishness and weakness. Unto Thee alone shall be the
glory that Thou art the mighty, all-
wise and merciful God, and this Thy
glory is shown forth when through
Thy holy angels Thou helpest us,
that we defeat the devil. Unto this
ever help us, Lord God. Amen.

140.

In Temptation.

L ORD, Jesus Christ, we pray
Thee for strength of mind and
heart, and that by Thy grace Thou
wouldst remove all timidity from us.
Help that we may wholly submit

ourselves under Thy hand in true faith; and if it be Thine and the Father's good pleasure to visit judgment upon us in this our life on earth, for the merit of our sins, that we may be submissive, with patient hearts accepting all as coming from Thee alone, in order that under these things we may learn better to know ourselves, heartily to repent and bear true sorrow on account of our manifold sins. That we may never be severed from Thee, grant also that we may have strength to bear the well-merited correction of our sins and all that Thy grace shall send us. O ever faithful Shepherd and Bishop of our souls, maintain what is Thine, and the things of the Holy Ghost; also all revealed truth and whatsoever Thou hast hitherto vouchsafed unto us for knowledge of

Thee and of our everlasting salvation. Let the light Thou hast kindled,
—even though it yet shineth in dark
places—never be snuffed out, O
Lord, Jesus Christ. Let us not again
be led into our former blindness,
idolatry, and error. Give us peace,
Lord. Grant us peace for the sake
of that eternal peace which Thou
hast earned for us with Thy precious
blood upon the cross. Let us use all
Thy gifts more gratefully than we
have hitherto done, that we may
know Thee, our Lord, aright, without dissimulation, and serve Thee
and the Father on that account.
Fight Thou our battles with us,
strengthen and console our hearts in
times of danger, and carry the issue
to victory and everlasting life: for
we know that all things are in Thy
hand, and we believe that in answer

to our prayer Thou wilt grant us all
things salutary for us, and wilt not
leave us.　Lord, Jesus Christ, be
gracious unto us and grant us Thy
mercy.　Amen.

141.

Short and Good Counsel to be Frequently Considered by Those who are in Deep Straits and Grievous Temptation.

1. Stand not unto thyself, and
govern thyself not according to
thy feelings; for he that dependeth upon his own heart is
a fool.

2. Dwell not upon thine own
thoughts nor sink and entangle
thyself into them, else thou castest thyself into the camp of the
enemy that besieges thy soul.

3. Keep not thy sufferings thyself; but seek and confide fully and quickly in thy more experienced pastor.

4. Cleave unto the words which are spoken to thee in God's name. Consider them in thy heart. Repeat them again and again and direct the thoughts and emotions of thy heart to them.

5. Especially, let nothing make thee forget nor doubt these three passages:

a) The word of Isaiah, 49:14— 16; concerning God's faithful remembrance of us:

"Zion said, the Lord hath forsaken me, and my Lord hath forgotten me. Can a woman forget her sucking child, that she should not

have compassion on the son
of her womb? Yea, they
may forget, yet will I not
forget thee. Behold, I have
graven thee upon the palms
of my hands; thy walls are
continually before me."

b) The word according to John
10:28; concerning the security
of the soul in the hands of
Jesus:

"I give unto my sheep
eternal life; and they shall
never perish, neither shall
any man pluck them out of
my hand."

c) The word according to
Matthew 10:28—31; con-
cerning the security of the
body in the hands of Jesus:

"Fear not them which
kill the body, but are not able

to kill the soul: but rather fear him which is able to destroy both soul and body in hell. Are not two sparrows sold for a farthing? and one of them shall not fall on the ground without your Father. But the very hairs of your head are all numbered. Fear ye not therefore, ye are of more value than many sparrows.''

6. In moments of sore temptation, above all other times, neglect not the preaching of the gospel, which is the power of God, rejoicing the soul.

7. Neglect not to pray, even if it seem unto thee as if thou wert attempting to draw a load that is too heavy. James says, 5:13: ''Is any among you afflicted? let

him pray." Especially pray the
51st Psalm vv. 12—14: "Uphold
me with Thy free spirit;" and
Psalm 142.

8. When thou feelest as if courage
were at an end, begin to sing
Psalms and spiritual hymns.
This is very offensive to Satan
and exerts a wonderful power
upon troubled souls. Especially
to be recommended are the
Hymns of Praise. The prayer of
praise will oft' attain what no
prayer of entreating sighs may
gain. At times it immediately
draws one out of his distress.
If thou canst not thyself sing,
let others sing for thee.

9. When thou prayest take heed
lest thou in any wise desire to
be released of thy trial without
or against the will of God. Say

joyfully, or at least firmly, "If I shall drink this cup, dear Father, let Thy will be done."

10. Do not for one moment conceive that thou art the only one under so great trial. In Peter's first epistle, 4:12, thou learnest that such trials are common; and, in the same epistle, 5:8, 9, that like sufferings come upon thy brethren which are in the world. When a man begins to imagine that he alone is suffering, or that his sufferings are greater than those of others it is a sign of secret vanity.

11. Thou shalt thank God for His visitation upon thee. Temptation teaches to give heed unto the Word, and blessed is the man that endureth. (James 1:2, 4. 12.) Many one, if he but

knew how great good unto him
is hidden under his trials, would
gladly give up all his days of
joy for them.

12. Meet thy temptations not idly.
Idleness breeds and multiplies
many temptations which had
otherwise never come, nor abode
long if they came. Small is the
hope for recovery of an able
man tempted, if, when his temptation comes, he leaves the work
of his calling undone or but half
done.

13. When thou art tempted, flee
from solitude and seek the com-
panionship of godly, joyful
people. Few people can, without injury to themselves, live
constantly in great companies,
and less are they who can live
in constant solitude without

harm. God created men for each
other.

14. Many trials have their origin
in a diseased body. If, therefore, an experienced pastor ad-
vises thee to seek the services of
a physician, do not neglect that
advice; but use the treatment
prescribed with a prayer for
God's benediction upon such use.

15. Consider these recommendations
diligently. Let them guide and
comfort thee; and may God
grant thee peace. Amen.

142.

Prayer of an Anxious Soul That Knows Not the Source of Its Anxiety.

O LORD, since I know not whence
arises this anguish which
troubles and oppresses me in body

and soul, whether from heaven or hell, or from mine own weak and diseased body, I flee unto Thee, Father of all mercy and God of comfort, to seek renewal and relief in Thee. Say unto me "Be of good cheer, my son, (daughter,) thy sins are forgiven thee," and grant me confidence that this unrest in my members cometh neither by Thy curse nor wrath. So speak unto me that I may find that peace which passeth all understanding; and I shall bow under every anguish which Thy mighty hand sends me, and be at peace in the midst of unrest. Have mercy upon me, O great God, have mercy upon me for Jesus Christ's sake. Amen.

143.

Prayer of a Troubled One Who Knoweth Not Whether His Trouble Cometh From the Devil or From His Own Body.

O LORD, since I know not whence cometh this grievous anguish and pain that oppresses and troubles my body and soul, whether from the devil or from mine own weak and diseased body, I commit the cause of all my suffering unto Thee and seek my help from Thee alone, O Lord, God of peace that passeth understanding. Take away, for the sake of Him, Who in Gethsemane and on the cross did suffer all human pain and anguish; take away, for the sake of Christ my only Savior, Who is the eternal covenant between Thee and me; take away my fear-filled heart,

for His dear sake, and so bring quiet
unto my body and soul. If it be
Thy will, however, O God, that I
continue in pain and anguish, grant
unto me a sure haven of rest within,
from whence I may overcome all
things. Grant me Thy peace and the
surety of Thy grace in Jesus Christ;
and, when it shall seem to me that
I am not able to suffer more nor to
overcome my sorrow, then uphold
Thou me and cause me to stand.
Suffer me not to be tempted above
what I am able; but with the temptation also make a way to escape
that I may be able to bear it. O
Thou, Who after the darkness and
noonday heat of Good Friday gavest
an evening of rest and peace, Thou
wilt grant a morn of peace after a
night of tears; through Jesus Christ.
Amen.

Bear Thou me up; for I will not leave Thee. Uphold me, O my Light and my Consolation, for I will not leave Thee.

Ever quiet and more quiet let me grow, O peaceful Lamb, content under trial and content in peace, content until my days shall end. Amen.

144.

No. 144 is omitted from the translation because it is fully covered by other prayers in the book.

145.

Petition Against the Devil and the Powers of Evil.

ETERNAL Lord, Mighty Son of God, Who art come to crush the head of the serpent, and his dominion, and to destroy the works of the devil, we render Thee hearty thanks that by Thine almighty hand Thou de-

liverest us from the devil, through
Thy Word and Holy Baptism, and
consecratest us to be holy temples
and sanctuaries undefiled; and, we
beseech Thee, that by Thine almighty arm and invincible power
Thou wilt no more permit Satan to
desecrate Thy house and defile Thy
temple, nor suffer him to have any
power over us; O Thou Who lovest
and defendest us: one unconquerable
God and Lord, praised forever.
Amen.

Pray also: "A mighty fortress is our God," etc.

146.

THY kingdom come, and with us be
    Both now and in eternity.
The Holy Ghost to us impart,
With gifts divers for home and heart.
The devil's wrath and pow'r allay
And shield from him Thy Church, we
        pray.

Into temptation, gracious Lord,
Lead Thou us not, but help afford,
That we, assailed on ev'ry hand,
May in the evil day withstand,
Sustained by faith 'mid Satan's host
And solaced by the Holy Ghost.

147.

L ORD Jesus Christ, we pray to
       Thee,
Wilt Thou our true Protector be,
That Satan, who our souls would
       harm,
May be restrained by Thy strong
       arm.

For, Thine inheritance are we,
Redeemed with Thine own blood by
       Thee.
'Twas from eternity decreed
That Thou shouldst own us, Lord,
       indeed.

So let Thine angel for us care
And shield Thy people ev'rywhere.
Yea, let Thy watch around us stay
To keep the evil foe away.

148.

BID not Thine angel vanish,
   Let him abide with me.
But Satan from me banish,
That I may never be,
In this dark vale of woe,
By him, my foe, attended,
But, till my life is ended,
Go safely to and fro.

149.

O LORD, destroy the devil's
      pow'r,
And quench his work within us.
Lend us Thy strength at ev'ry hour,
That Satan may not win us.
Help us that we may watchful be,
Lest, being made from Satan free,
He should again possess us.

150.

(Psalm 91.)

HE that dwelleth in the secret place of the most High shall abide under the shadow of the Almighty.

I will say of the Lord, He is my refuge and my fortress: my God; in Him will I trust.

Surely He shall deliver thee from the snare of the fowler, and from the noisome pestilence.

He shall cover thee with His feathers, and under His wings shalt thou trust; His truth shall be thy shield and buckler.

Thou shalt not be afraid for the terror by night; nor for the arrow that flieth by day;

Nor for the pestilence that walketh in darkness; nor for the destruction that wasteth at noonday.

A thousand shall fall at thy side, and ten thousand at thy right hand; but it shall not come nigh thee.

Only with thine eyes shalt thou behold and see the reward of the wicked.

Because thou hast made the Lord, which is my refuge, even the most High, thy habitation;

There shall no evil befall thee, neither shall any plague come nigh thy dwelling.

For He shall give His angels charge over thee, to keep thee in all thy ways.

They shall bear thee up in their hands, lest thou dash thy foot against a stone.

Thou shalt tread upon the lion and adder: the young lion and the dragon shalt thou trample under feet.

Because he hath set his love upon Me, therefore will I deliver him: I will set him on high, because he hath known My name.

He shall call upon Me, and I will answer him: I will be with him in trouble; I will deliver him, and honor him.

With long life will I satisfy him, and shew him My salvation.

Glory be to the Father, and to the Son, and to the Holy Ghost; as it was in the beginning, is now, and ever shall be, world without end. Amen.

151.

For the Church, Against Her Enemies.

ALMIGHTY and Ever Merciful God, look upon all the oppression and persecution which Thy

beloved Christendom is made to
suffer at the hands of the devil and
his followers. Behold how constantly and zealously Thine enemies seek
our destruction both physical and
spiritual! Loving Father, have
mercy upon us for Thy Name's
glory. We have not sinned against
Thine enemies but against Thee
only; therefore, judge us according
to Thy loving-kindness and grace,
and not according to our deserving.
Despite all our sins and weaknesses
we are and remain Thy heritage
which Thy beloved Son, our Lord
Jesus Christ, has purchased and won
by His own precious blood. For
His sake, Holy Father, Thou wilt be
gracious and merciful and not permit those who are enemies of Thee
and of us to outrage us with pernicious doctrines or persecution. Thou

art the Mighty God who causest the wicked and mighty of this world to fall by their own counsels. Let Thy will be done. Bring to naught all evil purposes of Satan and his followers who assemble and conspire against Thee and Thy holy, saving Word. We commend ourselves wholly to Thy care and protection. Assist and comfort us in these perilous times. Preserve us from shameless unbelief and from all dreadful falling away from Thy gospel. Maintain us steadfast in Thy Word. Grant us strength unto faith, truth, love, and perseverance under the cross; through Thy beloved Son, Jesus Christ, our Lord Who, together with the Holy Ghost, liveth and reigneth with Thee, world without end. Amen.

152.

Common Prayer in Time of War.

ALMIGHTY and gracious God, Who didst cause the light to shine and bringest peace, Who stillest the roarings of the deep, the noise of its waters and the unrest of the nations, Who makest wars to cease unto the ends of the earth, destroyest the bow, breakest the spear asunder, and burnest the chariots with fire, we beseech Thee, O very God of peace, so to rule and govern the hearts of them that bear rule over us, that, in Christian unity one with another, they may follow after peace; that the church, the schools, and all government be preserved in prosperity, and we may serve Thee all our days in pure knowledge and holy lives without fear. Preserve

us from war, sedition, and bloodshed.
Defend us against every counsel of
evil men who follow not after the
ways of peace, but always go about
pregnant with disaster, destruction
and harm. Cause their machinations
to be confounded, their disasters to
come upon their own heads, and
their mockery to rest upon their own
shoulders. Disperse the nations
that love to war, and grant us peace
from all our enemies; that each
may dwell under his own vine
and fig-tree without fear, and none
may rise up against us. Fasten
Thou the bars upon our gates and let
no fear come upon them that bear
rule in the land. O God of Peace,
give peace within our borders. Always and everywhere grant peace to
our country, that we may rest in
safety, with none to make us afraid.

Grant us grace that the dissensions
and bitternesses which have arisen
be again stilled through peaceable
means and orderly counsels. Our
country trembles, and all who dwell
therein. Lord, uphold Thou her
pillars. Awake and send us saviors
who shall help and save us that we
may dwell in our homes as before.
Hear us in the day of our great need,
and let Thy holy Name be our
defence. Send us help speedily
from out of Thy sanctuary; and
from Thy sacred dwelling-place
strengthen Thou us. Let honor
abide in our land and all her cities;
that loyalty and goodness may kiss
each other; that fidelity increase in
the earth, and righteousness look
down from heaven. Arise, Lord, to
judge; and help all the oppressed
and miserable of the earth. Arise,

and help us with Thy good right
hand. Do good unto the nations
among whom Thy Word dwelleth,
and let not the vineyard Thou hast
planted among us be destroyed. O
Lord, abide with us, the day is far,
spent, the evening is at hand.
Strengthen Thy kingdom which Thou
hast established among us, and preserve us and all posterity in the true
faith. Have mercy upon us, O God.
Help us in every need. Let Thy mercy be upon us as our trust is in Thee.
Graciously grant us these our sincere
petitions, O Merciful and Gracious
God, for the sake of the precious
merits of Thine only-begotten, well-
beloved Son, the Prince of Peace,
Who, in unity with the Holy Ghost,
liveth and reigneth with Thee, true
God, glorified forevermore. Amen.

Prayers for Peace.

153.

O GOD, Author of peace and Source of all love, whoso confesses Thee shall live, and whoso serveth Thee shall reign. Defend the humble and preserve them against every onslaught of their enemies, that we, who rely on Thy protection, may fear no weapon of enmity; through Jesus Christ, Thy Son, our Lord. Amen.

154.

LORD God, Heavenly Father, Who workest in us an holy zeal, good counsel and just works, grant unto Thy servants that peace which the world can not give; that we may give our hearts unto Thy commandments, and, under Thy protection,

live out our days in rest and quiet-
ness from our enemies; through
Jesus Christ, Thy Son, our Lord.
Amen.

155.

O LORD God of Hosts, make us
to be quiet and peaceable, in
our hearts, our congregation, our
country, and our homes; and, in the
day of salvation, take us into Thy
quiet, still, and peaceable country of
eternal joy and glory. Amen.

Prayers for Peace in the Home.

156.

MAY the Divine Housefather,
Who prepares His house and
vineyard early, grant His blessing
unto our house and all that belongs
thereto.

May the Lord Jesus Christ, at

Whose entrance the house of Zachaeus experienced salvation, enter our house also in grace, that no evil befall.

May the Holy Ghost, Who planteth unity and great love, well-pleasing before God and man, in the home, now, and at all times, rest upon this house with all His consolations, that we may here rest under the temporal benediction of God, and look forward patiently in hope to the eternal blessings of heaven. Amen.

157.

DEAR Father, Thou hast vouchsafed unto me wife and child, house and home. For these I plead Thy promises; and, for Thy sake, I go before them in the way. It is my desire, therefore, so far as in me lieth,

to do what ever may lead us aright;
and, when all does not go according
to my desire, I pray for patience to
submit and let the outcome be according to the proverb: — Come
what may, as God will, so will
I go. If all go well, I will render
the praise unto Thee, O Lord, for it
is after all not my care, my work,
my toil, nor my labor, but of Thy
gift and grace when things go aright.
I pray Thee that by Thy help and
grace all things may ever go right.
. Amen.

158.
Prayer for Peace.

(To be repeated at evening time when one returns
to his house.)

ALMIGHTY, Ever-Gracious Father, Thine only-begotten Son
had not on earth where to lay His
weary head. By Thy grace, we have

houses and homes to which we can
go, when storms come or wild beasts
threaten, and whither we retire from
the unrest of the masses, and from
the cares of our calling. Grant, that
by Thy grace our body may here
rest in peace, freed from labor, and
yield unto the soul that it may rise
into Thy most holy rest; and
through Thy peace, let all things
abide still, quiet, and in peace.
Nothing can be more like unto Thy
divine and most holy nature than a
composed heart and mind; therefore, ·
Thou hast called us out of turmoil
unto a safe haven, from the world
unto eternal peace, which is greater
than all the world can understand.
May the peace of our Lord Jesus
Christ be and abide upon this house,
and upon all who dwell therein,
for ever and ever. Amen.

Evening Prayers.
159.

MAY the Lord grant us peace; a realization of our sins; and the amendment of our sinful lives through true faith in Jesus Christ; and, after this life, the life eternal. Amen.

I beseech Thee, Lord Jesus Christ, abide with me this night, so that when my body rests my soul may be alert to keep Thee ever before my heart and mind, to guard me from all evil. Let Thy holy angel guard me that the enemy come not nigh unto me; but that Thou, O Lord, abide alone with me. Let also all that Thou hast given me be so commended unto Thee, and receive all under Thy guardianship to defend them against all evil and preserve them unto eternal life. Amen.

160.

ETERNAL, Gracious, and Great God in heaven, Who through abounding grace and paternal care hast permitted me to complete this day in good health, I heartily render thanks unto Thee as is meet to do. Since I have not lived all this day unto Thy glory and honor, nor to the benefit of my fellows, because my whole nature ever inclines to evil rather than to the good, help me, who am conceived in sin, O most faithful God, that I may rightly acknowledge my weaknesses and become a partaker of Thy divine grace. Teach me often to dwell upon my latter days that I may compose myself thereunto through true repentance; and, when the end draweth nigh, may I gladly depart from this vale of sorrow to be translated with all believers into Thy heavenly paradise. In the meanwhile, so long as I am yet to abide here, receive me under Thy protection and graciously defend me against all harm and danger of body and soul, for Christ's sake. Amen.

161.

O LORD, my God, at evening time I lift up my hands unto Thee. Come unto us like the latter rains that make the earth fruitful. Abide with us, for the day is far spent, the evening is at hand, and in the darkness there is no one to defend us except Thou alone, O God. Hasten to uphold us. Defend us this night lest our souls fall into the sleep of sin and our bodies be overcome with evil. Awake us again in due time, and make us to hear joy

and peace, for we love Thy word
and Thy testimonies, which are the
delight of our souls. Let our ears
be saved from all messages of sorrow,
and turn all anguish from our souls;
for, Thou alone canst prosper all
that liveth, and fill it with Thy blessing, in Jesus Christ, our Lord.
Amen.

162.

LORD, Jesus Christ, Savior of the
World, Eternal Word from the
Father in heaven, by Whom all
things were made, and without
Whom nothing was made that exists,
and without Whom nothing is preserved that liveth; years, seasons,
and months, day and night were
made by Thee, and by Thee all
are governed and maintained: we
miserable creatures who are ever in

danger from our enemies, beseech
Thee, O gracious Lord, protect us
this night under the wings of Thy
mercy, that we fall not away from
Thee, nor let the evil one make us
afraid. Help us that even in the
darkness we may behold the light,
Thou, Who art eternal Light, Who
livest and reignest together with the
Father in heaven, and the Holy
Ghost, now, henceforth, and forevermore. Amen.

The Lord's Prayer.

The Creed.

Psalm 3,

and, The Gloria Patri.

4.

WEDNESDAY.

"For to me to live is Christ, and to die is gain. But if I live in the flesh, this is the fruit of my labor: yet what I shall choose I wot not. For I am in a straight betwixt two, having a desire to depart, and be with Christ; which is far better: nevertheless to abide in the flesh is more needful for you." (Phil. 1: 21 —24).

While here I grieve,
To Thee I cleave,
O God, my stay!
And this I pray:
If dark to me
Thy ways must be,
That still I may
Be blest for aye
Through Jesus Christ, my Savior. Amen.

Wednesday Morning Prayers.

163.

SING unto the Lord a new song. Sing unto the Lord, O earth! Sing forth the honor of His Name. Let day proclaim unto day the salvation of our God. O come, let us sing unto the Lord our God a new song. May He bless and preserve me,—The Father, Who created me, The Son, Who redeemed me, The Holy Ghost, Who sanctified me. Amen.

God the Father, God the Son, and God the Holy Ghost, blessed and most holy Trinity, abide with me this day and at all times. Let me now, together with all the elect of God, arise unto **one** faith and **one**

confession thereof in like confidence
and hope of God. Let me arise from
all my sin and sorrow to the grace
and comfort of God and unto eternal
life in Jesus Christ. Amen.

164.

UNTO Thee, Lord, God Almighty,
do I this day commend my
body and soul, all my goods, my
wife, child, father, mother, and all
my thoughts and words, my heart,
my ambitions and all my purposes.
Again, I commend unto Thee also
my tongue and all my words. All
my acts also I commend, that the
same may serve unto Thy honor and
the welfare of my fellow men. Let
me be this day a vessel of Thy grace
and an instrument of Thy mercy.
Bless all my undertakings, make my

business to prosper, and prevent everything that could hinder these things. Amen.

165.

ALMIGHTY and Everlasting God, as Thou hast so graciously preserved me throughout the past night and caused me to awake from the darkness and from the semblance of death unto the light of day, I beseech Thee, grant me grace this day also, that I may live through the same in acknowledgment and fear of Thee, to praise and glorify Thee, and to render thanks unto Thee for all Thy loving-kindness which Thou showerest upon me. Let mine duties of office be discharged by Thy help and support, that all be done unto the honor of Thy holy Name and the

salvation of my soul, for the sake of
Thy well-beloved Son, Jesus Christ,
my Savior. Amen.

166.

GRACIOUS and Almighty God,
Merciful Father in heaven,
with my whole heart I render
unto Thee all praise and laud and
honor that Thou hast preserved
me throughout the night now past
under the protection of Thy holy
angels, and permitted me to see the
light of this day in health and
strength. I beseech Thee, Heavenly
Father, to Whose will I submit all
things begun or ended by me, and all
that I may do or leave undone, grant
me Thy continued grace; and, by
Thy Holy Spirit, so rule and govern
all my thoughts and purposes, my

heart, mind, energies, and desires, together with every word and deed, that I may ever recognize what is good and what is evil; so that I may this day walk here amid this evil and perverse world, free from all transgression, keeping in mind the hearty desire toward my heavenly home, which Christ, my Savior, has obtained and merited for me, and that I may never by an evil and sinful life forfeit the same. Unto all this help me graciously by the love and power of Thy Holy Spirit, for the sake of Jesus Christ, Thy well beloved Son. Amen.

The Lord's Prayer.

The Creed.

Psalm 73.

The Gloria Patri.

THE NOONDAY OF LIFE.

167.

Retrospection.

(A prayer of thanksgiving.)

ALMIGHTY and Eternal God, Who art my life, my prosperity, and my salvation, I, a creature of the dust of the earth, undertake to come into Thy presence to praise Thee. Spurn not my unworthy praises, O Lord, but graciously accept my thanks, through Jesus Christ. Thou hast provided and nourished my life in body and soul, from the hour of my birth until now. From innumerable dangers to body and soul Thou hast guarded and saved me. Though I have greatly erred by the way, sunk into many grievous sins, shamed and disgraced

Thy honor, become a source of vexation in all the world, and abundantly deserved Thy displeasure, yet, hast Thou not condemned me in my sins, but hast suffered me in all forbearance. Though I hesitated both to hear and to obey, yet, without ceasing, Thou hast in manifold ways continued to admonish me unto the way of salvation. Neither didst Thou cease ere Thou hadst set me aright. With great mercy Thou overcamest my evil and hast turned my steps into the paths of the Christian life. All this hast Thou done for me for the sake of Jesus Christ, Who gave Himself into all sufferings, punishments, and guilt, even unto death, that I might at length rejoice with Thee in everlasting blessedness. What can I render unto Thee, O God and Father, for all Thy mercies and Thy faithfulness unto me? How shall I render thanks unto Thee, Lord Jesus, Thou meek, humble, and gracious Lamb of God, Who by Thy great merit feedest and nourishest me, a miserable sinner, with life and peace, yea, even with Thine own Self? I command no good thing: how, then shall I thank Thee? Thou Who gavest me all that I have and am, grant that I may in return offer my insufficient thankfulness, and yield unto Thee again all that I am and all that I have; nor seek any more to rob Thine altars of my offering, so long as I may live. Let Thy holy will alone be done with me, in me, and through me, and, unto the last, let my life be devoted unto Thy glory. To this help me by Thy great love. Amen.

A CONTEMPLATION OF THIS PRESENT LIFE.

168.

Faithful and Upright Preserve Thou Me, For in Thee Do I Trust.

Proverbs 30:7 ff.

TWO things have I required of Thee; deny me them not before I die: Remove far from me vanity and lies: Give me neither poverty nor riches; feed me with food convenient for me: lest I be full, and deny Thee, and say, Who is the Lord? or lest I be poor, and steal, and take the name of my God in vain.

169.

Prayer of a Housefather for Strength to Fulfil His Paternal Duty.

ALMIGHTY God, Gracious Father, Who hast called me to be a housefather for the sake of Thy

Son, unto Whom all the household
of Thy Christian people is commended, I beseech Thee, grant me
wisdom that I may govern my wife,
children, and servants with Christian
charity, and bring them up in all
good order and the admonition of
Thy word. Bless my living, and
cause Thy beloved angels to watch
over my home. Except Thou build
the house and bless our labor and
industry, all our care and labor is in
vain. Help us, O Father, through
Jesus Christ. Amen.

170.
Prayer of a Housemother for Strength to Fulfil Her Duties.

L ORD Jesus Christ, very Son of
God Who has given unto me my
husband, my children and mine own
hearthstone, graciously help me

that, according to Thy command, I may be submissive unto mine own husband and train my children in reverence and fear of Thee. Grant unto me also that I may ever faithfully administer whatever my husband by Thy blessing does earn; and that I live in peace with all; that I may make my calling sure, and praise Thee with my works, Who art also the Savior of believing women, and makest them to be partakers of Thy grace, blessed unto all eternity. Amen.

CARE FOR THE FUTURE.

171.

For Calmness.

TAKE from me, Lord, what grieveth Thee,
Though precious it may be to me.

Give me whatever pleaseth Thee,
Though it should grievous be to me.
When Thou takest, I am giving,
Poor I grow, though rich I be;
When Thou givest, I am taking
Life and wealth in poverty.
Draw us to Thee, that we
Thy followers may be.   Amen.

172.

Prayer for Christian Steadfastness in Faith.

GREAT, Unchangeable, Eternal God and Father, Who art faithful, just, holy, and righteous, I come to lament my heart's instability before Thee. I am moved as easily as are the waters; now by fear, and again by the favors of men; now by riches and honors, and again by poverty and oppression; now by pleasure, and again by this world's vexations which turn me from Thy word and command. Though my spirit is willing, I realize that my flesh is weak. Forgive me this my sin and reckon it not unto me. Turn from me Thy just judgments, Who hast said:—"The Lord has no pleasure in them that turn aside, but will cast them out with the evildoers." Though so often I have strayed from Thee, depart not Thou from me. Cast me not away from Thy presence, though I have frequently disregarded Thee and Thy Word. Take not Thy Holy Spirit from me, though I have often grieved Him; but let me hold fast Thy true, steadfast, and joyful spirit. Establish my heart with divine power. Grant me good courage that I may prefer Thy riches and glory before all the riches and honors of this world, and not be drawn away from faith, patience, and every Christian virtue, but, daily increase in the same. Grant me grace to overcome the world and her lusts, and subdue in me the desire of the flesh, that I may not be offended by the ingratitude of the world nor by any tribulations which may befall me because of godliness and Christian virtue. Grant that I may rest secure in Thy promises, for Thou hast vouchsafed that no one shall take away Thy sheep from Thee, and Thou wilt send the Comforter Who shall be with us always, for Thou hast prayed for us that our faith cease not. Now I know God is faithful Who has promised. Therefore grant me a ready, heavenly mind that I may prefer eternal before temporal things, and fear no power that may rise up against me. Grant that I may not exult in good fortune nor despair if evil befall. Cause me to be firm, that I undertake what is good and carry it out, and not allow myself to be hindered therefrom. Grant me Thy Spirit of Power that I may love and confess the truth, and stand for righteousness without any hesitation, to advocate and defend it until death, even that for its sake I may gladly suffer without murmuring at Thy will; that for Christ and the confession of His dear Name I may not fear, dread, nor flee from any danger, ever witnessing a good confession as did Christ, my Savior, before Pontius Pilate. Let not Satan's craft turn me away from Thee and Thy divine truth. Grant that I may

overcome all his fiery darts, and
establish Thou me on the firm foundation which abideth and has the
seal "God knoweth them that
are His." By Thy divine might,
preserve me unto salvation. Cause
me to spend my days in the power
of God, my Lord, to be strong in
the Lord and in the power of His
strength. O Lord, my strong defence, maintain the good work which
Thou hast begun in me, and complete it unto the day of Jesus Christ.
Cause me to be ready, strengthened,
established, and founded, that I may
be found pure, without blemish in
faith and holy living, filled with the
fruits of righteousness which are by
our Lord Jesus Christ unto the
glory and honor of God; that rendering true service, retaining a good
conscience and faith, I may finish

my course, keep the faith, that
the crown of righteousness be laid
up for me, which that just judge,
Jesus Christ, shall give unto me and
to all who love His coming. Amen.
In the name of Jesus. Amen.

To Live for Christ Alone.

173.

BLESSED Lord Jesus, most
heartily do I beseech Thee, by
Thy great mercy according to
which Thou, Lord, hast redeemed
me from eternal death, make tender
my hard and stony heart by the
anointing of the Holy Ghost, that I
may always have a broken and a
contrite spirit before Thee. In love
to Thee, let me die unto the world
that I sorrow not exceedingly for
temporal things, nor rejoice exceedingly therein; that I fear

nothing temporal, nor yet inordinately love the same, but have all my desire, my love and my joy in Thee, and rejoice in every other thing only with Thee. Amen.

174.

WE magnify and confess, honor and praise Thee, Lord Jesus Christ, King of all grace, and Prince of victory, for Thine elect. Thou art come to destroy all dominion and power of the devil in us and about us, thereby calling our bodies and souls, our faculties and understanding unto the knowledge, glory, honor, and service of Thee. O most merciful Savior, let us mortals never forget Thy loving-kindness. Preserve our hearts, tongues and lips, yea, our whole lives in service and obedience to Thy holy will, that by our

words and deeds and godly lives we
may proclaim the power and virtue
of Thy word, and remain Thy beloved children, the sheep of Thy
pasture. Amen.

175.
Nearness of Death.

IN the midst of life we see
    Snares of death surround us.
Who, then, shall our refuge be,
Lest the foe confound us?
    O Thou alone, our Savior!
We mourn our grievous sin which
       hath
Stirred the fires of Thy wrath.
Holy and souvereign God,
Holy and mighty God,
Holy and all-merciful Savior,
Thou eternal God,
Suff'r us not to perish
In the bitter woes of death.
       Kyrieleison.

In the midst of death we see
Hell, with all its raging.
Who is he that sets us free,
All our fears assuaging?
  O Thou alone, our Savior!
It moves Thy tender heart to see
All our sin and misery.
Holy and sovereign God,
Holy and mighty God,
Holy and all-merciful Savior,
Thou eternal God,
Keep our hearts from fainting
At the thought of burning hell.
    Kyrieleison.

Into hell's deep agony
By our misdeeds driven,
Whither shall we sinners flee?
Who takes us to heaven?
  O Thou alone, our Savior!
For, lo, Thy precious blood is spilt,
Cleansing us from sin and guilt.

Holy and sovereign God.
Holy and mighty God,
Holy and all-merciful Savior,
Thou eternal God,
Let us not abandon
Faith's true staff that comfort lends.
Kyrieleison.

176.

Prayer for a Blessed Death.

MERCIFUL God, teach me to remember that I must die and have here no continuing city. When my hour cometh, grant me a blessed departure in grace, that I may rejoice to die, having a conscious end in the true confession, and that my mind and my senses be not disturbed so as to make me speak foolish words or to blaspheme against Thee, my Lord, or against my salvation. Save me from an

evil death and everlasting condemnation. Let not my last hour come
suddenly and unexpectedly upon me,
but that I may first have prepared
for the same in true repentance and
faith; and, when it cometh, make
me to be ready and joyful unto
temporal death which openeth unto
me the gates of life eternal. And so
let Thou Thy servant depart in
peace. Grant that my last words
may be like unto those which Thy
beloved Son spake upon the cross:
"Father, into Thy hands I commend my Spirit," and, when I can
speak no more, hear my last sighings, through Jesus Christ. Amen.

177.
In Contemplation of the Judgment Day.

O THOU Great, Merciful, and Gracious Lord, I confess unto Thee that I have sinned against Thee in manifold ways and abundantly deserve Thy righteous condemnation. No repentance of mine can atone for this; but Thy mercy exceeds my transgression. Therefore, I flee unto Thee and pray Thou wilt not reckon my sin and the shortcomings of my repentance and sorrow unto me, nor enter into judgment with Thy servant, but according to the multitude of Thy tender mercies blot out my transgressions. Woe is me, a sinner, should the Day of Judgment come when the records of conscience shall be opened and all men shall say of me: "Behold this

man and his works." Lord, God,
what shall I do in that hour when
heaven shall reveal all my sins, and
the very death shall rise up against
me? Behold, I could answer nothing,
but to hang my head in shame and
stand in fearful hopelessness. O
have mercy upon me, Lord, my God,
lest I fall into grievous doubt; for
though, indeed, I have done much
evil for which Thou shouldst justly
condemn me, yet, Thou hast great
store of grace from which Thou canst
help and lovest to help such as I
am. Lord, Thou desirest not the
death of a sinner, nor hast Thou any
pleasure in the destruction of them
that die; yea, even therefore didst
Thou Thyself suffer death, and by
Thy death didst rob death of his
power, that the dying might have
life. Therefore, I beseech Thee,

reach out unto me from heaven Thy
mighty and gracious hand to save
me from the hand of mine enemies
that they rejoice not over me in
mine anguish, nor have pleasure in
executing their will upon me, and
saying: Now will we destroy him
entirely. Who, O Lord, can despair
of Thy mercy? While we were yet
sinners Thou didst redeem us with
Thy precious blood, and hast reconciled us to our heavenly Father.
Permit me now to approach the
throne of grace under the shadow of
Thy mercy, that I may sue for grace
and cease not to knock and to
cry until Thou hast had mercy upon
me. Thou hast Thyself called us
unto the feast of pardon when we
sought it not; how much more then
shall we not find forgiveness when
our souls have become exceedingly

anxious in their quest for it? I come seeking Thy mercy. Mercy! O Thou Judge of the world, Who comest and bringest with Thee the reward. Mercy! for all my life, short or long as its days may be permitted to be. Mercy! in the hour of death. Mercy! in the day of judgment. Mercy! O Lamb of God, by Thy bitter sufferings and death. Amen.

178.

In Contemplation of Eternal Life.

AS the hart panteth after the water-brooks, so panteth my soul after Thee, O God. My soul thirsteth for God, for the living God: when shall I come and appear before God? O, Fountain of Life, Thou Well of Living Waters, when shall I come away from this miserable, erring, pathless, and desert

world to the sweet waters of Thy
beauty that I may behold Thy power
and majesty and quench my thirst
in the fountain of Thy grace and
mercy? Thinkest Thou that I shall
see that great day—the day of joy
and gladness? O that glorious,
happy day which knoweth no night
nor waning, when I shall enter into
the beautiful mansions of my God
and into His joy and the enjoyment
of His unfathomed miracles without
number! There shall be no enemy,
neither opposition, nor vexation. No
evil and deceptive temptation shall
come nigh, but only harmless, continuing safety to the soul, holy rest,
pure, peaceful joy, a blessed eternity,
and everlasting blessedness; yea,
the Most Holy Trinity, and the
blessed beholding of Deity Itself,
which is the joy of the Lord our

God. O when shall I come and appear before God? I rejoice that my day on earth is declining. Hasten the evening, O Lord Jesus. Come and lead me forth from this my prison house unto eternal joys; out of the darkness of this life to the light of never ending day. Come, Thou desire of the gentiles, make me to behold Thy countenance, that my heart may revive. from the sorrows of this life, and my soul live forever. Amen.

Evening Prayers.

179.

I LAY me down to sleep in the Name of the Lord Jesus Christ, the Crucified. May He bless, defend, and lead me unto eternal life. Amen.

Unto Thee, Lord, Heavenly Father, I render praise and thanksgiving for all Thy loving-kindness which Thou hast this day so graciously shown unto me. I pray Thee, protect and defend me from evil this night. Keep from me the devil and every vexation, that I may rest safely and sleep in peace. Let me not be overcome by an evil death this night, without a recognition of Thy beloved Son; but, let me with joy arise from sleep to acknowledge Thy grace, to praise Thy holy name, and to render thanks unto Thee; through Jesus Christ our Redeemer and Savior. Amen.

180.

ALMIGHTY and Most Gracious God, I give thanks unto Thee that Thou hast this day so graciously guarded me from all evil and danger in body and soul. By Thy divine grace, I beseech Thee, cover over all sins I have this day committed in thought or word, and especially my transgressions against Thee and Thy holy law, and leave not me, Thy creature, whom Thou hast purchased at so great a price with the blood of Thy Son, Jesus Christ; but shield me this night under the wings of Thy grace against the evil one who cometh abroad like a roaring lion to devour me. Cause me to rest and sleep in the shadow of Thy mercy, that the evil one come not nigh nor be able to harm me. `Amen.

181.

LORD, I am about to close mine eyes in sleep, but Thou, Who keepest Israel, slumberest not nor sleepest. Thou dost guard me in body and soul. Darkness has fallen round about me. Let the light of Thy countenance be over me and be gracious unto me. Sorrow and care are now laid aside, but let me not forget Thee while I sleep. As my lips now sink into silence, let my soul still pray to Thee when I sleep. Lord, bless my rest. Cleanse my soul that no impure dreams defile my heart nor trouble Thy spirit. Be Thou my dream, my joy and my glory, that I may awake to praise Thy name, so holy, so gracious, so wonderful. Amen.

182.

LORD Jesus Christ, the darkness descends upon us, to whom shall we flee? Unto Thee I come, O Heavenly, Eternal Light. Shine Thou round about me that mine eyes fall not into the sleep of eternal death. Banish from my presence the evil spirit and all his angels and whatsoever else is at enmity with my soul. Cause me to sleep in peace, to rest in safety, and to awake again in joy, to live a Christian life, and, at last, to die a blessed death. Let Thy grace be with me now and at all times, unto all eternity. Amen. O Son of David, have mercy upon me and forgive me all my transgressions. Amen. The Love of God the Father, the grace of our Lord Jesus Christ, and the communion of the Holy Ghost be with me and with all believers. Amen.

The Lord's Prayer.

The Creed.

Psalm 23.

The Gloria Patri.

5.

THURSDAY.

He that dwelleth in the secret place of the most High shall abide under the shadow of the Almighty. I will say of the Lord, He is my refuge and my fortress: my God; in Him will I trust.

The Lord is thy refuge; even the most High is thy habitation; there shall no evil befall thee, neither shall any plague come nigh thy dwelling.

Because he hath set his love upon Me, therefore will I deliver him: I will set him on high, because he hath known My name. He shall call upon Me, and I will answer him: I will be with him in trouble; I will deliver him, and honor him. With long life will I satisfy him, and shew him My salvation. (Ps. 91: 1, 2, 9, 10, 14—16).

Morning Prayers for Thursday.

183.

LORD, hear my prayer and let my cry come unto Thee. Hide not Thy face from me for I am poor and needy. Incline Thine ear unto me. When I cry unto Thee, hear me and answer me.

Under Thy good pleasure, O Lord Jesus Christ, I submit all that I do or leave undone, my beginnings and my endings, and commend unto Thee my body and soul, my kin and acquaintances, together with all my possessions. By the guardianship of Thy holy angels Thou hast this night protected me; and, I beseech Thee, condescend this day also to guard and defend me from all evil. Vouchsafe unto me and all my relatives and friends whatsoever we

need unto the maintenance of this
temporal life; and, as a merciful
father, care for us. Save us from
war and pestilence, from famine and
from evil trials, and, at last, receive
us into Thy eternal kingdom, the
heavenly paradise. Amen.

184.

GOD the Father, God the Son,
God the Holy Ghost, Thou
most blessed Trinity, unto Thee do
I commend my body and soul from
this day forth and forevermore. I
thank Thee most heartily that Thou
hast not permitted the evil one to do
me injury during the night now
past. Thou hast kept me in health
and strength through the protection
of Thy holy angels. How shall I
reward Thee? How shall I thank
Thee? I will offer unto Thee an

anxious and contrite heart, scarlet in sin, filled with remorse and sorrow. Condescend to accept it. Cleanse it with the blood of my Savior that it be white as snow, and hide it in His divine and innocent wounds, and thus graciously vouchsafe unto me the remission of my sins. As I can not know when Thou comest or how and where Thou wilt call me hence, grant that I may always be in such a state of Christian preparedness that I may enter into Thy eternal bliss. I ask this, O gracious God, for the sake of Jesus Christ. Amen.

185.

TO Thee, O God, Eternal Father, Who hast created me, and to Thee, O God, the eternal Son, Who hast redeemed me, and, to Thee, O God, the Eternal Holy Ghost, Who hast sanctified me in baptism, do I this day and all the days of my life commend myself. Eternal Deity, True Humanity, Holy Trinity, and Undivided Unity, Eternal Power, Unfathomable Wisdom, prepare me this day and at all times as Thou wouldst have me to be yonder in eternal blessedness. Amen.

Glory be to Thee, O God, my Defence Eternal, Who desirest so much to do good unto Thy servant, and hast again shown forth Thy lovingkindness beyond every ability to merit·during the night that is now past, I lift up mine eyes unto the hills from whence cometh my help. My help cometh from the Lord, Who made heaven and earth. Lord forsake me not nor leave me. Enlighten mine eyes that I this day walk not in forbidden paths. Save

me from evildoers and them that
thirst for blood; from sin and from
all harm. Let my heart rejoice in
Thee. Glory be to Thee on high,
and, on earth, unto me and to all
that love the Lord, be all grace and
peace and a blessed end. Amen.

186.

I N the break of day I will arise in
the Name of God. Lord Jesus,
let Thy passion and death be my
rod and my staff. Beloved Jesus,
Lord, Thy blood, Thy wounds defend me this day and always. Help,
that the fiends of hell, whom Thou
hast overcome and bound, be and
remain imprisoned this day and
evermore, that they obtain no power
over me. Amen.

Lord Jesus Christ, Almighty and
True Light, the source whence

cometh all other light; that of the
sun and of the day; Light that en-
lightenest all men that are born into
the world; Light, by which all
things become bright and glorious;
Eternal Wisdom of the Father,
unto Thee I cry. Enlighten my heart
that I, being blind to all else, may
behold only what is well pleasing to
Thee, and abide in Thy paths, desiring and loving none other. O
Lord, enlighten mine eyes that I
sleep not the sleep of death, and mine
enemy rejoice that he has overcome
me; Who livest and reignest with
the Father and the Holy Ghost, true
God, world without end. Amen.

The Lord's Prayer.
The Creed.
Psalm 5.
The Gloria Patri.

PRAYERS IN OUTWARD ANXIETIES.

187.

In Lingering Distress.

GRACIOUS God, most mighty to help, have regard to my pain and distress wherein I weep and complain so long, and help me. Thou canst not have forgotten me. I am Thy beloved child, Thy lamb that is marked with the blood of Thy Son Jesus Christ. My soul is troubled at the withholding of Thy help. For days and months,—a long time have I waited for Thy salvation, and as the hart panteth after the water brooks, so has my desire been unto Thy grace. Thou makest my soul to wait long in this vale of sorrow. Mine enemies exult over my misery. Lord, remember mine affliction.

Hasten to help me. How long must my soul be troubled, and how much more shall I hope for Thy help? O Lord, remember how lonely and miserable I am; how long I continue under this cross to wait for Thee, and daily, yea, hourly look for Thy help. O hear me in mine anguish when I cry unto Thee. Thou wilt yet remember me. My soul tells me Thou wilt yet hear me and answer me. Thou wilt not forget the needy forever, and the trust of the miserable will not always be in vain. Thou hearest the needy when they cry; their heart is certain that Thine ear will regard their cry. Help me, O God of my salvation, that I become not as they who go down into the pit. Then will my heart rejoice in Thy help and my soul shall be exceedingly glad. Amen.

188.

Prayer When the Peace of the Family is Threatened.

LORD God, Thou hast granted that I should be a husband, and hast given me a wife. We stand in this world, in this weak flesh and blood, surrounded by devils and them that disturb all conjugal fidelity and love. Therefore remove not Thy blessing from us, nor let any offence come between us. Let all disturbances be turned far from us, that all harm may be avoided and finally overcome by the gracious blessings with which Thou hast deigned to surround the marriage bond. Amen.

189.

In Time of Drouth and Famine.

MERCIFUL God, Heavenly Father, Thou seest our need and misery. Our great need which has now befallen us is not hidden before Thee. Our grievous sins have indeed merited not merely this temporal but eternal punishment, and Thy just wrath as well. O spare us, dear Father, for the sake of Thy beloved Son, Jesus Christ. Turn Thy righteous curse from us. Bless again our land that we may receive our daily bread and enjoy the same with grateful hearts, while we praise Thy loving-kindness here, in time, and henceforth to all eternity. Amen.

190.

When an Epidemic Threatens.

O LORD God, merciful and gracious, great in kindness and
faithfulness, we acknowledge Thy
righteous anger which we have
called forth with our sins. Spare us,
dear Father, for the sake of Thy
beloved Son, Jesus Christ. Consume
us not in Thine anger nor correct
us in Thy wrath. Lord, have mercy
upon us, be gracious unto us according to Thy goodness, and blot out
our transgressions according to Thy
great mercy. Turn Thy wrath
from us. Help us for the sake of
Thy loving-kindness. Heal and restore all who are sick and weak.
Leave them not in the hour of their
need. Succor them and let them
see Thy salvation. Have regard

unto their souls, and forgive them
all their transgressions. Teach us
all to remember that we must die,
that we become wise and choose
rather to fall into Thy hands than
into the hands of men. When our
last hour comes, let us hold fast to
Thy Word, departing in peace, that
we may never taste death. Hear us
and answer us. Hear our prayer, O
God, Father, Son, and Holy Ghost,
blessed forevermore. Amen.

191.
In Danger from Floods.

O LORD, Great God, mighty in
counsel and powerful to do,
Who holdest in Thy hand all
creatures, heaven and earth, seas
and oceans, and canst command
them with a sign; have regard unto
our great need and the extreme dan-

ger into which we have now come.
Be with us, that the floods do not
drown us nor the deeps swallow us
up. Lord, Jesus Christ, Thou art
He Whom wind and wave obey.
Rebuke the threatening of the
waters and the noise of the high
waves for us now. Speak but the
word, and we are saved, and we will
give thanks unto Thee for Thy grace
and the miraculous help which Thou
shewest unto the children of men,
praising Thee now and to all eternity.
Amen.

192.
In Danger of Fire.

L ORD God, gracious and full of
mercy, longsuffering and full
of goodness and faithfulness, with
heartfelt sorrow and repentance we
acknowledge that in Thy sight we
have richly deserved the now threat-

ening danger of fire which can easily gain mastery and destroy everything, wiping us out as were Sodom and Gomorrha, and leaving us desolate as were Adama and Zeboim. Since Thou, however, desirest not our destruction, but rather that sinners repent, and turn unto Thee and live, we do heartily beseech Thee graciously to turn away from us this well-merited punishment for our sins, together with all destructive winds and storms; remembering Thy grace and mercy in the midst of Thine anger, and command and say to this threatening fire, ''It is enough.'' We ask it for the sake of Thy dear Son, Who has released us from Thy just wrath and punishment, bearing the guilt of our sins, suffering and paying the whole price thereof. Lord hear us. Lord,

have mercy. Lord, hear and act,
and withold not, for Thine own
sake, O Lord our God. Lord God,
the Father in heaven, have mercy
upon us. Lord God, the Son, Redeemer of the world, have mercy
upon us. Lord God, the Holy Ghost,
have mercy upon us. Be merciful
unto us and spare us, good Lord. In
this great danger from fire, protect
us, good Lord. O Christ, Thou
Lamb of God, Who takest away the
sins of the world, have mercy upon
us. O Christ, Son of God, have
mercy upon us. Then are we Thy
people and the sheep of Thy pasture,
and, unitedly, with due obedience
and earnest amendment of our sinful lives, we will render unto Thee
eternal thanksgiving and publish
Thy glory for ever more. Amen.

(M. John Gottfried Olearius.
Prayers for Home and Church, 1670.)

193.
In Time of Great Storms.

ALMIGHTY God, in Whose hand
and power are all things which
are and move and have their being,
Thou hast caused the winds to come
forth from their secret chambers,
that they rush over the land with
great destruction in their wake, and
we, timid creatures, fear that Thou
hast given power to the destructive
fiend of hell to carry out Thy judgments upon our manifold sins and
transgressions. O tarry, Lord God
of mercy and grace! For the sake
of the Mediator Who is interceding
for us, even Jesus Christ, forgive us
our transgressions and let Thy grace
abound over Thy justice. Let the
terrible howling and storming of the
winds be stilled, and fill our
trembling hearts with the peace of

Thy Holy Spirit Who shall dwell
in us, and keep us in childlike fear
and humble thanksgiving forever
more. Amen. For Thine only Son,
Jesus Christ's sake. Amen.

194.

Prayer During a Thunderstorm.

M OST Mighty God, let all the
mighty of the earth praise and
worship Thee, O God, for Thou art
Lord in the highest throne, and all
are Thy subjects. All things acknowledge Thee as their creator, and
tremble before Thy divine majesty.
Great mountains and the deeps fear
Thy wrath. The whole earth
trembles. Oceans and seas flee
from Thy wrath. Most merciful
God, preserve us from Thine anger.
Make Thy face to shine upon us and
be gracious unto us. Protect our

bodies and lives, our house and our home from the threatenings of the storm, from its fiery flashings, from its thunders and from every destruction. Save also the fruits of the field from hail and tempest, from waters and from every harm. Holy Lord, save us from an evil death. May God, the Father Who permitted His Son to suffer the pains of the cross in my stead, keep me. Jesus of Nazareth, King of the Jews, preserve me. Holy Ghost, Who hast set me apart by Thy baptism and the sign of the sacred cross, defend my soul that no evil befall me. Amen.

195.

HEAVENLY Father, Almighty, Everlasting God, oft as we hear Thee in the voice of the terrible storms, and thunders, and lightnings

of the clouds under the heavens, it
is Thou Who dost ring the bells
unto repentance, to awaken us from
the sleep of our security unto a
knowledge of our sins. Thou art a
mighty, terrible God. In one flash
Thou canst ruin and destroy all the
earth. Thou alone art the Great
God, Who, as Isaiah saith (chapt.
30), lettest Thy glorious voice be
heard amidst terrible threatenings,
in consuming flames, with great rain
and hail storms, that each and all
may behold and see Thy mighty,
outstretched arm. How terribly
Thy thunders roll from high heaven.
In Thy hand is our life and our
death, our strength and our destruction. Lord of Lords, we bow before
Thy majesty. Enter not into judgment with us, for before Thee there
is none who liveth that is holy.

For Thy most holy name's sake, and
for the merit and intercession of
Jesus Christ, have mercy upon us.
Spare us, and we will render thanks
unto Thee for Thy great mercy now
and to all eternity, evermore fearing
to trespass against the word of the
Almighty. Grant us grace, that
many sinners be turned from their
godless ways by Thy word and the
manifold signs and wonders which
Thou dost perform, and be converted
unto Thee with their whole hearts.
Let Thine angels protect the homes,
cities, and fields of Thy poor. Save
our goods and possessions from fire,
and shield Thou the fruits of the
fields against destruction by hail or
tempest. Help us always to remember the coming again of Thy beloved
Son, Jesus Christ, that we be prepared to receive Him with joy, and

to serve Thee with pure hearts; for, as the lightnings flash from the rising to the going down of the Sun, even so shall be the coming of Thy beloved Son. Lord, hear us. Lord, have mercy upon us poor sinners, in body and soul, both in this life and in the life to come. Amen.

PRAYERS IN INWARD STORMS OF LIFE.

196.

For Grace to be Patient Unto Death.

O LAMB of God that bearest the sins of the world, Lord Jesus Christ, by Thy holy passion we beseech Thee to grant us true patience under every cross and trial, that we keep our lips from blasphemy and our hands from vengeance. Bless our needful susten-

ance that we, miserable pilgrims,
may obediently wait upon Thy
pleasure and enjoy eternal life with
Thee in glory. To our bodies and all
our members grant sweet rest in
the earth, that, in the day of Thine
appearing, these may rise again in
joy, and our souls, clothed again
with our risen bodies, may finally
enter upon everlasting life, together
with all the congregation of Thy
saints. Amen.

197.
Prayer for Help.

LORD Jesus Christ, Victor over
Satan and the gates of hell, I
beseech Thee, by Thy great mercy,
let the cries and desires of the poor
come before Thee. Spurn not the
pleadings and the tears which fall
from the eyes of the oppressed.
Stretch out Thine arm over us for

our help, and turn again our sorrow. Awaken us, who lie dead in sins unto a recognition of our great danger which threatens us because of our enmity, and which we seldom consider aright. Make it to be known unto us that nothing is so high, so broad, so deep, nor yet so burdened but that Thy grace, mercy, and inestimable love can reach it, and that Thou canst, and art ever ready to help us free from every need; that we may praise and magnify Thee without ceasing, henceforth, forever more. Amen.

198.

For the Guidance of the Holy Ghost Through This Restless Sea of Life.

HOLY Spirit, true Leader and Guide of all the elect, with my whole heart I pray Thee to dwell in me and abide with me eternally. Guide and lead me, that, by the governance of Thy power and might, I may attain to that inconceivable glory of eternal life where eternal peace, eternal sunshine, eternal strength, and eternally increasing joys shall be. Here we are upon wild and stormy waves, in an evil world; but help Thou us through this all, that we may finally attain to heaven and come to the fatherland with joy after all these great tribulations. Grant this, O Thou, Who art blessed together with the Father and the Son, world without end. Amen.

199.

Prayer for the Joy of the Holy Ghost Amid the Trials of This Life.

GOD has given and sent us His Son to be our Lord and Christ, for Whose sake He will be gracious unto us, to forgive our sins, to grant us His Holy Spirit, and to receive us graciously as the children of everlasting life. O Lord, Jesus Christ, with my whole heart I pray Thee, evermore speak this joy of heaven unto my heart, and write it in golden letters of faith upon my soul, that, as a child of God and heir of eternal life, I may, in the midst of trials, always have Thy joyful comfort in my heart, and a peaceful conscience in my body, to the end that I may overcome all temptation and adversity with joyful patience, bear all adversity in my calling joyfully, and, at last, in Thine own good time, end my days in gladsome hope. Amen.

200.

Prayer for Cleansing of the Soul.

RIGHTEOUS God, turn my desire and thoughts, that I may fear and serve Thee in love with all my soul. Sanctify me wholly, and turn away from me all that is not purely Thine. So sink my life in Thyself that my will may ever yield to Thine, to be governed by Thee; for neither mine own nor the help of any creature can give me counsel. Grant that I neither fall into nor remain in sin. Quench my thirst for things temporal. Uproot in me all self-love and selfishness. Banish evil passions and covetous desires. Destroy all lusting and cleaving unto the

things of this world. Gather my
soul unto Thee, and retain in me a
pure and peaceful conscience unto
my latest breath. Praise, glory, wisdom, thanks, honor, power, and
majesty be unto Thee, O God, forever more. Amen.

Evening Prayers.
201.

UNTO Thee, O Gracious God, I
render thanks, glory and honor
for Thy goodness and loving-kindness which Thou hast this day
shown unto me, even though I am a
sinner, unworthy to be called Thy
child . I know that Thy mercy is
very great,—greater far than my
sins and the sins of all the world.
Therefore, I confess unto Thee all
my sins and transgressions which I
have this day, or even all my days

from my youth up, committed
against Thee, and beseech Thee,
pardon and blot out all these, and
have mercy upon me, through Thy
grace, as Thy beloved child. Give
Thy holy angels charge concerning
me, that I may this night and all the
days to come be defended against
all harm to body or soul. Unto Thee
I commend myself wholly, in life and
in death. Let me ever be and remain with Thee. Amen.

202.

MOST Merciful, Longsuffering
God, Eternal Father, great is
Thy sincere love and paternal providence toward me, a miserable sinner,
that Thou hast condescended, from
my youth up even unto this moment,
so graciously to defend me against
every danger and harm from Satan

and this evil world: I humbly beseech Thee, by the great love which
Thou bearest to me, that Thou wilt
not now nor evermore remember
against me what I have this day
sinned against Thee; but wilt remit
it unto me for the sake of Thy beloved Son, Jesus Christ, Who died
and became my strength with Thee.
Defend me and mine everywhere
this night from harm and destruction
by fire or water, from pestilence and
every danger, and from an evil
death. I, therefore, commend myself, body and soul, and all that I
have unto Thy fatherly care. Let
Thy holy angels be round about
me, that I fear no evil. Amen.

203.

O GOD, and Father, darkness
and thick clouds oppress our
hearts, if these be not illumined by

Thy light. The beautiful sun is the light of this natural world, but the light of our spiritual world is Thine eternal wisdom, by which the light has risen upon our souls. When the day departs and the night comes apace with silent tread, Thou hast ordained the lesser natural lights to illumine the darkness, but unto our souls Thou hast given Thy Word, brought unto us by Thy Son, for a healing balm against every fear and the uncertainties of the night. Thy word is a lamp in our darkness and a light unto our fearsome paths. Let this true light shine upon me that I may rejoice in its glory. Let me recognize my everlasting light, the Lord Jesus Christ, and evermore praise Him unto His face, saying, O Lord Jesus, sweetest comfort living or dying, I am Thine.

Whether I live, I live unto Thee,
whether I die, I die unto Thee; for
to this end didst Thou taste death,
that I might have life everlasting.
Sustain me in Thy love and embrace me with the arms of Thy
grace. Let me be Thine own, here
and to all eternity. Amen.

204.

LORD Jesus Christ, cover me
this night with the mantle of
Thy gracious, blood-bought merit.
Be with me when I pray. Strength-
en me in my prayer even as the
angel from heaven strengthened
Thee on Olivet against Thine anguish
of death. Be with me when death
overtakes me, and strengthen Thou
me that neither devil nor world may
bring any evil against me. Amen.

The Lord's Prayer.
Psalm 4. The Gloria Patri.

In Remembrance of the Holy Sacrament of the Altar and Its Institution on a Thursday Evening.

HE that eateth My flesh, and drinketh My blood, hath eternal life; and I will raise him up at the last day. For My flesh is meat indeed, and My blood is drink indeed. He that eateth My flesh, and drinketh My blood, dwelleth in Me, and I in him. As the living Father hath sent Me, and I live by the Father: so he that eateth Me, even he shall live by Me. (St. John 6: 54—57.)

———

6.

FRIDAY.

Behold the Lamb of God, Which taketh away the sin of the world. (John 1, 29).

God so loved the world, that He gave His only begotten Son, that whosoever believeth in Him should not perish, but have everlasting life. (John 3: 16).

All they that be fat upon earth shall eat and worship: all they that go down to the dust shall bow before Him: and none can keep alive his own soul.

The meek shall eat and be satisfied: they shall praise the Lord that seek Him: your heart shall live forever. (Ps. 22: 29, 26).

May the soul of Christ sanctify me. May the body of Christ preserve me. May the blood of Christ nourish me. The water that flowed from His riven side, may it cleanse me. In Thy holy wounds let me hide. O Lord, help me that I be never separated from Thee. Defend me against the evil one. In the hour of death set me down by Thee, that I may with all Thy holy angels evermore praise Thee. Amen.

205.
All Hail.

A LL hail! King of mercy. Hail! Thou Who art the life, the joy and the hope of our souls. We miserable children of Eve cry unto Thee. We long for Thee, sorrowful and weeping in this vale of tears. Hail, therefore, O Lord Christ! Thou Who dost intercede for us with God, turn Thine eyes, beaming with mercy, upon us, and show Thyself unto us, Thou blessed Son of God and of Mary, when the days of our misery shall have passed, O gracious gentle, sweet, and lovely Jesus Christ. Amen.

Morning Prayers for Friday.
206.

I N the Name of the Father, and of the Son, and of the Holy Ghost. Amen. In the Name of the Lord

Jesus Christ Who has redeemed us with His precious blood, I do now arise. May He defend me against all evil, and preserve my body and soul; granting me also whatsoever shall prosper and confirm me in all good, unto eternal life. Amen.

207.

IN Thy Name, O crucified Lord Jesus Christ, I, a miserably great sinner, have risen. O Thou, Who in my stead hast meekly suffered the most painful death on the holy cross as a truly meek Lamb of Sacrifice, and with Thy crimson blood hast redeemed me from all my transgressions, from death, the devil, and from hell: direct me and so govern my heart by Thy Holy Spirit that it may be revived and refreshed with the heavenly dew of

Thy grace. By Thy divine love, preserve me through this and all the days, and hide me, body and soul, within Thy holy wounds. Cleanse me from all sins. Keep me in all good works. And finally lead me from this vale of sorrow into eternal joy and glory, O most faithful Redeemer, Jesus Christ, my only comfort, hope, and life. Amen.

208.

GOD, and the Father of our Lord Jesus Christ, Who art known of none save alone of them unto whom Thou hast revealed Thyself most graciously in Christ Jesus, I beseech Thee, beside all Thy manifold blessings, deny me not the greatest: that my soul be freed from the sleep of sin and from the darkness of this world. As Thou hast now awakened my body from slumber, grant also that the same, my body, may in this life be the faithful companion of my soul and its servant unto a godly walk in life. If in such service it, at last, fall into the grave, then I know that what men call death is only to sleep in Thee, and Thou wilt, in Thine own good time, afterward, raise up also this my mortal body unto immortality, and bring it into the communion of eternal joys. Therefore, my heart rejoiceth, and my honor is secure, for even my flesh shall rest in safety. With body and soul I will rejoice forever in the living God. Hallelujah! Amen.

209.

I WILL call upon God; and the Lord shall save me. Evening, and morning, and at noon, will I pray, and cry aloud: and He shall hear my voice.

Glory, and honor, and praise be unto Thee, O Almighty and Merciful Father, for the gracious watch Thou hast this night exercised over me and mine through Thy holy angels. Bless and preserve me this day from sin and all evil. Grant me grace that I may live circumspectly, peacefully, and quietly, cleaving unto that which is good, that it may please Thee to preserve me, together with all the children of God, rejoicing with all angels, and with my Redeemer to have eternal life. Even so shall my last day on earth be my first in the Kingdom of heaven. Amen. The Lord's Prayer.

The Creed.

Psalm 22.

The Gloria Patri.

210.

Adoration of Jesus, the Crucified.

(Isaiah 53.)

WHO hath believed our report? and to whom is the arm of the Lord revealed?

For He shall grow up before Him as a tender plant, and as a root out of a dry ground: He hath no form nor comeliness; and when we shall see Him, there is no beauty that we should desire Him.

He is despised and rejected of men; a man of sorrows, and acquainted with grief: and we hid as it were our faces from Him; He was despised, and we esteemed Him not.

Surely He hath borne our griefs, and carried our sorrows: yet we did esteem Him stricken, smitten of God, and afflicted.

But He was wounded for our transgressions, He was bruised for our iniquities: the chastisement of our peace was upon Him; and with His stripes we are healed.

All we like sheep have gone astray; we have turned every one to his own way; and the Lord hath laid on Him the iniquity of us all.

He was oppressed and He was afflicted, yet He opened not His mouth: He is brought as a lamb to the slaughter, and as a sheep before her shearers is dumb, so He openeth not His mouth.

He was taken from prison and from judgment: and who shall declare His generation? for He was cut off out of the land of the living: for the transgression of my people was He stricken.

And He made His grave with the

wicked, and with the rich in His death; because He had done no violence, neither was deceit in His mouth.

Yet it pleased the Lord to bruise Him; He hath put Him to grief: when Thou shalt make His soul an offering for sin, He shall see His seed, He shall prolong His days, and the pleasure of the Lord shall prosper in His hand.

He shall see of the travail of His soul, and shall be satisfied: by His knowledge shall my righteous Servant justify many; for He shall bear their iniquities.

Therefore will I divide Him a portion with the great, and He shall divide the spoil with the strong; because He hath poured out His soul unto death: and He was numbered with the transgressors; and

He bare the sin of many, and made intercession for the transgressors.

Prayer to Our Lord, Jesus.

211.

At this place Loehe quoted one of the ecstatic adorations of the Son of the Virgin Mary, as originally used by Bernhard of Clairvaux. The translator has felt that it would be burdening the book unnecessarily for an American use to publish this at length. It is therefore omitted.

212.

O LORD, Who when Thou didst redeem me and suffer for me, didst not turn away Thy face from shame and mockery: I beseech Thee, be gracious unto me, and hide not Thy face from me.

213.

I KNOW, Lord, that I owe my being unto Thee, for Thou art my creator, and, since Thou hast purchased me, and wast incarnate

for me, I owe Thee more than myself, if I but had more, yea, so much
more as Thou art Thyself greater
than he for whom Thou gavest Thyself. Behold, I have nothing more,
and what I (am and) have I can not
give unto Thee without Thyself;
but accept Thou me, and draw me
unto Thee that I may be Thine, to
love and follow Thee, as I am even
Thine by creation and my very ex-
istence; Who livest eternally. Amen.

(Augustine.)

A Remembrance of the Sufferings of Jesus.

214.

O LORD, Jesus, Who by Thine
holy and innocent suffering
hast wrought out grace for us poor
and lost sinners, from the Heavenly
Father, and purchased us unto eternal life; from the depths of our

hearts we thank Thee for Thy love, Thine anguish and misery, and for Thy vicarious death. We praise Thee for Thy holy passion, and we beseech Thee, preserve us eternally by Thy love, and grant us grace to realize the eternal benefit of Thy redemption, with grateful hearts. Cause us to be strengthened by the same in faith, and ever to become more joyful in hope, zealous in love, comforted unto patience, consistent in obedience, and die daily unto sin. Help, O Lord, Jesus Christ, that in the end we may be comforted and rejoice in everlasting salvation by Thy bloody death. Amen.

215.

FOR the sake of Thy passion and death, we beseech Thee, Lord Jesus Christ, sustain us in that bitter hour when hearts do break

and soul and body are sundered. Be
Thou then our life. Impart to us
Thy saving comfort. Shorten and
assuage for us the anguish of death.
Help us to bow our heads in Thy
Name. Let us joyfully realize the
power of Thy passion, and make us
to be partakers of Thy glorious
merit, that, in the comfort of Thy
bitter pain and death, we may joyfully and blessedly overcome all our
sin, need, misery, anguish, and even
death itself; heartily and ever confidently commending our poor souls
into Thy gracious hand, and rendering our praises and thanksgivings
unto Thee for Thy saving grace evermore. Amen.

216.

O HIGH and Mighty Prince and
Bishop of Life, Lord Jesus
Christ, Who wast lifted up upon the

cross that Thou mightest draw the
sheep of Thy fold unto Thee, I have
comfort in Thy beloved cross, and
mine eyes behold in it, by faith, a
glorious altar, whence Thou dost
preach unto me and to all Christians,
and whence Thou dost bear testimony of the eternal, unspeakable
love of our Heavenly Father toward
a lost mankind, and where, also,
Thou dost show me what horrible
things are sin, and hell, and the
eternal wrath of God, which no
creature in heaven or in earth could
appease, except alone the shedding
of Thy blood. O let it be unto
me the power unto my salvation.
Amen.

217.

L ORD Jesus, I behold Thee hang-
ing upon the cross with outstretched   arms.   Thy   painfully

outstretched hands are to me an evidence of Thine earnest desire to embrace me and all believers, in grace; to press us to Thy bosom, and to bear us up into the community of Thine everlasting kingdom. By Thy hands and Thy feet wert Thou nailed to the cross: from which I gladly realize how faithful and true Thou art toward me; how faithfully and truly Thou wilt remain and be with me in every need, every cross, and every trial. Thou didst hang between earth and heaven, as the only redeemer and mediator between God and man. Cause me to realize Thy love and majesty, O Lord, Who hast promised to draw all men unto Thee when Thou shouldst be lifted up from earth upon the cross. Amen.

218.

UNTO the poor malefactor wrestling with death, Thou, O Lord Jesus, didst say: "Verily, this day shalt thou be with Me in paradise." Now, Lord Jesus, I also cry, believe, and with the Church of old confess:

"He that pitied e'en a thief
Will not let me come to grief."*

Thou Who didst graciously regard even the late repentance of the thief, let Thy grace receive also me, who am coming late; yet, praised be Thy name, not too late, unto Thee. Strengthen my faith, O Mighty Prince and Savior, that, like the malefactor, I may embrace Thee, and never more turn from Thee; but keep myself · by faith and a

---

* Qui latronem recepisti,
Mihi quoque spem dedisti.

lively hope ever unto the power of Thy death. Amen.

219.

LORD Jesus, I regard Thy bowed head upon the cross, as the sign that Thy head is ever graciously inclined to hear me and all poor sinners in our need. Hear, therefore, the poor contrite hearts and minds, who, in these latter evil days, sigh and cry unto Thee without ceasing. Their hearts are assured that Thine ear is open unto them, and Thou wilt not let them cry in vain; for Thou wilt answer them quickly, "here am I, here am I." Thou wilt save and grant them life and full satisfaction. Amen.

220.

O LORD Jesus Christ, Son of the Almighty Father, our only, eternal High Priest, Who gavest

Thine immaculate body a sacrifice
upon the altar of the cross, and
didst die for our sins, and by Thy
death didst remove power from him
who had the power of death, who is
the devil, and didst redeem them
who for fear of death were enslaved
all their days: I pray Thee, grant
me grace ever to be truly grateful
for Thine innocent death, and to find
comfort therein. Help me in this
life that I so subdue all my members
that they be dead unto sin. Grant
also that my last word may be the
same which Thou didst pronounce:
"Father, into Thy hands I commit
my spirit." Amen.

221.

O LORD Jesus, from Thy wounded side flowed water and blood.
Therefore, there comes one proclaim-

ing with a loud voice: "This is He Who cometh by water and blood, not by water alone, but by water and blood." Thou hast offered me the gracious water of life and the cup of salvation,—the New Testament in Thy blood. Unto me Thou art a fountain of grace. Grant that Thy redeeming love be not attested to me in vain by the streams of blood and water from Thy heart. Help me to apprehend them in true faith, that I be purged and totally cleansed therein. Amen.

222.

M OST beloved Lord Jesus Christ, reconcile me with the Father; intercede for me His grace; wash me thoroughly from my sins; protect me against the evil spirit; save me from the power of hell; defend

me against eternal damnation; and,
finally, translate me to eternal glory.
O, Crucified Jesus, hear me, for I
trust in Thee; despise me not, for I
love Thee; reject me not, for I revere
Thee: even the bitterness of death
shall not sunder me from Thee.
Amen.

223.

O CHRIST, Who canst cause men
to be blessed, make me blessed
whom Thou hast redeemed by Thy
cross and Thine own precious blood.
O my God, help me this day and at
all times. Most holy, immortal God,
have mercy upon me, a poor sinner,
and keep me both in body and soul
unto everlasting life, now and evermore. Amen.

224.

Thanksgiving for Christ's Sufferings.

W E give thanks unto Thee, Lord
Jesus Christ, true God and
man, that by Thy holy sufferings,
death, and the shedding of Thy
blood Thou hast redeemed us poor,
sinful and condemned beings, who
are without any works, merit or
worthiness in ourselves. O Lord
Jesus Christ, how great were Thy
sufferings, how bitter Thy pain,
how manifold Thy burdens, how
deep Thy wounds, how bitterly painful Thy death! Unspeakable is the
love by which Thou hast reconciled
us with the Father in heaven, when,
on Olivet's mountain side, in anguish
of death, Thou didst sweat drops of
blood which fell upon the ground,
and, deserted of all Thy disciples,

didst willingly yield Thyself up
unto the treacherous Jews and the
wicked multitude for our sake, to be
bound without pity, and led from
one unjust judge to another. Thou
wast falsely accused and condemned,
mocked, spit upon, and stricken with
fists in Thy face. Thou wast wounded for our transgressions, and for
our sins wast Thou smitten, scourged,
crowned with thorns, and abomin-
ably treated like a poor worm that
has no likeness to man. So despised
and disregarded, so full of sorrows
and misery wast Thou, that even a
heathen heart was moved with pity
to exclaim: "Behold the Man." For
our transgressions Thou wast ad-
judged among malefactors, and for
a curse wast crucified in the midst
of two of them, pierced in hands and
feet by cruel nails, and, in the height

of Thine agony and thirst, they offered Thee vinegar and gall.   In
great agony Thou gavest up Thy
spirit, that Thou mightest pay the
price of our debt, and we be healed
by Thy wounds.   O Lord, Jesus
Christ, for these and all Thy martyr
sufferings and pain, we render praise
and thanksgiving unto Thee, and beseech Thee, let not Thy sacred and
bitter passion be lost upon us; but,
grant that we may at all times be
heartily comforted and honored in
the same, so contemplating and considering them that all evil passions
may be quenched and destroyed in
us, and all virtues be implanted and
prospered instead; so that we, being dead unto sin, may live righteously, following Thine example left
unto us, to walk in Thy footsteps,
bearing evil patiently and suffering

injustice even with a good conscience. Amen.

For Increasing Love to Christ.

225.

JESUS, my Lord, beloved Jesus, true God and searcher of the secrets of the heart, Thou knowest I love Thee better than the earth and all that is in it. Thou art dearer to me than heaven and earth. My heart desires to love Thee more. Lord, grant and permit me to love Thee so much as I desire and ought, so that all my undertakings, my deeds and thoughts be directed toward Thee, and I may alway so live and do as will be well pleasing unto Thee, and, finally, behold Thy face with joy. Amen.

226.

O SWEET and beloved Jesus, dear and lovely is Thy name. I pray Thee, fill my heart with Thy love, that, as a consuming fire, I may entirely glow with love to Thee. Lord, let my love for Thee be such that for very love I will resign the great burdens which oppress my soul, and all the fleshly lusts and passions of this earthly life, and, by Thy guidance, follow after Thee, without hinderance, into eternal glory. Amen.

Evening Prayers.

227.

THE Lord defend my soul. The Lord deliver me from all evil. The Lord preserve my going out and my coming in from this time forth and even forevermore. Amen.

Lord God, heavenly Father,

whether we wake or sleep, live or die, we are Thine. I heartily beseech Thee, care Thou for me, and let me not fall into destruction through works of darkness; but, let the light of Thy countenance arise in my heart, that, by faith, true knowledge of Thee may increase in my soul, and I may ever do Thy will. Guard and defend me against every deception of the evil one. Preserve me from all evil visions and horrid dreams, and let me this night rest peacefully in Thee, to attain unto the morning in joy and health, and to fulfil my calling unto the glory of Thy holy Name and the salvation of my soul. Amen.

228.

DEAR Lord Jesus Christ, I thank Thee that for my sake Thou didst condescend to this earth, really becoming true man, and hast tasted all manner of human misery and trial for my good and comfort. Heartily do I thank Thee also for Thy holy, painful sufferings, for the drops of blood, and for the shameful death which Thou didst suffer upon the cross for me, a poor, miserable, sinful being; thereby redeeming me from eternal death and God's just displeasure. I beseech Thee, Lord Jesus Christ, let not Thy holy and bitter pains and death be lost upon me, a miserable sinner; but, in my latter end, let them support and comfort me. O glorious God, grant me a blessed hour in which to die peacefully, and to rise again in joy. And now, when I lay me down to sleep, receive me into Thy hands and unto Thy bosom, and grant that I may rest peacefully in Thee. Amen.

229.

ALMIGHTY, gracious, merciful, and eternal God, Who hast said, "Call upon Me in the day of trouble and I will deliver thee," I pray Thee, have mercy upon me and forgive my sins. Let Thy Holy Spirit come upon me to fill my heart at all times with divine comfort. Whether I wake or sleep, whether I go or stand, help me as Thou best knowest to help my needs of body and soul. Thou knowest all things. Thou canst do all things. Thou art God and Lord over all, and in Thy hand are all things. Remember Thy mercy and Thy promises. Yea, remember the perfect obedience of Thy beloved Son, Jesus Christ, by Whom I am wholly reconciled to Thee. For His sake, have mercy upon me now and ever more. And

if it were Thy will that I should
taste of danger, a cross, or any misfortune, even death itself, visit Thy
divine comfort, blessing, and grace
upon me. Without Thine assent, O
Lord, nothing can befall me. Though
I walk in darkest night, Thou art
with me; Thy rod and Thy staff,
they comfort me. Thou hast numbered the very hairs of my head;
why should I then be afraid? Living or dying, I am Thine; therefore,
I am not lost, but saved forever
through Jesus Christ. Amen.

230.

LORD Jesus Christ, patient Lamb
of Sacrifice, and holy Propitia-
tion for my sins, not mine alone, but
the sins of the whole world; once
again I thank Thee with my whole
heart that Thou hast this day so

paternally defended me with Thy
protection in body and soul. I pray
Thee, graciously pardon and forgive
all my sins which I have this day
committed through the weakness of
my evil nature or through precipi-
tation, and which now oppress my
heart and conscience. I am about to
lay me down to rest and sleep.
Cause Thy grace to overshadow me
that, sheltered thus, I may this night
rest my limbs in peace but with the
soul be evermore awake unto Thee.
Cause me also to realize Thy glorious
coming again unto judgment, and
eagerly to await Thee even unto the
day when, at last, I shall pass hence
unto Thee in Thy salvation. To all
this help me, gracious Redeemer,
Who, together with the Father and

the Holy Ghost, art praised and
glorified forever. Amen.

The Lord's Prayer.

The Creed.

Psalm 15.

The Gloria Patri.

———

7.

SATURDAY.

There remaineth therefore a rest to the people of God. For he that is entered into his rest, he also hath ceased from his works, as God did from His. Let us labor therefore to enter into that rest. (Heb. 4: 9—11).

Be careful for nothing; but in everything by prayer and supplication with thanksgiving let your requests be made known unto God. And the peace of God, which passeth all understanding, shall keep your hearts and minds through Christ Jesus. (Phil. 4: 6—7).

Morning Prayers for Saturday.

231.

JESUS Christ, Son of God, let me this day again commend unto Thee my body and soul, and, at last, when I depart from this vale of sorrow, grant me a blessed departure that I may appear faultless and pure in Thy holy sight, and permitted to hear Thy joyous voice saying, "Well done, thou good and faithful servant, thou hast been faithful over a few things, I will make thee ruler over many things: enter thou into the joy of thy Lord."

Ever faithful Father in heaven, It lieth not in the compass of my power or might sufficiently to thank and praise Thee for all Thy goodness which Thou hast shown unto me all my life, even down to this moment, for I am mere flesh and blood which can do no good thing. Without measure, Thou causest Thy grace to abound to me daily, and if Thou hadst not been my stay and shield this night, Satan's power had harmed me much, that I could not have risen again in health. By Thy gracious guardianship I have been wholly defended, and I beseech Thee most heartily to let Thy grace abound to me ward this day, and graciously defend me, Thy child, by the price of Christ's blood, henceforth unto everlasting life. Amen. Lord Jesus, receive my soul into Thy hands, and let it be commended unto Thee. Amen.

232.

PRAISE be unto Thee, O heavenly Father, that Thou lookest upon my miserable estate so paternally, and hast shown me, a poor, weak, and perishable creature who am worth naught because of mine inborn sin, so great grace, even unto this day. Grant that I may fully realize my imperfections, and how I, conceived and born in sin, would be eternally lost on account of my sins if, for Thy beloved Son's sake, Thou hadst not been mindful of me, so that I may ever thank Thee and never abuse Thy grace and manifold benefits. Defend me henceforth against every disaster to body and soul. Let me not fall into pride or presumption, but rather, teach me that I must die and that my life has its goal, so that I may be daily prepared, when mine hour cometh to depart from this misery, to fall quietly and peacefully asleep in the knowledge of Thee, and, with all believers, enter into eternal joy and glory. Amen.

233.

GRACIOUS and most merciful Father, Great and Eternal God, most heartily do I beseech Thee, look down upon me from Thy heaven above and turn Thy countenance unto me. Gracious Father, so lead and guide me this day that I commit no evil, nor sin and offend against against Thee. Almighty God, lead Thy poor lamb in Thy truth. Defend me, Lord, for in Thee do I put my trust. Thou only art my strength, my rock, my fortress, my shield and buckler. Righteous God, turn my mind and my lips thither, that I fear and serve Thee in love, with all my soul. Sanctify me within and without, and turn me from all that cometh not from Thee.

Hide me within Thyself, that my will subject itself entirely unto Thee, and I be freed from the dominion of self and of every other creature. Let me not be wholly possessed of mine own nature. Grant that the thirst for temporal things be quenched in my heart. Uproot all self-love and selfish desires. Banish all hatred and jealousy, and cut off passion and my attachment to the things of this world. Gather my soul unto Thee and preserve in me a pure and peaceful conscience. Glory, praise, wisdom, thanksgiving, honor, power, and might be unto our God for ever and ever. Amen.

(Joachim Muensinger von Freundeck's
Prayer-book, 1584.)

234.

A Prayer of Praise and Thanksgiving.

MOST humbly do I thank Thee, Lord God, Heavenly Father, for all Thy grace, goodness and truth which Thou hast shown unto me this day and all the days of my life. Great and innumerable are they. Thy mercy has been rich and great unto me. In Thine image Thou hast created me. By the blood of Thy Son, Thou hast redeemed me from death and accepted me an heir of Thine everlasting kingdom. Thou hast admitted me unto holy baptism, and afterward caused me to be taught Thy holy will from Thy Word, that I have learned to know Thee, and may call upon Thy Name without idolatry; and, in the Name of

Christ, I may call Thee Father. Praise be to God, I have learned to live a Christian life and to die a blessed death. For my comfort also, Thou hast instituted the exalted sacrament of the true body and blood of the Lamb of God, Jesus Christ, whereby Thou feedest, waterest, and dost nourish my soul, and givest me the assurance that Thou wilt dwell in me and I in Thee. For this spiritual treasure I render praise and thanksgiving unto Thee. Besides these, Thou hast caused me to be born of Christian parents, hast provided me with food, drink, and raiment, and hast most miraculously sustained me amid many dangers and misfortunes even to this moment. All which Thou hast done for me without any merit or worthiness in me; and for all which

benefits, I give thanks to Thee this
morning with a grateful heart;
especially, also, because during the
night now past Thou hast saved me
from all harm in body and soul.
Permit me, this beautiful day and at
all times, to be commended unto
Thine eternal, divine mercy, grace
and favor, and be Thou my defense
and shield. Save me from all evil, and
whatsoever is in opposition to Thee,
and from all that worketh my
destruction and condemnation.
From sin, shame, and blasphemy
save me. Against harm and danger,
accident and misfortune, Satan's
guile and every evil defend me. To
Thee, O Lord, alone, I commend my
defence and protection, for Thou
wilt comfort and strengthen me in
body and soul, in mind, conscience,
mood, and thought, and in all my

honor and possession. Thou, better than myself, dost realize, know, and observe my need and danger. Therefore, I commit my all totally unto Thee. Thou, my God in all things, help me in everything. Cast even the smallest grain of Thy grace from on high unto me, for that will be mightier and more able and potent to comfort, help, and overcome all misfortune for me, than all the sorrows of the world can inflict. Let me this day find grace in Thy sight, O God; that grace which has been found in Thy divine sight by all whom Thou hast loved from the foundation of the world. Let Thine anger be far removed from me; may Thy grace draw nigh unto me. Embrace me in Thy mercy this day. Hold me in the hollow of Thy hand, O Lord, and let me not fall into the hands of mine enemies. Guard me as the apple of Thine eye. Cover me with the shadow of Thy wings, that I may abide there in safety from all evil. Let Thy Holy Spirit dwell evermore in my heart, and teach me by the same rightly to know, fear, love, and trust in Thee; to call upon Thee in spirit and in truth, and to serve and magnify Thee all the days of my life. Sanctify my heart unto every Christian virtue; and grant me grace so to live here in time, that I may dwell also with Thee in eternity. Amen.

The Lord's Prayer.

The Creed.

The 90th Psalm.

The Gloria Patri.

(Revised Brandenburg Prayer-Book, 1679.)

FOR PENITENTIAL DAYS.

235.

Prayers at Confession.

I, A miserable sinner, acknowledge and confess unto Thee, O my God and Lord, that during my life I have grievously sinned against Thee and my fellow man in many ways, by evil thoughts, words, and deeds. I am by nature sinful, unjust, and unclean, inclined to all that is evil, and corrupt in body and soul, having thereby merited Thy divine wrath, temporal punishment, and eternal death. Nevertheless, since Thou, in Thy word, bearest testimony and assurest that Thou hast no pleasure in the death of the wicked, but that through penitence and sorrow he turn unto Thee and live, therefore I flee unto such Thy

promises, and to Thine unfathomable mercy, seeking and imploring
Thy grace. O God, be gracious and
have mercy upon me, a miserable
sinner, and forgive my sins and offences for the sake of the precious
merit of Thy beloved Son, Jesus
Christ, our Lord. Amen.

236.

L ORD God Almighty, Who provest the heart and bowels, and
knowest all my evil thoughts, passions, and deeds. I can repeat
nothing that Thou dost not already
know, and desire nothing that is not
naked and open before the eyes of
Thy divine majesty. Yet, I have no
rest and am tormented by my sins,
which I have so miserably and manifoldly committed against Thee, O
Father in heaven, and against my

fellow man here on earth. These are cause enough for me to come with open sinners, and with truly penitent heart to fall down before Thy gracious and merciful face, in true faith and confidence crying: "Have mercy, O God, upon me a sinner;" through Jesus Christ, Thy well-beloved Son, our Lord and Savior. Amen.

Prayers After Receiving Absolution.

237.

ALMIGHTY, Everlasting God, we have sinned against Thee in many ways, and for our sins have merited eternal condemnation; yet, since we believe that Thy beloved Son, Jesus Christ, our Lord, has wrought out for us the forgiveness of our sins and eternal salvation before Thee, and are now assured thereof by the holy gospel, and have our hearts strengthened by this holy absolution, we most humbly beseech Thee, grant us the power of Thy Holy Spirit that we may henceforth flee from sin, and lead a truly godly life in Thy calling; through Jesus Christ, our Lord. Amen.

238.

DEAR Lord, Jesus Christ, Eternal and Almighty Son of God, Who, by Thine own holy and perfect sacrifice of Thy body and blood, hast fulfilled the holy will and counsel of Thy Heavenly Father; and by the same, those also are sanctified for whom Thou hast ordained Thy true body and Thy precious blood to be offered and to be eaten and received by us in the Holy Sacrament; with what earnest, heartfelt sorrow and

repentence for our sin, what trustful
desire and reverence shall we approach and receive Thy Holy Supper? Because of the sin that
cleaves unto us, we human beings
are much too insignificant, weak, and
unworthy of ourselves to fulfill Thy
will and command, or to receive the
same to our benefit. Therefore, most
precious Lord and Savior, do Thou
sanctify our bodies and souls by Thy
Holy Spirit, and make us ready to
come worthily to this heavenly feast.
Whatsoever in our weakness, we
lack in true repentance, sorrow, and
regret for our sins, or in firm faith
and childlike, sincere resolve to better our lives, add Thou most graciously unto us through the riches and
merit of Thine own bitter sufferings,
pain, and death. These things grant
us, that we, who, in this world's

pilgrimage, desire to enjoy Thee, our only comfort and salvation, in the form of the Holy Sacrament, may at length behold Thee face to face in that true, eternal fatherland, and stand before Thee, Who livest and reignest with the Father and the Holy Ghost, true God, world without end. Amen.

PRAYERS AT THE CLOSE OF THE WEEK.

Widowhood.

239.

O LIVING God, the Comforter of all who sorrow, I have lost the dearest of earth's treasures, and feel as if Thou hadst torn from me a part of mine own heart. Yet, I believe that all this has not come to pass without Thy knowledge or permission. Thou gavest me my wife, and didst permit me to have her for a time; and hast again taken her from this estate of sorrow unto Thyself, for she acknowledged Thy Son and called upon Him. Comfort me, a sorrowing and distressed widower, and help me to bear my grief; to raise my little children; and vouchsafe unto me and all whom Thou gavest me a gracious day when we shall be reunited in new joys and everlasting love before Thy face: who canst turn our sorrows to eternal joy and pleasure, glorified forever more. Amen.

240.

ALMIGHTY, merciful, eternal, and just God, since it hath pleased Thee to afflict me by taking my beloved and pious husband unto

Thine eternal joy and blessedness, and left me a widow, I beseech Thee most heartily, to grant me grace to set all my hope in Thee, and to hold fast to Thee alone by prayer, both day and night. Preserve me against the shameful lusts of this world, against shame and disgrace, against pride, covetousness, deceit and all wantonness. Grant me grace, with patience and humility to bear and overcome this bitter cross which Thou hast laid upon me. Give me wisdom also and understanding that I may administer my stewardship to Thy glory, to the amendment of my life, and so to use my goods and possessions that they may serve the good of my neighbor. Such, and all other benefits mercifully vouchsafe unto me, O God, for the sake of Jesus Christ. Amen.

241.

LORD Jesus Christ, since Thou art come unto the comfort and salvation of all poor, miserable souls, I beseech Thee come also unto me and dwell with me in my poverty and dire distress. Fill my miserable heart with the beauties of Thy comforting presence, my poor dwelling with Thy rich blessings, and my whole life with Christian modesty. Amen.

242.

Longings for a Quiet and Peaceable Life.

DEAR Lord, how miserably unreasonable it is that while the kingdoms of this world flourish and are sustained by the prayers of Thy Church, yet, at the same time, these 'do oppress and recklessly tread under foot Thy poor Church by

whose prayers, faithfully offered,
they are helped. For it is the
Church alone, O God, whom Thou
hast commanded to exercise care and
diligence to pray for all in authority,
as St. Paul has counselled (I Tim. 2);
and, Thou hast so commanded because man needs peace, order, dis-
cipline, and safety to spread Thy
word, and by the word to gather
the Church. Grant, therefore, beloved Father, that under our government we may lead quiet and peaceable lives in all godliness and
honesty, as may be well pleasing to
Thee. Amen.

243.
A Longing for the Recovery of the Soul.

LORD Jesus, Son of God, true and
ever to be desired Anchor of
Grace, Who camest into the world

to save sinners, my soul rejoices in
Thy salutary Name. By Thy great
mercy, I pray Thee, order my life
well pleasing unto Thee. At all
times graciously hinder and turn
from me all that worketh harm to me
or is displeasing to Thee, and grant
me those things that are beneficial to
me and well-pleasing to Thee. Lord,
Thou alone canst cleanse the things
that are conceived of unclean seed.
Thou alone art almighty and Thy
goodness is without end: Who
justifiest the sinner, and revivest
them that are born in sin. Therefore, take away from me also all that
is opposed to Thee, all that pains
Thine eye to see. Lord, my weakness and my strength are all in Thee
alone. Lord, Who revivest the
weak, and upholdest what Thou hast
revived, Who with a look of Thine

eye canst set the fallen upright
again, heal me also, a poor sinner,
and I shall be made whole. Bless
Thou me and I shall be blessed
indeed. Amen.

244.

Prayer for the Service of Angels Unto Us.

MOST gracious, everlasting God,
merciful Father, Thou hast
not ordained us unto wrath, but,
that by Thy grace we might be
sustained and blessed. Therefore,
we do heartily beseech Thee, dear
Lord and God, support us throughout our whole lives and give charge
to Thy holy angels, who serve before
Thy face continually, that they
watch over and care for us, to defend
us in body and soul against the
craft of the devil and his angels;

that we abide with Thee unto the
end; and all our enemies, both
visible and invisible, be put to
shame, through Thy beloved Son,
Jesus Christ, our Lord and Savior.
Amen.

245.

Thanksgiving for all God's Benefits.

Praise the Lord of Hosts: for the Lord is good;
for his mercy endureth forever. (Jeremiah 33:11.)

I will greatly praise the Lord with my mouth;
yea, I will praise Him among the multitude.
(Psalm 109:30.)

I WILL give thanks unto Thee, O
Lord God, Heavenly Father, that
by Thine almighty and divine power
Thou didst create me an intelligent
human creature, unto the praise and
glory of Thy holy Name.

I will give thanks unto Thee, O
Lord and Savior, Jesus Christ, that

by Thy passion and bitter death, and through the gracious shedding of Thy blood, Thou hast redeemed me from sin and everlasting condemnation.

I will give thanks unto Thee, O Lord God, the Holy Ghost, that by Thy rich grace Thou didst lead me unto holy baptism that I might be a Christian and heir of the kingdom of God; and, hast supported me and defended me from evil, even from earliest infancy unto this hour.

Vouchsafe unto me, O Thou One God in Three Persons, grace, henceforth to live according to Thy good pleasure, in holy desire for my soul's salvation, a Christian and godly life, continuing in obedience to Thy voice to the end of my days; and, at last, to die blessed in Thy grace, to rejoice with Thee forever. Amen.

246.

PRAISE and glory be unto Thee,
O Lord God, Heavenly Father,
Who by Thine almighty power hast
created me and all things from
nothing.

Praise and glory be unto Thee,
O Lord, the Son of God, Jesus
Christ, true God and true man, Who
by Thy precious blood hast redeemed
me and all the world.

Praise and glory be unto Thee,
O Lord God, Holy Ghost, Who by
Thy gracious gifts hast sanctified me
and all Christians.

———

O God, the Father in heaven,
have mercy upon us and keep us.

O Jesus, Son of God, Redeemer
of the world, have mercy upon us
and keep us.

O God, the Holy Ghost, Comforter and Teacher of all Truth, have mercy upon us and bless us.

O Holy Trinity and everlasting Unity, God the Father, God the Son, and God the Holy Ghost, three divine persons in one essence, have mercy upon us, and establish what Thou hast wrought in us.

We praise and magnify Thine inexpressibly mighty power by which all things were created; and Thy wonderful, unfathomable wisdom by which all things are governed; and Thy tender, inexhaustible goodness, by which all things are sustained and prospered.

O Most Holy Trinity, by Whom, and through Whom, and in Whom are all things; with my whole heart, with all my soul, with all my power, and with all my mind's capacity to love and praise, I praise, laud, magnify, worship, and desire but Thee. Grant, O Creator, Redeemer, and Comforter, Thy divine grace unto me, that I may rightly understand and fulfil Thy will, and neither live nor die otherwise than according to Thy good pleasure, and unto the glory and salvation of my soul. Praise, glory, and honor be unto the Father, and to the Son, and to the Holy Ghost, as it was in the beginning, is now, and ever shall be, world without end. Amen.

247.

O LORD, Holy Father, Almighty, Everlasting God, great is Thy goodness and mercy: Thou hast created man in Thine own image, and ordained him to be lord over all visible creation; but, Satan

shamefully deceived our first parents
and led them out of light into darkness, from righteousness into sin,
and from life into death. And,
though all the angels and archangels
had come, they could not have helped
us. Therefore, unto Thee, Almighty,
Everlasting God, we give thanks
that Thou hast not permitted us to
die and be destroyed, but hast be-
holden us with eyes of mercy, for
Thou gavest us Thine own dear Son,
born of the Virgin Mary, and of Thy
wonderful counsel and unfathomable
mercy ordained Him to be our
Redeemer and Mediator, and hast
deigned, for His sake, to accept us
again unto grace. O be merciful
unto us for Thy Son's sake. Gather
from among us an everlasting congregation unto Thyself. Direct and
keep us by Thy Word. Let us not

follow the thoughts and inclinations of our own hearts, but let our course be made sure by Thy Word, that sin have no more dominion over us. Let our way be upheld in Thy footsteps, that our feet glide not; lest we fall into sin and shame. Amen.

Lord Jesus Christ, terrible are the judgments that shall fall upon the ungrateful! For thus doth the Holy Spirit testify: "They who give not thanks for benefits shall not prosper;" and likewise, "He that rendereth evil for good, from his house evil shall not depart." Therefore, Lord Jesus, save me from ingratitude, and strengthen my soul that I may daily render thanks unto Thee for all Thy benefits, and receive and enjoy every temporal and spiritual blessing at Thy hands with thanksgiving and praise. I praise

and magnify Thee that Thou camest
unto our first parents in their sorrow, and there, in paradise, didst
reveal Thy gracious will unto them;
and afterward, in the fullness of
time, didst present Thyself in the
flesh, a bloody passover for us,
reconciling the wrath of God, over-
coming Satan, despoiling hell, taking away everlasting death, and
maintaining Thy Holy Church
against every tyranny of men to
this day. Let Thy mercy continue
unto us. Maintain temporal peace
among us. Give us our daily bread,
even as from our youth up Thou
hast nourished and fed us most abundantly from Thy gracious bounty.
Punish us not in Thy wrath. Redeem Thy Church, and lead her even
unto Thy Heavenly Father, and we

will praise and thank Thy majesty forever. Amen.

O Holy Ghost, Fire of God, True Comforter of all who are forsaken, Who proceedest from the Father and the Son, and wast visibly poured out upon the apostles, we render thanks unto Thee that Thou preparest our hearts to hear God's word with firm and joyful courage, and to receive the same by faith; that Thou leadest us to call upon the Lord God in truth, and unto all good works; and workest in us such joy, that we rely in and upon God with confidence to ask and receive all manner of benefits. We beseech Thee, keep us steadfast in all reasonable knowledge and worship of God, even as it is written of Thee and Thine office, "I will pour out upon you the Spirit of grace and prayer." Be

Thou our continual support, our faithful Intercessor, our Comforter in every undertaking, in wearisome trials, and in every need; and so enkindle our hearts that we may evermore glorify, honor, and praise the Father of our Lord Jesus Christ, His Son, our Savior and Redeemer, together with Thee, the Holy Ghost, by true obedience. Grant also that we may always love our neighbor and render him gratitude and good, as becometh us. Strengthen our faith that all our help and solace may be drawn from Thee in every need, and we magnify and praise Thee without ceasing, forever more: Who livest with God the Father and the Son, true God, forever. Amen.

248.

At the Passing of the Week.

MERCIFUL God and Father, most heartily do I thank Thee that by Thy grace I have been permitted to pass through another week, approaching a few days nearer the hour of death. With heartfelt sorrow I confess unto Thee that in the past week I have manifoldly sinned, both consciously and unconsciously, against Thee, and merited Thy just wrath by the doing of evil as well as by leaving undone the good I might have done. Lord, have mercy upon my transgressions according to Thy never ending grace, and let me enjoy the precious benefits of the passion-week of Thy beloved Son; that I may honor and praise Thee here and to all eternity. Amen.

249.

ALMIGHTY and Everlasting God, gracious, beloved, Heavenly Father, another week is past, and time treads rapidly upon his own heels, and I am passing with each day unto that hour set for me which I can not escape. Therefore, have mercy upon my sinful and imperfect life, and in Thy fatherly grace forgive and remit unto me all things by which, during the week past, I have by thought, word, or deed pained Thee. Unto Thee, and in Thy sight, O Lord and Father, ɪ confess my evil and perverse nature, and that my evil will has in many ways run counter to Thy will, which alone is good and right, and by which opposition there results to me a continuation of much lack of peace, of anger, disobedience, disorderliness, and a perverse and most miserable life: all which, however, Almighty Lord and God, Thou wilt not reckon for ill against me, for the sake of Thy beloved Son. In whatsoever the activities of my life and stewardship have, in the past week, fallen into error and disorder, help me, dear Father, to set the same again in order, to uproot all evil, and to right the same as may be well pleasing to Thee; that my whole life may become one continuous day of preparation for the promised rest that shall come, and for eternal peace and blessedness. All which I pray Thee, Everlasting God, in the Name and through the merit of Thy dear Son, my Lord, Redeemer, and Savior, Jesus Christ. Amen.

250.

The Evening Cessation from Work.

HEAVENLY Father, I praise Thee that, by Thy grace, I have been permitted to put another week of trials behind me, and have not been cast away in my sins together with the godless. O Lord, my God, Who ordainest and changest times and seasons, change also my heart and mind, by Thy Holy Spirit, that this week may mark a true change of time for me, to turn me from my former impenitence, my love for the world, and my lusting desires, unto Thee alone, through faith and love, so that, if this had been my last week on earth, I might lay aside this corrupt and sinful life, and put on the incorruptible, holy life in Christ. Amen.

PREPARATION FOR THE LORD'S DAY.

Prayer to the Holy Ghost for His Gifts.

251.

HOLY Ghost, Almighty, Ever-lasting God, Who didst fill the hearts of the apostles with the richest comfort of heaven, we beseech Thee, have mercy upon us. Send down the bright beams of Thy glory upon us and grant us the sweet consciousness of Thy presence. Without Thee there is nothing that can be called good in us. Cleanse us from every impurity. Sprinkle and revive what has dried up. Strengthen what has become weak. Correct that which has erred. Bind up our wounds and heal our sicknesses. Rekindle what has grown cold. Direct

again what has become perverse.
Grant unto all who put their trust
in Thee great power at all times to
do that which is good, and to avoid
that which is evil, that we increase
and continue in the good always, and
finally receive grace joyfully to depart and be eternally blessed. Amen.

252.

LORD God, the Holy Ghost, Who
art the faithful and only true
support of all who are in any need,
the Spirit of Truth and Promise, the
Finger of God, the Water of Life,
a Heavenly Fire to enkindle with
true love unto God the hearts that
have grown cold, Thou hast revealed
Thyself unto the apostles amid the
sound of wind and in the miraculous
spectacle of flaming tongues of fire.
We beseech Thee, come also into

our hearts, strengthen and rejoice
our burdened conscience, maintain
and sanctify us with Thy blessings,
and be Thou ever the holy earnest of
our salvation and blessedness. Amen.

253.

O HOLY and Everlasting Spirit,
we pray Thee, come into our
troubled hearts, revive us by the
power of Thy divine Word, cleanse
whatsoever is unclean in us, by the
blessings of sanctification, renew
our inclinations and our minds, grant
us holy thoughts, abide with us in all
times of anguish and need, be our
salvation, our consolation and our
help against every enemy of our
souls. Thou art the faithful doorkeeper of the fold of Jesus Christ.
Thou carest for the flock of the congregation of the Lord for their good.

Therefore, do we now yield and entrust ourselves entirely into Thy care and love. O Gracious Spirit, grant that we may nevermore depart from the household of the elect of God. Open wide the gates of mercy to all erring and penitent sinners, that, by Thy guidance, they also come and earnestly abide with the company of them that are blessed of God, and be saved. Let us continue evermore in Thy grace, that we find life and all satisfaction in the super-abundant fields of the saving gospel, unto all fruitfulness and amendment in their use. Amen.

254.
A Pastor's Prayer.
(Dr. Martin Luther.)

O LORD God, Thou hast set me to be a bishop and pastor in Thy Church. Thou seest how unfitted I am 'to bear such great and responsible office; and had not Thy counsel hitherto sustained me, I had long since brought all to ruin. Therefore, I cry unto Thee: gladly will I submit and give my lips, my tongue, and my heart unto the teaching of the people, and ever learn and occupy myself in Thy word to consider the same diligently. Use me as Thine instrument: but, dear Lord, leave me not; for were I to be left unto myself, I would quickly bring all to ruin. Amen.

EVENING PRAYERS.

255.

G OD, be merciful unto me and forgive me all my sins and transgressions, in the name of Thy beloved Son, Jesus Christ. For there is salvation in none other, and there

is none other name under heaven
given among men whereby we must
be saved, except alone the name of
Jesus Christ, Thy Son; and we
believe that through the grace of the
Lord Jesus Christ we shall be saved,
even as were all our fathers. (Acts
15: 11.)

Merciful God and Father, most
heartily do I praise Thee and give
thanks that Thou hast so paternally
cared for me all the days of my life,
and hast this day and during the
whole week, even to this moment,
graciously defended me against
every evil to body and soul. By the
grace which all repentant sinners
find before Thee, I beseech Thee,
cover and remember no more the
sins which I this day and all this
week have consciously or unconsciously committed against Thee or

against my neighbor. Graciously
grant, that I may step out of this
dying week into a new Christian life,
to be acceptable unto Thee and all
the elect in heaven. And in the darkness of the night now falling, let me
be commended into Thy most gracious arms, to rest and sleep in peace,
and rise again refreshed and strong
unto Thy further glory. And when
my last day comes, receive me unto
Thee, Lord Jesus Christ, for I am
Thine and Thou art mine. O how
gladly would I come soon and dwell
with Thee. Amen.

256.

IN the Name of Him with Whom I
began this day and this now
passing week, let me also end the
same. Lord God, Father of my life,
save me. Lord God, the Son, my
Savior, defend me. Lord God, the

Holy Ghost, preserve me that mine eyes close not in the sleep of death. Amen.

O Blessed, Holy Trinity, God the Father, Son, and Holy Ghost, unto Thee I commend my all, body and soul, and all that is mine, and beseech Thee, send Thy holy angels to watch over me this night, to defend and save me, and keep from me the devil, so that he add no evil unto me. Keep me in Thy pure and all-saving word and let me not sink into the darkness of this world; but enlighten my heart to know what is good and what is evil. Blot out all my sins which, consciously or unconsciously, I have committed against Thee during this week. Let me begin a new life, acceptable before Thee, unto the glory of Thy Name and the salvation of my soul. Amen.

257.

ALMIGHTY God, Holy and Merciful Father, Who in six days didst create heaven and earth, and all that is in them, and didst rest on the seventh day, grant Thy grace unto me, Thy servant, that in true faith I may partake of the rest which Jesus Christ, Thy Son, merited for me. Let my conscience be at peace from all painful, spiritual, and physical trials; and, when I have labored sufficiently in this vale of sorrow, release me according to Thy gracious will and lead me into Thy rest against the day when, with all Thy saints, I shall rejoice in one sabbath of peace after another. Grant me this, O God and Father; through Thy Son Jesus Christ, in the Holy Ghost. Amen.

258.

BLESSED be the God and Father of our Lord Jesus Christ, Who hath blessed us with spiritual blessings in heavenly places in Christ; in Whom we have redemption through His blood, the forgiveness of sins, according to the riches of His grace; wherein 'He hath abounded unto us, and made us to know the mystery of His will, according to His good pleasure: in Whom also we have obtained an inheritance and are sealed with the Holy Spirit of promise, which is the earnest of our inheritance until our redemption as His purchased posses-sion, unto the praise of His glory. May He fill us with the knowledge of His will in all wisdom and spiritual understanding, that we walk worthy of our Lord unto all pleasing, being faithful in every good work, and increasing in knowledge of God; strengthened with all might, according to His glorious power, to the glorious day of our Lord Jesus Christ, unto the honor and glory of God. Unto Him, the only true God, Eternal King, immortal, invisible, and omniscient, be honor and glory forever. Amen.

The Lord's Prayer.

The Creed.

Psalm 146.

The Gloria Patri.

(Remark.)
The Christian's Time.

A Christian lives his days **with Christ** and in contemplation of Him.

His **Days** pass in remembering the sufferings of Jesus. When the clock strikes eleven, he knows that the bells are ringing in the noon hour of his Redeemer, when thick darkness overshadowed him. In the afternoon at three o'clock, he breathes a grateful prayer of joy, for the Lord has finished. Every stroke of the clock calls upon him to consider what Christ did and suffered in that hour.

His **Weeks** are pictures of Christ's life. Sunday, at each return, is the brother of the Easter Day, the most joyful day of the week. It is preceeded by days of repentance and suffering. Wednesday already brings the memory of the unholy bargaining of Judas with the high priests and murderers of Christ. Thursday divides the mind between the struggle in Gethsemane and the blessed institution of the Lord's Supper. Every Friday is a weekly "Good Friday." Every Saturday is a sabbath of the rest of Christ in the grave.

As is the week so also the **Year**: It recalls the life, suffering, and death of the Christ, an ever new experience of what the gospels narrate: itself a very gospel of Christ our Lord.

(Concerning this, see Number IV.)

IV.

THE CHURCH YEAR

His foundation is in the holy mountains. The Lord loveth the gates of Zion more than all the dwellings of Jacob. Glorious things are spoken of thee, O city of God. Selah. (Ps. 87:1—3.)

Make a joyful noise unto the Lord, all ye lands. Serve the Lord with gladness: come before His presence with singing. Know ye that the Lord He is God: it is He that hath made us, and not we ourselves; we are His people, and the sheep of His pasture. Enter into His gates with thanksgiving, and into His courts with praise; be thankful unto Him, and bless His name. For the Lord is good; His mercy is everlasting; and His truth endureth to all generations. (Ps. 100).

The Christian's Service:
    Faith.
    Charity.
    Hope.
    Cross.
    Prayer.
    Thanksgiving.

Four of these cease with this life. Love and Thanksgiving alone remain to all eternity.
(I Cor. 13).

259.

A Table of the Movable Festivals.

ALL movable festivals depend on the time of Easter.

Easter always falls upon the Sunday after the full moon of March 21st, or next after that date. Should the full moon occur on Sunday, then Easter is celebrated on the next succeeding Sunday. Therefore, Easter can not occur earlier than March 22nd, nor later than April 25th. In 1845 it occurred upon March 23rd; in 1848, on April 23rd, and in 1886 on April 25th. According to this any one may easily calculate on what day of the year Easter will be. If the date for Easter is fixed, one can easily compute the dates for all the other movable festivals of the Church year:

1. Septuagesima comes 9 weeks before Easter.
2. Sexagesima comes 8 weeks before Easter.
3. Quinquagesima, or Esto Mihi comes 7 weeks before Easter.
4. Ash Wednesday comes 46 days before Easter.
5. Invocavit comes 6 weeks before Easter.
6. Reminiscere comes 5 weeks before Easter.
7. Oculi comes 4 weeks before Easter.
8. Laetare comes 3 weeks before Easter.
9. Judica comes 2 weeks before Easter.
10. Palmarum comes 1 week before Easter.
11. Dies Viridium, or Holy Thursday, occurs Thursday before Easter.
12. Dies Parasceues, or Good Friday, occurs Friday before Easter.
13. D. D. F. Resurrectionis, or Pascha, is the Easter festival.
14. Quasimodogeniti occurs 8 days after Easter.
15. Misericordias occurs 2 weeks after Easter.
16. Jubilate occurs 3 weeks after Easter.
17. Cantate occurs 4 weeks after Easter.
18. Rogate, or Sunday of Prayer occurs 5 weeks after Easter.
19. D. F. Ascensionis, or Ascension day occurs 40 days after Easter.
20. Exaudi occurs 6 weeks after Easter.
21. D. D. F. Pentecostes, or Whitsunday occurs 7 weeks after Easter.
22. D. D. F. Trinitatis, or Trinity Sunday occurs 8 weeks after Easter.

For convenience there is inserted here a table of days on which Easter occurs from 1900 to 2000.

1900	April	15	1926	April	4
1901	April	7	1927	April	17
1902	March	30	1928	April	8
1903	April	12	1929	March	31
1904	April	3	1930	April	20
1905	April	23	1931	April	5
1906	April	15	1932	March	27
1907	March	31	1933	April	16
1908	April	19	1934	April	1
1909	April	11	1935	April	21
1910	March	27	1936	April	12
1911	April	16	1937	March	28
1912	April	7	1938	April	17
1913	March	23	1939	April	9
1914	April	12	1940	March	24
1915	April	4	1941	April	13
1916	April	23	1942	April	5
1917	April	8	1943	April	25
1918	March	31	1944	April	9
1919	April	20	1945	April	1
1920	April	4	1946	April	21
1921	March	27	1947	April	6
1922	April	16	1948	March	28
1923	April	1	1949	April	17
1924	April	20	1950	April	9
1925	April	12	1951	March	25

1952	April	13		1977	April	10
1953	April	5		1978	March	26
1954	April	18		1979	April	15
1955	April	10		1980	April	6
1956	April	1		1981	April	19
1957	April	21		1982	April	11
1958	April	6		1983	April	3
1959	March	29		1984	April	22
1960	April	17		1985	April	7
1961	April	2		1986	March	30
1962	April	22		1987	April	19
1963	April	14		1988	April	3
1964	March	29		1989	March	26
1965	April	18		1990	April	15
1966	April	10		1991	March	31
1967	March	26		1992	April	19
1968	April	14		1993	April	11
1969	April	6		1994	April	3
1970	March	29		1995	April	16
1971	April	11		1996	April	7
1972	April	2		1997	March	30
1973	April	22		1998	April	12
1974	April	14		1999	April	4
1975	March	30		2000	April	23
1976	April	18				

260.

Table of Fixed Festivals in the Church Year.

Month	Day	Festival
January	1	D. D. F. Circumcisionis, Festival of the circumcision.
January	6	D. F. Epiphanias, Epiphany.
January	25	The Festival of the Conversion of Paul.
February	2	D. F. Purificationis, Purification of the virgin.
February	24	St. Matthew's Day.*
March	25	D. F. Annunciationis, Festival of the annunciation.
May	1	St. Phillip and St. James' Day.
June	24	Birthday of John the Baptist.
June	29	St. Peter and St. Paul's Day.
July	2	D. F. Visitationis, The Visitation of Mary.
July	22	Mary Magdalene.
July	25	St. James the Elder.

Month	Day	Festival
August	10	St. Laurentii, M. 258.
August	24	St. Bartholomew.
November	21	St. Matthew.
September	29	St. Michael the Archangel.
September	28	St. Simon and St. Jude.**
October	1	All Saints' Day.
November	30	St. Andrew.***
December	21	St. Thomas.
December	25	D. F. Natalium, Christmas.
December	26	St. Stephen.
December	27	St. John's Day.
December	28	Festival of the Innocents.

* In leap-year, February 25th.
** Reformation Festival is celebrated either on June 25th, the day of the presentation of the Augsburg Confession, or on October 31st, or the Sunday next following either of these dates.
*** Advent occurs upon the Sunday nearest to St. Andrew's Day.

ADVENT.

Prepare ye the way of the Lord. Hallelujah!
Make straight the path before Him. Hallelujah!

261.

EVER faithful and merciful God, praise and thanksgiving we render unto Thee, that, by Thy beloved prophets Thou hast promised to the patriarchs of old the gift of Thy beloved Son, Whom Thou didst send into the world in the fulness of time, that, by Him, Thy holy will and counsel might be fully revealed unto us. He crushed the serpent's head and has redeemed us from sin and death. All generations wait upon Him, and in Him are all the nations of the earth blessed. Prepare us, Good Lord, that we may serve Him with undefiled hearts; and, when He cometh, to receive Him with joy; and, for this, we will thank Thee eternally in heaven. Amen.

262.

O GOD, our Father in heaven, grant unto Thy beloved congregation that, remembering her own unrighteousness and corruption, she may take no offence at the lowly presence and the despised word of her only King, the Just, the Helper, Jesus Christ; but always rejoice in His wonderful advent, and receive and accept Him in pure and ready hearts, gladly rejoicing in Him, and rendering all praise and glory to Thee for ever more. Amen.

263.

L ORD Jesus Christ, all Thy holy Christendom rejoices this day to celebrate Thy holy advent. As a bride sings the Church beloved, for

Thou, the heavenly bridegroom, comest unto her. We, poor, erring lambs, leap for joy that Thou, O Shepherd and Bishop of our souls, causest Thy gracious presence to be realized among us. We, being sick, rejoice because Thou, O blessed Physician of mankind, visitest us. We, being poor, rejoice because Thou art a very rich Lord and deignest to come among us so fraternally, bringing such great gifts. O Lord depart not from us with Thy grace, but let us gratefully realize this gracious day of Thy visitation, that Thy coming may ever be salutary and full of grace unto us. With all Thy pure word, Thy holy sacraments, Thy wisdom, support, favor, blessing, and grace, visit us daily in our churches, our schools, our courts, and our dwellings. As

Thou art come into our hearts—of which we are conscious by the infallible testimony of the Spirit bearing witness within us unto our great comfort—so let us nevermore tire of Thee nor lack the consolation of Thy presence. Finally, since Thou wilt come at last to judge the quick and the dead, do Thou so rule and govern our hearts that we be ready to end our course, rejoicing in Thy coming, not as a just Judge before Whom we tremble, but rather as the kind Redeemer, with Whom we shall be joint heirs of the kingdom. Amen.

CHRISTMAS.

Unto us a child is born.   Hallelujah!
Unto us a son is given.   Hallelujah!

264.

HELP us, Lord God, that we, being released from our old sinful birth, may be made partakers of the new birth in the flesh of Thy beloved Son, and ever continue in the same; through Thy Son, Jesus Christ, our Lord. Amen.

265.

A LMIGHTY, Everlasting God, we beseech Thee, grant that we, whom Thou hast graciously enlightened by the light of Thy newly incarnate Son Jesus Christ, may show forth in our deeds what we believe with our hearts and profess with our lips; through the same, Thy beloved Son, Jesus Christ, our Lord. Amen.

266.

A LMIGHTY God, we bless Thee that Thou hast had compassion upon our miserable estate, and for us hast given Thine only begotten Son to become man. We beseech

Thee, graciously enlighten our hearts rightly to apprehend this comfort; to enjoy the same in every need and temptation; to praise Thee with all angels, and let us have peace that we may heartily rejoice, and so overcome all anguish and sorrow of this world. Amen.

267.

WELLBELOVED Emmanuel, Lord Jesus Christ, Son of the Highest, and Son of the Virgin, we give thanks unto Thee that, having so heartily compassioned our sinful birth, Thou hast come to us from the Father's throne into this misery below, taking upon Thyself our flesh and blood, that so we might be made partakers of Thine own divine nature. Now, indeed, has the Heavenly Father shared His loving heart

with us. Now is come great joy
without ceasing; and in Thee is His
wrath assuaged. By Thy holy birth,
we are born again unto heaven, and
Thou art become the veritable gateway of heaven for us; and by Thee
have we access unto the Father, and
abundant entrance into Thy kingdom. O then help, dear Lord,
gracious Emmanuel, that we may
rightly realize the mystery of Thy
revelation in our flesh; ever remembering Thy condescension unto
us, Thy poverty and distress, and
rejoice heartily in Thy gracious
birth, unto a realization of all its
mighty power. Lift up our hearts.
Open our lips. Unloose our tongues,
that with all the angels, unto whose
friendship we are now restored, we
may worship, praise, and magnify
Thee, and in Thee, the Beloved be

acceptable unto the Father; and
finally, be and abide with Thee in
the everlasting joys of heaven.
Amen. Blessed be the Lord God of
Isreal. Blessed be His Holy Name.
All the earth is full of His glory.
Amen. Amen. Amen, Hallelujah!

(**M.** J. G. Ol.)

268.

A Preface for Christmas.

IT is truly meet, right, and salutary,
that we should at all times, and in
all places, give thanks unto Thee, O
Lord, Holy Father, Almighty Everlasting God, for in the mystery of the
Word made flesh, Thou hast given us
a new revelation of Thy glory; that
seeing Thee in the Person of Thy
Son, we may be drawn to the love of
those things which are not seen.
Therefore, with Angels and Arch-

angels, and with all the company of heaven, we laud and magnify Thy glorious Name; evermore praising Thee, and saying: Holy, holy, holy, Lord God of Sabaoth; Heaven and earth are full of Thy glory; Hosanna in the highest.

Blessed is He that cometh in the Name of the Lord. Hosanna in the highest.

NEW YEAR, THE DAY OF CIRCUMCISION.

The Spirit and the Bride say: Come. Amen, Even so, Come Lord Jesus.

269.

GENTLE Lord Jesus Christ, Who wast circumcised on the eighth day, shedding the first drops of Thy blood for our sins, to redeem us from the grievous burden and awful curse of the law, we call upon Thee with

our whole hearts, to circumcise our
hearts, taking away the veil of our
unbelief and choking out all sinful
lusts and desires of the flesh, that we
may become new creatures, comforted in every time of need by Thy
most Holy Name; and, as children of
the new covenant, love one another
until we shall all be finally gathered
unto Thee, our Savior. Amen.

270.

LORD Jesus Christ, Redeemer of
the World, we give thanks to
Thee with our whole hearts that for
us Thou hast so humbled Thyself, as
to clothe Thyself in our flesh and
blood, being subject to the law; and
even in tenderest youth didst submit
Thyself unto pain that Thou mightest be called our Jesus, our Redeemer. O Lord Jesus, as Thy Name,

even so has Thy glory gone out unto
the ends of the earth. Great are
Thy works and the thoughts which
Thou hast revealed unto us. In these
we rejoice and speak of Thy truth
and salvation, praying Thee to
reckon the merit of Thy circumcision
unto our faith for righteousness, and
grant us Thy holy Spirit that we
may humbly yield our hearts circumcised unto Thee. Thou, Lord, wilt
create in us new hearts and renew
a right spirit within us, that we may
henceforth serve Thee in a new life,
rejoicing before Thee for Thy
mercies, which are new before us
every morning; ever praising Thee,
and finally, through Thy merit, be
made worthy to celebrate the eternal
New Year with Thee in the heavenly
Jerusalem. Grant this, most heartily beloved Redeemer, for Thy most

blessed and holy Name—Jesus.
Amen. (M. J. G. Ol.)

271.

ALMIGHTY Lord, our God, Holy
Father, we give thanks unto
Thee that during the past year Thou
hast so graciously preserved and
defended us. We beseech Thee,
grant us a peaceful, joyful, and
blessed new year. With Fatherly
kindness, keep and bless us in body
and soul; but, above all, grant us
grace that with the old year we may
lay off also the old man of sin and
put on, instead, the new man which
is renewed in knowledge of the
image of the holiness of the Creator,
until we shall be translated from this
old world into the new Jerusalem,
where, with new voices, we shall
glorify Thee, world without end.
Amen.

THE FESTIVAL OF EPIPHANY.

Arise, shine; for thy light is come. Hallelujah!
The Gentiles shall come to thy light. Hallelujah!

272.

LORD God, Heavenly Father, Who, by a star, didst reveal Thine only begotten Son, Jesus Christ unto the Gentiles this day, graciously grant that we who have by faith acknowledged Him, may also be led to behold Thy divine majesty and glory, through the same Jesus Christ, Thy Son, our Lord. Amen.

273.

O GOD, Father of all grace and mercy, we praise Thee that Thou hast revealed the Redeemer of the world unto us poor Gentiles also, and hast enlightened us to realize that He is the light of the Gentiles and Thy salvation unto the ends of the earth. We pray Thee, grant us divine grace to walk worthily of our heavenly calling, bringing offerings of the pure gold of faith, incense of prayer, and the priceless myrrh of patience in suffering and death, unto our King, Jesus Christ, Who with Thee, and the Holy Ghost, liveth and reigneth, world without end. Amen.

274.

KING of Heaven, Jesus Christ, we render thanks unto Thee, that from among Jews and Gentiles Thou hast gathered unto Thyself a church, and hast prepared praise unto Thyself out of our mouths. Keep us in that heavenly wisdom which Thou hast revealed unto the wise. Grant us Thy Holy Spirit that we may reverently seek Thee and Thy kingdom. Help us to follow after Thy Word as our miraculous guiding star. Cause us to confess Thy Holy Name before friend and foe. Govern us by Thy Holy Spirit, that the Christian joy kindled in our hearts may ever increase. Hear our sighings and our prayers. Accept the offerings which Thou hast Thyself given us, the gold of faith, the frankincense of prayer, and the myrrh of our contrite hearts. Save us from all shameful paths of sin, and let Thy good Spirit lead us in paths of pleasantness. After this life, grant us all to attain that great New Year, the jubilee of everlasting life: then will we be praising Thee and the Father, together with the Holy Ghost, forever and forever. Amen.

275.

Preface for Epiphany.

IT is truly right, meet, and salutary, that we should at all times and in all places, give thanks unto Thee, O Lord, Holy Father, Almighty, Everlasting God; for Thine only begotten Son hath renewed us according to the light of His immortal being, having appeared unto us in the body of our mortality. Therefore, with Angels and Archangels, with all thrones and principalities, and with all the company of heaven, we laud and magnify Thy glory, evermore praising Thee and saying: Holy, holy, holy, Lord God of Sabaoth; Heaven and earth are full of Thy glory; Hosanna in the highest.

Blessed is He that cometh in the Name of the Lord. Hosanna in the highest.

THE FESTIVAL OF MARY.
CANDLEMAS.

Lord, now lettest Thou Thy servant depart in peace.
For mine eyes have seen Thy salvation.

276.

BELOVED Lord Jesus Christ, Who art the true light, enlightening all men who come into the world, we beseech Thee so to enlighten our hearts by Thy grace that, with the sainted Simeon, we may recognize Thee as our Redeemer; and, after the darkness of this world, abide with Thee in eternal glory; Who livest and reignest together with the Father and the Holy Ghost, from everlasting to everlasting. Amen.

277.

ALMIGHTY, Everlasting God, we heartily beseech Thy majesty, that like as Thy Son was this day

offered incarnate in the temple, even
so wilt Thou cleanse us, that with
holy thoughts and pure minds we
may be offered unto Thee. Amen.

278.

L ORD Jesus, kindly and bright
Light of the Gentiles, Who,
with Thy beloved mother, didst this
day journey to the temple, we give
Thee thanks that for our sakes Thou
didst submit Thyself under the law.
We pray Thee, enlighten us that we
may offer ourselves unto Thee, a
˙ holy, acceptable sacrifice, holding
ourselves with earnest reverence
toward Thy holy temple. Grant us
to be cleansed of all our sinful lusts
and desires; and, since we are so
impotent unto such works, do Thou
Thyself cleanse our sinful natures by
Thy Holy Spirit and Thine innocent

blood. Grant that with eyes bathed
in innocency we may behold Thee as
the Light of the World, never to
walk in darkness, and to lay hold
upon Thee with true faith, embracing
Thee in our hearts, and be comforted
in Thee alone in every time of trial
and temptation, and in all moments
of terror of conscience. Kindle in
us the light of the knowledge of Thy
divine will, and the earnest prayer of
faith that shall shine before men in
good works, that they may praise
God in heaven. By the light of Thy
glory, banish all darkness and weakness from our minds, that we may
daily be renewed by Thy grace, and
not be found unclean in Thy sight.
Enlighten our eyes that we sleep not
the sleep of death; and, when our
last hour approaches, hold us, O
faithful Redeemer, safely in Thy

holy arms that we may nevermore
fall from Thee, nor that Satan, with
all his temptations, may ever tear
us away. Like unto Simeon of old,
vouchsafe unto us a quiet, joyful, and
peaceful departure, that our death
may be turned into a sweet sleep,
and we behold Thee with all the
saints in Thy eternal light. Amen.

Lord Jesus Christ, I am Thy
servant. I will depart in joy and
peace, for death will be my gain.
Amen.

THE FESTIVAL OF THE AN-
NUNCIATION.

The word was made flesh. Hallelujah.
And it dwelt among us. Hallelujah!

279.

ALMIGHTY, Everlasting God,
Who hast willed that, in the
womb of the virgin Mary, Thy Son

should take unto Himself human
nature, we beseech Thee, grant that
our sinful conception may be
cleansed by His holy conception;
through the same, Thy Son, Jesus
Christ our Lord. Amen.

280.

I GIVE thanks unto Thee, dearly
beloved Lord, Jesus Christ, in the
counsels of the upright and in the
congregation. I am glad, and rejoice
in Thee, O Emmanuel, and I praise
Thy Name, O Most High. I will
praise and sing unto Thee, Who for
my comfort and salvation didst take
upon Thyself true human nature in
the womb of the blessed virgin, and
becamest true man, my beloved
brother; that, by Thy humiliation, I
might be exalted, and partake of
Thy divine nature, be cleansed from

my sinful conception and become a
child of God. O Lord, I am totally
unworthy of all Thy mercy and Thy
faithfulness which Thou hast shown
unto me! Nevertheless, I am heartily comforted by Thy holy incarnation, sinful and unholy though I be;
for I know, since Thou hast esteemed
me so highly, Thou wilt, Thou canst
not hate Thine own flesh. Therefore,
I flee unto Thee in every time of
need and trouble with such confidence, and beseech Thee heartily,
ever to sustain me in such faith
that, above and contrary to all my
understanding, I may, with the
mother of the Lord, look up unto
Thee alone, to be comforted always
by Thy love and grace; and be Thine
forevermore. Amen.

(**M.** J. G. Ol.)

281.

AWAKE my soul! Rejoice in God thy Savior. Praise God Who has fulfilled all His promises of salvation and sent forth His Son in the flesh. Rejoice in thine exaltation. God is made flesh, and has done great things for thee. Who shall sufficiently praise the condescension of God which He has shown forth in the sending of His Son? O Lord Christ, most gracious Friend of Man, I give Thee thanks that in the tender, pure, and blessed womb of Mary Thou didst take our nature upon Thee, and hast reconciled us with the Father, though, in very deed, we neither merited nor deserved the same. What a blessed journey Thou didst undertake, coming from heaven into Mary's womb; from that womb into this world;

from this world to the cross; from
the cross into the grave; and from
the grave back again into Thy kingdom of heaven! And all this for the
sake of us poor sinners; for Thou
camest from Thy throne unto us in
order that we might finally be exalted into Thy heavenly glory. Thou
didst greatly humble Thyself that
we might reign forever. Thou hast
greatly honored us all, becoming our
brother, that we might be the children
of God. Thou didst not despise us
who are but dust and ashes. Greater
love it had been impossible to show
forth unto us. Sweet Redeemer,
Emmanuel, I do most heartily rejoice in these things, and truly hope
Thou wilt not be angry with me,
nor hate Thine own flesh and blood.
Though I am sinful and unclean, I
am comforted at Thy glory. By

Thine incarnation Thou hast established an eternally unbreakable covenant between God and us. Being true God, Thou didst take human nature upon Thyself to be able to intercede as a true mediator with God for us, to reconcile God, to realize our need, and to comfort abundantly. O kindly Brother, Jesus Christ, come unto me also with Thy grace; for I am Thine and desire to remain Thine forever. Where my flesh and my blood reign, surely there, through Thee, will I also reign eternally. Amen. (S. S.)

HOLY THURSDAY.

As often as ye eat of this bread and drink of this cup, Ye shall proclaim the Lord's death.

282.

ALMIGHTY, Everlasting Lord God, Who hast commanded us to remember and proclaim Thy sufferings in the institution of Thy blessed Sacrament, grant that we may so' employ the Sacrament of Thy Body and Blood that we may daily realize Thy salvation in fruitful hearts: Who livest and reignest with the Father and the Holy Ghost, forever and ever. Amen.

283.

LORD Jesus Christ, Who hast given us the joy of Thy bread to eat and Thy cup to drink in remembrance of Thy sufferings, we pray Thee, enlighten us that by true self-examination we may worthily receive that Sacrament, in true discernment of Thy presence. Amen.

284.

LORD, Eternal God, grant unto Thy people here assembled before Thee in the Holy Spirit, that, though distressed by the fiery darts of Satan, they be not overcome; but strengthened, and at all times increased by Thy power, through Jesus Christ. Amen.

285.

O LORD, unworthy though I be that Thou shouldst enter my house, yet, I stand in need of Thy help and greatly desire Thy grace. I come, therefore, with no other plea than that I have heard Thy tender invitation to me to come to Thy table, and hast promised me, unworthy being that I am, that through Thy body and precious blood which I eat and drink in this sacrament I receive the forgiveness of sin. O Precious Lord, I know that Thy word and promise are true. Of this I have no doubt, and upon that word and promise I eat and drink with Thee: let it be unto me according to Thy word. How glorious this sacrament! How precious its mystery! O Lord Jesus, I can not sufficiently adore the great wealth of this glorious grace, that in the New Testament, besides the word of reconciliation, Thou hast prepared us such sacrament of grace, dispensing therein so great treasures unto us. What more couldst Thou have done, or how more tenderly comfort our hearts? O God, what a glorious testament Thou hast made! What great riches Thou hast appointed! When other lords die, they leave lands, money, goods, and possessions for an heritage. Frequently they build great houses and beautiful sepulchres unto their own memory; yet all these pass away. But Thou,

Lord Jesus, hast imparted Thyself to us for a memorial, and ordained Thy body and Thy blood to be a nourishing food and drink unto us. Yea, Lord, this is Thy Holy Supper, which Thou hast Thyself instituted for us Christians; this is the glorious table which thou hast spread for Thy children, where Thou dost feed us with Thine own true and holy body, and the cup that we bless and drink is the communion of Thy true blood. Happy, blessed are we! We also are called to the feast of the Lamb which the Lord God of Sabaoth, our Redeemer, has prepared in His holy mountain before all people, a precious, glorious feast to satisfy the desire of all believers who hunger for the bread of life. We will hasten to come and buy without money and without price. Here is the Lord, The

Bread of Life. Whoso cometh to Him shall hunger no more, and whoso believeth in Him shall not thirst again. Let us, however, beware, lest we approach unworthily, and profane the body and blood of the Redeemer, and, instead of life, we become partakers of death.

Lord Jesus Christ, Thy flesh is the true bread, and Thy blood the true cup. Grant us to have earnest desire thereto in Thy feast. Feed Thou us, and give us to drink, O Lord. Abide in us that we may remain in Thee. Satisfy us with Thy comfort and fill us with Thy treasures, that in Thee we may live, be satisfied, rejoice, and be blessed. May Thy most holy body, which suffered bitter death for our sakes, and the precious treasure of Thy most holy and innocent blood by

which we are purchased and redeemed, now feed us, give us to
drink, sustain, guide, and lead us
unto everlasting life. Amen. Amen.

(Comp. Number 90.)

GOOD FRIDAY.

Christ was wounded for our transgressions,
He was bruised for our iniquities.

286.

ALMIGHTY, Eternal God, Who
for us hast caused Thy Son to
suffer the pains of the cross, that
Thou mightest put away the power
of the enemy from us, grant so to
observe the memory of His suffering that we may attain to the forgiveness of sin, and the surety of
release from eternal death, to serve
Thee in everlasting righteousness,
innocence, and blessedness. Amen.

287.

GRACIOUS GOD, Who delightest rather to be gracious than to pour out Thy wrath upon any, grant unto Thy chosen ones, by the sufferings of Thy Son, that they hate their sins and receive comfort of Thee; through Jesus Christ, Thy beloved Son, our Lord, Who liveth and reigneth with Thee, in unity with the Holy Ghost, world without end. Amen.

(See also Prayers for Friday.)

288.

Preface for the Passion Season.

IT is truly meet, right, and salutary, that we should at all times, and in all places, give thanks unto Thee, O Lord, Holy Father, Almighty Everlasting God, Who on the tree of the Cross didst give salvation unto mankind; that whence death arose, thence life also might rise again: and that he who by a tree once overcame, might likewise by a tree be overcome, through Christ our Lord; through Whom with Angels and Archangels, and with all the company of heaven, we laud and magnify Thy glorious Name; evermore praising Thee, and saying: Holy, holy, holy, Lord God of Sabaoth; Heaven and earth are full of Thy glory; Hosanna in the highest.

Blessed is He that cometh in the Name of the Lord. Hosanna in the highest.

EASTER.

The Lord is risen. Hallelujah!
He is verily risen. Hallelujah!

The Lord is truly risen. Hallelujah!
And appeared unto Simon. Hallelujah!

He was delivered for our sins. Hallelujah!
And is risen again for our justification. Hallelujah!

I know that my Redeemer liveth. Hallelujah!
He will, in the latter day, raise up me also from
the grave. Hallelujah!

289.

EVERLASTING God, Who by
Thine only begotten Son, Jesus
Christ, our Lord, hast opened unto
us the portals of eternal life, sealed
unto us the bond of reconciliation,
and, by His joyful resurrection, hast
granted hope and salvation unto the
whole world, we beseech Thee,
awaken in us a desire unto that
beauteous eternity, and grant us the
gift of perfect liberty, that we, being
released from the power of sin and
death, may ever serve Thine honor in
newness of life. Amen.

290.

ALMIGHTY God, Who by the
death of Thy Son hast destroyed
death, and by His resurrection hast

brought again innocence and eternal
life, that we, being redeemed from
the power of the devil, might live in
Thy kingdom: grant that we, with
our whole hearts, may believe; and,
in that faith abiding, evermore
praise and thank Thee, through the
same, Thy Son, Jesus Christ, our
Lord. Amen.

291.

L ORD God, Heavenly Father, Who
for our sins didst give Thine
only begotten Son, and for our justification didst raise Him up from the
dead, we beseech Thee in mercy to
awaken our dead hearts to newness
of life; and, with Christ, make us
ever to live by the power of the resurrection of Thy Son, our Lord, Jesus
Christ, Who, with Thee, in unity of
the Holy Ghost, liveth and reigneth,
true God, forevermore. Amen.

292.

BELOVED Lord, Jesus Christ, Almighty God, Great, Victorious Prince, Who hast broken the bonds of death, in great majesty and glory to rise from the grave and become the first-fruits of them that slept; on this memorable day we praise Thee for Thy holy sufferings, death and resurrection; for all this is come to pass for our sake. Like a true and mighty Samson, Thou didst powerfully lift up and destroy the gates of the portals of hell, that we might pass our days in everlasting liberty. With mighty hands hast Thou led us up out of the hellish Egyptian bondage and dominion of death, whose power Thou hast taken away, and redeemed us from eternal servitude. As our Head and our Shepherd, Thou art risen from the dead, and come forth with power that we, Thy members and the sheep of Thy fold, might not remain dead in the grave but, through Thee, arise unto everlasting glory. Therefore, with joyful voice, we this day cry: "Blessed be God Who hath given us the victory through Jesus Christ our Lord."

We pray Thee also, let Thy holy resurrection evermore be our comfort, unto our firm reliance in faith that in Thy grave Thou didst deeply hide our sin and guilt, that it be hidden from the Father's face and never shame us again. In the assurance of the resurrection of our bodies, help us finally to overcome with joy every anguish and pain of death; and when Thou shalt call by the voice of the archangel, "Arise from the dead," open Thou our

graves that we may enter into joy
with Thee. So shall we behold Thy
face with joy; and even as Thou with
Thy disciples didst hold converse
after the resurrection, so will we in
heaven hold many hearty, joyful,
loving conversations with Thee, and
praise Thee, together with the
Father and the Holy Ghost to all
eternity. Amen.

293.

GRACIOUS Lord, Jesus Christ,
Triumphant Easter King, we
laud and magnify Thy unspeakable
love wherein Thou didst greet Thy
friends on the day of Thy resurrection, and didst comfort their sorrowful hearts with mighty comfort. We
pray Thee, be our companion also
through the pilgrimage of this life.
Be our guest in the home, and bless

our bread. Be thou the treasure of our hearts, and enlighten them through the glory of Thy saving word, that they glow with love and burn with faith. When our life's sun shall set, and the day of this world declineth, abide with us in Thy grace, and lead us from this vale of sorrow to the heavenly Jerusalem, that we may ever behold Thee, in Thy glory, together with the Father and the Holy Ghost, face to face. Amen.

294.

Preface for Easter Day.

IT is truly meet, right, and salutary, that we should at all times, and in all places, give thanks unto Thee, O Lord, Holy Father, Almighty Everlasting God, but chiefly are we bound to praise Thee for the glorious Resurrection of Thy Son Jesus Christ our Lord: for He is the very Paschal Lamb, which was offered for us, and hath taken away the sin of the world; Who by His death hath destroyed death, and by His rising to life again, hath restored to us everlasting life. Therefore with Angels and Archangels, and with all the company of heaven, we laud and magnify Thy glorious Name; evermore praising Thee, and saying: Holy, holy, holy, Lord God of Sabaoth; Heaven and earth are full of Thy glory; Hosanna in the highest.

Blessed is He that cometh in the Name of the Lord. Hosanna in the highest.

ASCENSION DAY.

I ascend unto My Father and your Father. Hallelujah!
To My God and to your God. Hallelujah!

295.

LORD Jesus Christ, Son of the Highest, Who now no longer walkest on earth in suffering and humiliation, but sittest on the right hand of God the Father, mighty Lord over all that is in heaven and on earth; Who fillest immensity; we pray Thee, send Thy Holy Spirit unto us. Give us pious preachers of the Word. Endow them with rich gifts. Maintain them in Thy Word. Defend them against Satan and all Thine enemies. And maintain Thy kingdom on earth mightily until all Thine enemies shall be put under Thy feet, and we, through Thee, overcome sin and death, and all things. Amen.

296.

O GOD, Lord of peace and true love, pour out Thy loving spirit into our hearts, that we, who are assembled in Thy name, may praise Thee with one accord, through Jesus Christ, Thy Son. Amen.

297.

JESUS Christ, Almighty Lord and God, we praise Thee that upon Thy victory over all Thine enemies Thou didst, in great majesty, amid the triumphal rejoicings of the holy angels, ascend into heaven, and sittest on the right hand of the Heavenly Father. Thy cross and passion have attained a blessed end. Through death, Thou hast entered eternal glory. Dear Redeemer, Thou hast attained the shore; we are yet upon the wild waves. Thou art triumphant; we, militant. Grant us Thy grace, that with heart and mind we ever keep Thee in view, that our hearts be where our treasure is. Let all earthly things be put under our feet, that, with sincere prayers, and desires, and on the wings of true faith, we may rise to Thee on high. We verily believe and are comforted that Thou wilt not leave us, the members of Thy body, in misery; but, wilt, finally, when we shall have finished our course and kept the faith, also receive us even unto Thee; for, before Thy holy expiation, Thou didst pray the Heavenly Father and say, "Father, I will that where I am there shall also be whom Thou hast given me." And, since Thou art ascended not only to Thy Father, but to our Father also, and hast promised Thy disciples and us, "I

will come again and receive you
unto Me, that where I am ye may be
also," therefore, fulfill Thy comforting promise, dear Redeemer, and
bring us soon unto Thee: for our
hearts pant for Thee. How gladly
we would be with Thee in that heavenly fatherland, rather than journey
longer in this miserable pilgrimage
here. Gladly would we lay off our
earthly tabernacles, for we long after
our home in heaven, and that this
mortal might be overcome by life
and we be at home with Thee.
Every day we cry with David,
"When shall I come and appear before God?" Lord, we are waiting.
Until our day cometh, we will pass
on toward heaven in our thoughts,
and in our desires we will be at home
with Thee, Who art the joy of our

hearts, adored unto all eternity. Amen.

298.
Preface for Ascension Day.

IT is truly meet, right, and salutary, that we should at all times, and in all places, give thanks unto Thee, O Lord, Holy Father, Almighty Everlasting God, through Jesus Christ, our Lord, Who, after His Resurrection, appeared openly to all His disciples, and in their sight was taken up into Heaven, that He might make us partakers of His Divine nature. Therefore, with Angels and Archangels, and with all the company of heaven, we laud and magnify Thy glorious Name, evermore praising Thee, and saying: Holy, holy, holy, Lord God of Sabaoth; Heaven and earth are full of Thy glory; Hosanna in the highest.

Blessed is He that cometh in the Name of the Lord. Hosanna in the highest.

WHITSUNDAY.

Create in me a clean heart, O God. Hallelujah!
And renew a right spirit within me. Hallelujah!

299.

O GOD, Who hast taught the hearts of believers by the illumination of the Holy Ghost, and gathered together a Christian Church by Him, grant us also that Thy good Spirit cleanse our hearts, lead us into all truth, sanctify us, give us zealous minds, and comfort us in every time of need, that Thy Church may realize the promise of Thy beloved Son, Jesus Christ, our Lord, to conquer over all the gates of hell. Amen.

300.

FAITHFUL Redeemer, Jesus Christ, since Thou hast ascended up on high, leading captivity captive, and given gifts unto men; giving some to be apostles, and some prophets, and some evangelists, and some pastors and teachers, that we be henceforth no more children, tossed to and fro, and carried about with every wind of doctrine, by the sleight of men and cunning craftiness, whereby they lie in wait to deceive; we pray Thee, give Thy word free course among us, to increase and be preached with all soberness, that we, being retained in Thy truth, may be preserved in the same to all eternity. Amen.

301.

O LORD, grant us the grace of the Holy Spirit, that the dew of Thy mercies may fall upon our hearts, making them fruitful unto all good works. Amen.

302.

Prayer to the Holy Ghost.

O GOD, Holy Ghost, Spirit of wisdom, of understanding, of counsel, of strength, of knowledge and of the fear of the Lord; Comforter of the sorrowful; Leader and Guide of the errorladen; Teacher of them that are ignorant; Strength of the weak, fearful and timid souls; we laud and magnify Thee, upon this festal day of joy, as true God, together with the Father and the Son, and give thanks to Thee that in these latter days also Thou dost enlighten Thy Church and people by Thy divine grace, working in us mightily by Thy holy word and the ever sacred sacraments. Thou hast hitherto sustained us through manifold trials mightily, beyond all human comprehension. We pray Thee, graciously awaken these our cold and sleepy hearts, enlighten our understanding and all our purposes, lead us into all truth, sanctify us in body and soul, grant us deep earnestness in prayer, and comfort us in every time of need. As the warm showers of rain refresh the flowers and the grass, so let Thy comfort and divine blessing revive our souls. Sustain us, lest our faith disappear, our love grow cold, our hope vanish, our patience cease, or our hearts despair, under afflictions and temptations, and grant us to bear

every misfortune patiently in the
sure hope of eternal life. But,
chiefly, since the evil one constantly
attacks us so bitterly, seeking, by
sin and temptation, to draw us away
from God, do Thou unite us more
closely with our God by Thy holy
word, that we be nevermore separat·
ed from Him. Defend us against
this crafty enemy, and give us the
sword of the Spirit that we may
battle as good soldiers, and by Thy
might overcome every lust and evil
desire. And when our end cometh,
support us, strengthen our weary
souls, and plead for us with sighings
unspeakable, that we be comforted
to pass from this vale of misery into
the eternal fatherland. Amen.

303.
Preface for Whitsunday.

IT is truly meet, right, and salutary, that we should at all times, and in all places, give thanks unto Thee, O Lord, Holy Father, Almighty Everlasting God, through Jesus Christ, Thy dear Son, our Lord and Savior; Who ascending above the Heavens, and sitting at Thy right hand, poured out on this day the Holy Spirit, as He had promised, upon the chosen disciples; whereat the whole earth rejoices with exceeding joy. Therefore with Angels and Archangels, and with all the company of heaven, we laud and magnify Thy glorious Name; evermore praising Thee, and saying: Holy, holy, holy, Lord God of Sabaoth; Heaven and earth are full of Thy glory; Hosanna in the highest.

Blessed is He that cometh in the Name of the Lord. Hosanna in the highest.

THE FESTIVAL OF THE TRINITY.

We praise God the Father, and the Son, and the
    Holy Ghost. Hallelujah!
And from now, henceforth, eternally we will praise
    Him. Hallelujah!

304.

ALMIGHTY, Everlasting God, Who hast taught us to know and confess in true faith that, in three persons of equal power and majesty, Thou art one everlasting God, desiring to be worshipped as such, we pray Thee, sustain us steadfast in that faith against everything that may threaten the same: Who livest and reignest from everlasting to everlasting. Amen.

305.

ALMIGHTY, Everlasting God, Father, Son, and Holy Ghost, Who hast revealed Thy grace unto us abundantly; Who, as the Father Eternal, didst create us in Thine own image; as the Son Eternal, wast incarnate for our sake, and for our sins didst pay the debt upon the cross; and Thou, Holy Ghost Eternal, Who proceedest from the Father and the Son, to lead us into faith and to sanctify us by the holy gospel: we beseech Thee, the One, Everlasting, Almighty God, Father, Son, and Holy Ghost, keep us in the true knowledge of Thy Name, and in true faith unto the end; and, by Thy grace, save us: Who livest and reignest forever. Amen.

306.

O MOST Holy, Blessed, Undivided Trinity, eternal, unending, inconceivable, illimitable, spiritual unity of essence in threefold personality; praise, honor and glory be unto Thee for the divine revelation of Thy holy word in which we have life eternal, that we may know Thee, the Father, and Him Whom Thou hast sent, Jesus Christ, Thy beloved Son, through the power of the Holy Ghost.

O God the Father, Who art the first person in the Holy Trinity, I acknowledge, love, honor, praise, and worship Thee as my most beloved Father, Who art the Father of all in heaven and earth. Thy beloved Son has commanded me to address Thee as my Father, and promised "whatsoever ye shall ask

of the Father in My name, that will
He give you." Likewise He said,
"I ascend unto My Father and
your Father; to My God and your
God." O dearly beloved Father,
Thou gavest me two great and noble
gifts,—Thy Son and the Holy Ghost,
—and for such unspeakable love I
will ever praise and magnify Thee.

O God the Son, Who art the
second person in the Holy Trinity,
begotten from eternity, of the same
substance with the Father, God of
God, Light of Light, very God of
very God, in substantial likeness of
the Father, the reflection of His
glory, true, eternal God and everlasting Life, the beginning and end of
all things, through Whom all things
visible and invisible were made, and
all kingdoms and governments; by
Whom all things were made that are

made, and in Whom all things exist;
Who in time wast made man and
sent forth of the Heavenly Father to
seek and to save that which was lost;
Who art become flesh of my flesh and
blood of my blood, my brother, my
bridegroom; Who has betrothed me
in eternity, in judgement, in righteousness, and in faith; Who art my
Redeemer, Advocate, Throne of
Grace, High Priest, Emmanuel,
King, Light, Life, Mediator, and
Helper, my only Surety and Savior,
God and man in one perfect person;
Who sittest upon the throne of Thy
glory at the right hand of divine
majesty; Who hearest our prayers
and desires, and art with us always
even unto the end of the world: I
render praise, honor, and glory unto
Thee for all Thy great love, Thy

passion and death, Thy resurrection,
and Thy ascension on high.

O God the Holy Ghost, Almighty,
Everlasting God, co-equally eternal
and almighty with the Father and
the Son, Spirit, proceeding alike
from the Father and the Son; Who
makest us to be temples and dwelling places of the Holy Trinity; Who
makest us new-born and enlighten-
est, sanctifiest and comfortest us:
Thou art our most beloved and most
high Comforter, Who abidest ever
with us when this world and all
creatures forsake us: unto Thee be
praise, honor, and glory for my regeneration, enlightenment, and sanctification.

O Holy Trinity, distinguishable
as to persons, but indivisible in essence, God the Father, Son, and Holy
Ghost, of the same divine substance,

of the same everlasting divinity, we acknowledge three persons, co-equally eternal, holy, glorious, and incomprehensible. Therefore, with the seraphim, we say and sing, "Holy, Holy, Holy, Lord God of Sabaoth," Holy is God the Father, Holy is God the Son, Holy is the Holy Ghost; and, with Saint Paul, we confess that, "Of Him, and through Him, and to Him are all things, to Whom be glory forever. Amen."

O Holy Trinity, come unto us and deign to make us Thy temple; for, Thou art above us all, and through us all, and in us all. O Lord Jesus, he that beholdeth Thee beholdeth the Father, for Thou art in the Father and the Father in Thee. Thou hast instituted our blessed baptism in the name of the Holy

Trinity, and hast renewed the eternal covenant of grace in us by the same. Thou art our true blessedness, in whom and through whom we are blest in the Holy Trinity, even as Moses wrote: "The Lord bless thee and keep thee," that is, may God the Father defend us, together with all His children; "The Lord make His face shine upon thee, and be gracious unto thee," that is, God the Son, Who is the image of the Father, our light and the refuge of grace, enlighten us by His grace; "The Lord lift up His countenance upon thee, and grant thee peace," that is, God the Holy Ghost, through Whom we behold the fatherly countenance of God and enjoy peace, satisfy our hearts. Yea, God the Father, Who art love and mercy everlasting, the inexhaustible fountain of all goodness; yea, God the Son, my everlasting righteousness, wisdom, glory and blessedness, my light and my salvation; yea, God the Holy Ghost, my only and everlasting comfort, peace, joy, strength, and might, bring me into unity with Thee; possess and dwell in my heart; keep me as the apple of Thine eye; protect me under the shadow of Thy wing; bless, enlighten, and, in my final need, comfort me and receive my soul unto Thee. At the last day, awaken me unto eternal joy and let me behold Thy glory forever. Amen.

(Olearius, Gateway of Heaven.)

307.

Preface for the Festival of Trinity.

IT is truly meet, right, and salutary, that we should at all times, and in all places, give thanks unto Thee, O

Lord, Holy Father, Almighty Everlasting God, Who with Thine Only-begotten Son, and the Holy Ghost, art one God, one Lord. And in the confession of the only true God, we worship the Trinity in Person, and the Unity in Substance, of Majesty co-equal. Therefore with Angels and Archangels, and with all the company of heaven, we laud and magnify Thy glorious Name; evermore praising Thee, and saying: Holy, holy, holy, Lord God of Sabaoth; Heaven and earth are full of Thy glory; Hosanna in the highest.

Blessed is He that cometh in the Name of the Lord. Hosanna in the highest.

ST. JOHN THE BAPTIST'S DAY.

Prepare ye the way of the Lord. Hallelujah!
Make straight His paths before Him. Hallelujah!

308.

O GOD, Who hast made this day precious unto us by the birth of Saint John: grant unto Thy people to have spiritual joy, and draw the hearts of all believers in the way of eternal salvation, through our Lord Jesus Christ, Thy Son, Who liveth and reigneth in unity with Thee and the Holy Ghost, the only true God, world without end. Amen.

309.

LORD God, Heavenly Father, with our whole hearts we praise Thee for Thine abounding grace, that Thou didst not finish Thy work with the preaching and doctrines of the law alone, but gavest us the Gospel, and also Saint John, who directed men to Christ, and bore witness that through the Lamb of God alone we obtain pardon, holiness, and righteousness: we beseech Thee, enlighten our hearts by the Holy Spirit, that we may obey Saint John, to follow the Lamb whithersoever He leadeth, and be finally saved. Amen.

THE VISITATION.

My soul doth magnify the Lord. Hallelujah!
My spirit hath rejoiced in God, my Savior. Hallelujah!

310.

ALMIGHTY and Most Merciful Father, Who, of Thine abundant grace, didst move the virgin Mary, the mother of Thy dear Son, to greet Elizabeth, in the visitation upon John the Baptist, who was still hidden in the womb: we pray Thee, grant, that by Thy grace, we also may be filled with the Holy Spirit, released from all evil, and nevermore forget Thy gracious visitation in Christ. Amen.

311.

L ORD God, Heavenly Father, we most heartily beseech Thee, grant us the spirit of Thy grace, that, like Mary, we may increase in faith, love, humility, and obedience, and that we may glorify Thy Holy Name, and serve our fellowman according to Thy command. Amen.

312.

M Y heart is prepared, O God, my heart is prepared even that I sing and praise Thee.'' With these words, O most beloved Jesus Christ, which Thy beloved mother according to the flesh is said to have used,

as the spiritual daughter of David,
at the close of her earthly life, I also
now come before Thy holy presence,
and rouse up all that within me lies,
to magnify Thy Holy Name. With
my whole heart, I give thanks unto
Thee, that Thou hast so graciously
revealed Thyself through Mary, and
Elizabeth, and John the Baptist,
unto me also, and hast promised and
commended eternal salvation unto
them that accept and appropriate
Thy great work by faith. I rejoice
and am glad in Thy salvation, and
pray Thee, keep me steadfast in such
salutary and established doctrine;
strengthen and increase my faith;
work righteous fear of God and true
humility within me; and make me to
be a temple of the Holy Ghost, filled
with faith, love, peace, and joy at
Thy great mercies, so that I may

evermore declare, speak, and sing of
them, remembering Thee without
ceasing, never leaving Thine assemblies, and finally, be admitted
into the everlasting assembly of all
Thy saints before Thy father's
throne, as a joyful, believing Israel-
ite raised from out of the dust of
time's vanities. Then shall my
mouth be full of laughter, and my
tongue full of singing; then will I
sing and say, "The Lord hath done
great things for us, whereof we are
glad." And now, O Lord, my God,
I sing unto Thee, as best I may in my
weakness, but then, in glory, I will
thank Thee more fully, world without end. Amen.

M. J. G. Olearius.)

ST. MICHAEL'S DAY.

He shall give His angels charge over thee.
Hallelujah!
They shall keep thee in all thy ways. Hallelujah!

313.

O ALMIGHTY, Everlasting, Merciful God, Who hast most adorably ordained that the angels should serve us mortals: we beseech Thee, graciously grant that our lives on earth may ever be guarded and defended by those who do constantly stand in the presence of Thy divine majesty in heaven; through Jesus Christ, Thy Son, our Lord. Amen.

314.

LORD God, Heavenly Father, Who hast commanded Thine angels to be a shield and defence unto men against the tyranny of the devil and the evil machinations of the world:

we pray Thee, maintain unto us such
guardianship of the angels; and, by
Thy Spirit, help us that Thy will be
done by mankind on earth as it is
done by the angels of heaven, that
we may here live according to Thy
good pleeasure, and in heaven forever praise Thee.　Amen.

315.

GREAT and Holy God, we give
thanks unto Thee, that of Thy
divine wisdom and fatherly love
unto us Thou hast given command
to the hosts of heaven to be our
servants; and, by their guardianship,
hast hitherto surrounded us as with
a flaming wall and defended us
against every power of enmity.
From early youth Thou hast graciously shielded and guarded us from
serious accidents and many deceits

of the devil, and saved us from many
and grievous dangers. Dear Father,
let these, Thy mighty heroes, the
hosts of heaven, encamp mightily
round about us and Thy Church, to
the rout and defeat of every assault
from Satan, his hosts and servants.
Come Thou Thyself, with Thine
angels, into our temples and homes,
as once Thou camest unto Abraham
and Sarah. Let them accompany us
upon all our ways and journeyings
as they did unto Tobias. Let them
save us from dangers and death,
even as they saved the three men in
the fiery furnace, a Daniel from the
mouths of the lions, and a Peter
from prison bonds. When we go
upon paths of unrighteousness, cause
them to hinder us, as they once
hindered Balaam. In danger of war,
cause them to be as fiery horses and

chariots round about us, as they were about Elisha and the boy with him. Let us at all times rejoice in these guardians of our bodies at Thy command, and be diligent to obtain ourselves an angelic, holy, and pure life; that we drive them not away from us with our sins and shame, to make room for spirits of hell to have power over us. Let them have further charge concerning us to defend us against the devil in all our ways, in our need, and danger to body and soul, honor and possessions, in life and in death; and, at our latter end, let them serve our souls to bear them up into Thy hands; and, in the last of all the days, to gather us from out of our graves as worthy grains of wheat into the glowing garners of heaven; there to receive us into their holy, eternal company;

that, with them and all the elect, we
may evermore praise and give thanks
unto Thee. Amen.

THE FESTIVAL OF THE RE-
FORMATION, OR SAINT
MARTIN'S DAY.

Rejoice in the Lord alway.
And again I say, Rejoice!

316.

ALMIGHTY and Most Gracious
God, with our whole hearts we
thank Thee, that Thou didst lead us
and our fathers up out of the darkness of papacy, and in the latter
days of this world gavest the Fatherland such a mighty instrument,
Martin Luther, a great light kindled
by Thee. In the might of Thy
Spirit he cleansed the wells of Israel,
faithfully translating the Scriptures,
revealing Antìchrist in all his hide-

ousness, saving the rulers, and, doing
many more great deeds unto the
glory of Thy Name and the quieting
of many anxious consciences. O give
thanks unto the Lord of Sabaoth.
He is gracious and bestoweth great
gifts unto us. Praise the Lord, O
Jerusalem! Zion, praise thy God!
He giveth us His Word, together
with hosts of evangelists. Let all
that fear the Lord say: "Mercy and
Truth reign over us forever!" Thou,
O God, hast hitherto maintained
unto us the light of Thy word against
every storm of error and persecution. So establish it henceforth
also, and conserve that fountain of
salvation, Thy saving truth, unto
us and our children, that the city of
God remain glad with the river
thereof. Awaken us unto all godliness that we hold fast what we have,

and not fritter away our treasure
through ingratitude; but, in true
evangelical manner, live and move
worthy of the same, and praise and
magnify Thee, the Everlasting God,
for all Thy great benefactions, both
here and hereafter, for ever and ever.
Amen.

317.

MERCIFUL, Everlasting God,
the Father of our Lord Jesus
Christ, Who, in the fulness of time
gavest Thine only begotten Son unto
us, Who, at first, personally, and
afterward through the sacred office
of the ministry, declared unto us
what He heard in Thy bosom; we
praise and give thanks to Thee, with
hearts and voices, that Thou hast
enkindled the light of Thy gracious
Word, and hast redeemed us from

the Babylonian captivity and dark-
some kingdom of the Antichrist, and
hast graciously preserved until this
day the good work which Thou didst
begin through Thy servant, Martin
Luther . . . . years ago, that Thou
hast given Thy Word power to
withstand the rancor and opposition
of the devil manifested in church
and schools, and hast given to Thy
poor flock pure and zealous teachers
at all times. We confess that we are
unworthy of these Thy great benefits
unto us; and, by our manifold sins
we have merited that, according to
righteousness of judgement, Thou
shouldst have entirely removed from
us the candlestick of Thy pure Word,
and for our ingratitude, indifference,
and hypocrisy shouldst have decreed
a great famine of Thy Word. We
beseech Thee, of Thine unfathomable

grace, do not deal with us according to our sins, nor reward us according to our iniquities. Abide with us, dear Father, for the evening lowereth. Keep us and all posterity steadfast in the pure, saving gospel, and the right use of Thy Holy Sacraments. Let Thy temples be glorious in every land, that Thy kingdom increase, Thy Name be hallowed, Satan be trod under foot, and the son of perdition be finally slain by the spirit of Thy Word. Keep far from us all heresies, schisms, and false doctrines; and, let not ravening wolves, which spare not the flock, break into the fold of the Church Thine only begotten Son purchased at so terrible a price; but, send us, always, teachers who are able to bear the office of the New Testament, and be faithful stewards of Thy divine myseries; that, by the light of Thy truth, we be sustained unto everlasting life. Amen.

318.

The Day of Consecration.

MERCIFUL God, Everlasting Father, unto Thee we lift up our hearts and voices in thanksgiving, that Thou hast revealed unto us Thy pure and saving Word, and hast caused the same to be preached in truth and purity unto this congregation throughout another year, whereby the glory of Thy Name has been served, our souls instructed, and our salvation prospered. Furthermore, we beseech Thee, bless this congregation with Thy continued fatherly and faithful protection; and cause all things undertaken·in her to be acceptable unto Thee. Do Thou Thyself put the word upon our teacher's lips, and by Thy Holy Spirit seal it mightily in the hearts of all who hear, that they may fully believe and follow therein with perfect obedience. Reject not them who in the congregation appear before Thy face petitioning Thee for their own needs or with prayers for others; but let Thine eye ever be open over the congregation, and graciously hear our prayers. For the children who are here brought to Thee in holy baptism, we pray Thee, maintain them mightily in Thy covenant of grace. For their elders we pray: grant them true repentance and, by Thy grace, grant them true absolution from sin; and, cause them to receive the most holy Sacrament of the true body and blood of Christ unto the renewal of their oppressed souls, and the strengthening of their weak faith. For all who are betrothed, and, indeed, for all members of the congregation we pray: Grant them Thy gracious benediction, and cause Thy holy angels to surround and defend all who enter these courts from time to time. Bless the labors of Thy servants, the officers of the congregation; and under such benedictions let our last moments be spent, that by the same we may be translated into the glorious home of the heavenly Jerusalem, toward which our souls reach out with desire; and there, at last, grant us eternal joys; through Jesus Christ, our Lord. Amen.

319.
The Festival of Harvest.

WE render thanks unto Thee, Almighty, Bountiful God and Father, that Thou hast so abundantly crowned the year with Thy goodness, and madest the earth to yield her increase, and the fields to stand thick with grain. For these, Thy mercies, we praise and sing, and bring the fruits of the earth, together with all Thy gracious gifts, with rejoicing. Now thank we all our God, Who wondrous things hath done, in Whom the earth rejoices; Who, from our mother's arms, hath blessed us on our way, and still is ours today. Blessed be the Lord, Who blesses the fruits of the earth unto us, and maketh her yearly to yield her increase. O Faithful God, we heartily beseech Thee, grant us

Thy benediction, together with health, peace, and quietness of life, that we may enjoy these gifts with joyful hearts as in Thy fear; to acknowledge all Thy goodness; and to praise, laud, and magnify Thee for all Thy grace and faithfulness, both here and hereafter, eternally. Amen.

APPENDIX
320.

A Birthday Anniversary Prayer.

DEAR Father in Heaven, most heartily do I give thanks unto Thee, that Thou hast created me an intelligent being, and placed me here in the world; that I have been conceived and born of Christian parents, and received into Thy Church. This day is the anniversary of my birth, and I come to bring Thee hearty thanks for the return of the day. As I have been permitted to lay behind me another year of my pilgrimage, I rejoice and sing with the Psalmist "Bless the Lord, O my soul; and all that is within me, bless His Holy Name. Bless the Lord, O my soul; and forget not all His benefits: Who forgiveth all thine iniquities; Who

healeth all thy diseases; Who re-
deemeth thy life from destruction;
Who crowneth thee with loving-
kindness and tender mercies." (Ps.
103:1—4.)

O Loving Father, since each day
is a step nearer death, which may
overtake me ere this day wanes, yea,
even in this moment, I pray Thee,
so to rule and govern me every day,
which Thou yet graciously givest
unto me, that, according to Thy will,
I may walk as in the day, that is,
first of all, in Thy light, then also,
wisely, honestly, and conscientiously; in short, in everything as a true
Christian, according to my promise
which I made unto Thee my beloved
God, in the day of my baptism.
Should the year now beginning, and
this anniversary day of my birth be
the last on earth for me, I leave all

unto Thy gracious providence. If it be Thy will that my days shall have numbered their course, I shall be satisfied; for, if it be sufficient unto Thee, it will be sufficient for me. For those whom Thou gavest me, Thou wilt care, though I could no longer provide for them. Therefore grant me now my desire to enter anew under Thy protection and defence, under Thy great, eternal power. Should it please Thee to grant me to live another year, let me live unto Thee; if I die, let me die unto Thee, that I may live, move, and have my being in Thee; and, whether I live or die, be and remain Thine forever. Amen.

THE SEASONS.

"I will not again curse the ground anymore for man's sake; for the imagination of man's heart is evil from his youth; neither will I again smite any more everything living, as I have done. While the earth remaineth, seedtime and harvest, and cold and heat, and summer and winter, and day and night shall not cease." (Gen. 8:21, 22.)

—

321.

Prayer at the Opening of Springtime.

I GIVE thanks unto Thee, O God and Father, that, in health and joy, Thou hast caused me to see the delightful springtime of the year, when Thou causest the whole world to be renewed, the death-bound earth to revive again and be filled with creature life, to abound with grass and flowers. Most humbly do I beseech Thee, turn away now all destructive frosts and forefend every accident, that, during this year again, 1 may gratefully enjoy Thy bounty. Grant me grace also, constantly and filially to rejoice in Thy fatherly goodness and providence, and evermore to look forward with joy to the ultimate spring time which is the last of days. Then shall follow everlasting joy, unending beauty and glory upon the inconstancies of time. Then is the blessed resurrection from the dead, and my flesh shall again spring forth renewed, and my mortal body shall become like unto the glorified body of our Lord Jesus Christ. Even then will I laud, praise, and forevermore magnify Thee, together with Thy dear Son, and the much beloved Holy Ghost, for all Thy bounties. Amen.

322.

Prayer at the Beginning of Summertime.

BE Thou praised, O Lord, my God, for the unfathomable goodness which Thou deignest to bestow upon us with the beautiful summer time, wherein Thou coverest the earth so richly and abundantly with the delightful fruits which Thy hand has prepared. Most heartily I beseech Thee, cause me to use the time, in health, in peace, and with a good conscience, unto Thy glory and the furthering of my fellowman. Bless our land with fatherly gifts, and mercifully preserve us from destructive rains, from thunder, lightning, hail and storms. Above all, cause my heart to be conscious of all these Thy gracious benefits, to realize the penetrating thunders of Thy law as well as the graciously gentle rains of the holy Gospel. Renew and refresh my soul mightily with Thy comfort under the heat and burden of the cross; and let the contemplation of the passing grandeur of earth and these physical blessings serve me unto a recognition of the everlasting glory and blessed joys which eye has not seen, ear has not heard, and the heart of man has not imagined, the things which Thou hast prepared for them that love Thee. Finally, perfect Thou me, that in the day of the harvest of heavenly joys, and the bringing in of the sheaves into Thy glory, I may evermore truly praise and magnify Thee, my Heavenly Father, together with Thy dear Son and the blessed Comforter, the Holy Ghost. Amen.

323.

Prayer at the Beginning of the fruitful Autumn Season.

B LESSED be the Lord! He hath done wonderful things; and blessed is His Holy Name, Who, now, that the summer is past, has brought me in joy to behold the blessed autumn days. Lord, I am not worthy of all Thy goodness and mercy which Thou hast again showered upon me. Most humbly and heartily I beseech Thee, O Loving Father, turn away all dangerous storms and infectious diseases, and so bless me in my participation in Thy bounty, that with health of body, peace of mind, and a good conscience, I may thankfully enjoy Thy gifts, and use what Thou hast given me unto Thy glory, and the promotion of my fellowman's

happiness, and unceasingly bring to
Thee acceptable fruits of my life.
In these days of the ingathering of
the vintage, let me rejoice in Him,
Who alone truly treads the wine
press, the beloved Redeemer, Jesus
Christ. With the fading and falling
leaf, cause me to remember my
mortality, and to prepare while it is
yet time for a blessed end; to leave
this inconstant, passing world with
joy, whenever it so pleases Thee;
and, to enter Thy glory, there, with
angels and all the company of the
elect, to evermore laud, praise and
thank Thee for all Thy benefits.
Amen.

324.
Prayer at the Beginning of the Winter Time.

I HEARTILY thank Thee, O Lord, Ruler of heaven and earth, that Thou hast caused me to enjoy Thy goodness with which Thou crownedst the year even to this moment. And, since it hath pleased Thee, in divine wisdom, that seedtime and harvest, heat and cold, summer and winter, day and night cease no more, so long as the earth shall remain, I most heartily beseech Thee, grant us to be sustained through these cold, dreary and bleak winter days, and bless us with Thy fatherly peace, that our flight from the enemy be not in the winter, nor that we be disturbed by fire or water or other adversity, nor perish in the cold and snow. Be merciful unto all who are

in need, the naked, and them that
are distressed; and, so keep my
heart, that in these days when
wickedness stalketh forth triumphant, and love so easily grows cold, I
may earnestly withold myself from
all the works of darkness, and not
deny my soul the offices of mercy;
but, at all times willingly aid and
give, even as Thou hast prospered
me abundantly.

Lord, Lord, when at last mine
eyes grow dim, and all natural
warmth departs from my body, help
me to see the sun of righteousness
in the night of death; to be clothed
in the garments of salvation and the
mantel of the righteousness of Jesus
Christ, my Lord and Savior; cleansed
in His blood from all sin, that I be
found white as snow; so to escape
the pains of hell and outer darkness;

and, when comes the glorious spring time of the last of days, to enjoy Thine eternal kingdom of peace; forever to laud, praise and magnify Thee in that kingdom, O beloved God, Father, Son, and Holy Ghost. Amen.

V.

INTERCESSORY PRAYERS.

I exhort therefore, that, first of all supplications, prayers, intercessions, and giving of thanks, be made for all men.

For kings, and for all that are in authority; that we may lead a quiet and peaceable life in all godliness and honesty.

For this is good and acceptable in the sight of God our Savior; Who will have all men to be saved, and to come unto the knowledge of the truth. (I Tim. 2: 1—4).

325.

Prayer for Posterity.

O MOST Beloved Father, I beseech Thee through Jesus Christ, our only Propitiator, reveal Thy salutary gospel of grace, by Thy Holy Spirit, unto the beloved children which Thou hast given us; that, by the guidance of the Holy Spirit, they may understand and believe the teachings of Thy Son, and continue steadfast in such faith unto the end. All possessions of the world are nothing in comparison with such Christian faith. I have no desire to leave any other heritage to my dear children, nor any other gift than the true, unalterable faith of Thy holy Church. If they have that, they will be rich here and hereafter; though, in this life they were beggars all

their days with the holy gospel. By
the holy faith of the Christian we
have Thee, God, Father, Son, and
Holy Ghost, the only true God, for
our own, by the gracious merit of
Jesus Christ, Who, for our sake became man, that we might be Thy
children, and Thou be our gracious
Father for ever and ever. What
needs can distress us if we have but
Thee, the only true, living God, as
our Father, in . Jesus Christ, our
Lord! Keep us, O Lord, in Thy
fullness, and we will thank Thee
eternally. Amen.

326.

Prayer of Parents for Their Children.

DEAR Heavenly Father, in Thy
Name, let me bless my children.
Hear the blessing I pronounce upon

them, even in Thy high heaven. Confirm it, and let it descend upon my
children. For Thine own blessed
Son's sake, help and give grace that
my blessings may be even greater
than those of my own parents. Bless
Thou, O Lord, whom I bless. Let
the blessing begin upon the house of
Thy servant, that it be established
before Thee forever, For, whatsoever Thou blessest, is blest forever.

Hear my children in every need,
and protect them for Thy Name's
sake. Send them help out of Thy
holy temple, and give them strength
out of Zion. Grant them their
heart's desire, and deny not their
prayers unto them. Prosper them
with Thy goodness, and grant them
length of days, life, and enjoyment
forever and ever. Gladden them
with the favor of Thy countenance.

Grant them to have clean hands and
pure hearts, and not lift up their
souls unto vanity nor swear falsely.
Bless them with peace, and let Thy
mercy and goodness overshadow
them. Make Thy face to shine upon
them, that they may know Thy ways
in all the earth, Thy saving grace
among the gentiles. Bless them, O
God, our God, that they may ever
fear Thee. Make them to flourish
as the palm-tree, and to grow like
the cedars of Lebanon. Make them
to prosper in Thy courts, there to be
ever strong and fruitful, that they
proclaim how Thou, O God, our
Defense, art good, and that there is
no evil in Thee. Lord, bless their
going out and their coming in from
this time forth and even for evermore. Let my children sit about my
board, strong and healthy as olive

branches. As unto the children of Jacob, so grant them the dew of heaven, the fatness of the land, and corn and wine abundantly. Make their seed mighty, and their generation shall be called blessed; riches and plenty shall be in their homes; their righteousness shall abide forever, and their horn shall be exalted unto honor. Make my children and their children to be blessed of the Lord, Who made heaven and earth. Blessed be they that bless them, and may every curse be turned into a blessing upon them. In the name of the Father, and of the Son, and of the Holy Ghost, the only true God, from Whom cometh the blessing out of the throne of the Most High. Amen.

327.

Prayer of Sponsors Before Baptism.

O LORD Jesus, Thou only Savior and Redeemer of mankind, Who hast said, "Whosoever believeth and is baptized shall be saved;" and again, "Except a man be born again of water and the Spirit, he can not enter into the kingdom of heaven," I come unto Thee, giving hearty thanks that Thou hast called me to serve a little child unto baptism and regeneration by water and spirit. I go now, with joy, in the name and stead of this child, to renounce the devil and all his ways, and with heart and mouth and in true faith to confess Thee, the true God. I commend and consign the child, body and soul, here and forevermore, unto Thy gracious protection and care. Thou hast said: "Let the little children come unto me, and forbid them not; for of such is the kingdom of heaven." Therefore, I bring and commit to Thy charge this infant, for whom I speak, that Thou enlighten him (her) with the light of Thy fatherly mercies. Bless, defend, and turn not Thy countenance away from him (her); but receive him (her) into the covenant of Thy christendom; and keep him (her), both here and evermore in Thy grace; and, when this life is past, grant him (her) Thy continued joy unto all eternity. Amen.

328.

O LORD, Triune God, Who hast commanded Thy servants to go and baptize in the Name of the Father, and of the Son, and of the Holy Ghost, be present now with Thy

servants in the administration of
this sacrament, and open Thy heavens as Thou openedst them over
Jordan, that souls may daily be added unto Thy congregation who shall
be blessed. Rule and govern all who
are present at this baptism, that
they remember that baptism is from
heaven and not of man, though it be
applied by man's hands; in order
that all may be here present in
reverent humility, as at a work instituted by Thee. Maintain among
us always the sacrament of baptism
in unaltered purity. Let nobody's
child be denied the benefits thereof;
and, if at times some attain not unto
baptism, being overcome by death,
comfort their parents and friends by
Thy Word, that they may entertain
no doubt of salvation. Finally, since
we all believe in one Lord, one faith,

one baptism, one God and Father of all, grant that we be diligent to hold the unity of spirit in the bond of peace; and, together with all the baptized, complete our course in the oneness of the hope of our calling. Amen.

329.

Prayer for the Church.

FATHER of all mercy, Who, by Thy Word and Spirit, gatherest and maintainest one holy congregation and church upon earth, I pray Thee, support Thy little flock, the small company of those who have received, who honor, and who propagate Thy Word, by the Spirit, in the true, acknowledged, pure, and salutary doctrine, and the right use of Thy most blessed sacraments, against the rage of Satan, and against all the

machinations and tyranny of an evil
world.   Uphold Thy little vessel,
together with all Christians, upon the
storm-tossed sea, amid all the swell-
ings of the waves thereof; that it
sink not, nor be destroyed.   Cause
Thy Church to stand fast, immovable
upon the rock upon which she is
built.   O God of Sabaoth, turn unto
us: look down from heaven; behold
the vine, and tend it in the soil where
Thou hast Thyself planted it; the
vine   which   Thou   hast   sacredly
chosen, that it might increase and its
branches grow mighty.   Surround it
with the wall of Thy protection; and,
take us, the sheep of Thy pasture,
under Thy care, that no one tear us
away from Thy hand.   Save us from
those who seek to put away pure
doctrine that they might elevate
their false idolatries instead.   Let

Thy beloved word, the clear, unmistakable light that shineth here, never be hidden nor quenched among us; but, help us by Thy mighty, outstretched arm, and maintain Thy Church and people in the midst of so many offences; that, among us, here on earth, Thou mayest ever have a people which acknowledges, honors, and worships Thee. O Lord, Who, in times past, forgavest the iniquities of Thy people and didst cover up all their sins; Who, in times past, didst abate Thine anger and turn away from the bitterness of Thy wrath, let not our sins be reckoned unto us. Comfort us, O God, our Redeemer, and cease from Thy just wrath against us. Defend Thy christendom that trusteth in Thee. Do this, for Thy Name's sake, that the same be not blasphemed. Grant

this, for the sake of Jesus Christ,
Thy dear Son. Amen.

330.

Prayer for Our Pastors.

E VERLASTING, Gracious, Heavenly Father, for my pastor I
pray: grant him to speak Thy word
with joy, fearlessly against every
error, false doctrine, and abuse; that
he may declare and make plain to us
the mysteries of the gospel, and remove from our hearts all delusions.
Keep him steadfast in the true
doctrine and Christian life, that he
may be unto us a leader unto everlasting life. Guard his body against
sickness, that to our great benefit, he
may for a long time go before us and
preach Thy divine word without fear
or hesitation, without hypocrisy, not
of favor, hatred, jealousy, or for self

advantage, but proclaim the truth in
all its purity and fullness, and de-
nounce evils as becometh them, that
I and many more may be won for
Thy kingdom. Open my heart and
ears that I may listen to Thy word
with desire and love, with reverent
mind, and hearty attention; to walk
in accordance thereto in true faith,
and bring fruit unto Thy divine
glory. Save me from becoming tired
of hearing and from slothfulness of
soul; and instill in my mind a great
hunger and earnest desire for the
inestimable riches of Thy grace,
which is tendered to us in the sermon.
Grant me grace to know and esteem
my pastor as a servant and steward
of the divine mysteries, that I receive
Thy word from his lips without
offence, unto the bettering of my life,
the abhorrence of sin; and not let

correction pass me by unheeded, nor,
that I offend, or despise him by whom
the correction cometh. Preserve us
all in the true faith and a Christian
life, that we may daily grow and increase therein, remaining steadfast
unto our end, and be eternally saved;
through Thy beloved Son, Jesus
Christ. Amen.

331.

Prayers for the Heathen.

ALMIGHTY and Everlasting God,
Who desirest not the death of
sinners, but that they turn unto
Thee and be saved: graciously hear
our prayer, and save the heathen
from their dreadful idolatries.
Gather them into the Christian
Church, to the praise and glory of
Thy Name; through Jesus Christ, our
Lord, Who liveth and reigneth with

Thee and the Holy Ghost, true God forever and ever. Amen.

332.

ALMIGHTY, Everlasting, Gracious God, we pray Thee, touch the hardened hearts of all heathen and all unbelievers. Open their darkened eyes to behold their errors, to depart from the same, and be converted unto Thee. Thou, alone, O God, art God; and besides Thee there is none other God. Thou alone hast power to slay and make alive again. Thou canst wound, and Thou canst heal. There is none that can save from Thy hand; but, the idols, in whom the heathen trust, have no power. Therefore, O Lord, have mercy upon the heathen. Make them to hear the sound of Thy gospel; and, so many as please Thee, turn unto

Thyself, for the glory of Thy Name, that the same may be universally praised, honored, and magnified by all peoples in all this wide world, and in the paradise of heaven evermore. Amen.

333.
Prayer for the Country.

BELOVED Lord, Jesus Christ, make our country, this commonwealth, our city (community), to be and remain always like unto a garden which the Lord blesseth; as a fountain of sweet waters that never faileth; as a vineyard planted by the right hand of the Lord, watched over by Thine own eye, guarded day and night that no leaf thereof be missed. Cause our country, this commonwealth, and our city (community), to have the honor that Thou dwellest therein, unto the end of time. Grant,

that among the nations of the earth
we may be blest in Thee and Thou in
us. Make our land to be filled with
Thy glory now, that, in the last day,
the resurrection of the just may be
great in it. Hear us, O King of all
the earth, Lord Jesus Christ, and let
not our prayer come to naught before
Thee. Amen.

334.

For Our Rulers.

O HEAVENLY Father, vouchsafe
unto us at all times pious, god-
fearing, and Christian rulers and
governors, inclined to promote Thy
glory, with their person, honor, and
possession, to strengthen Thy Church
in matters pertaining to salvation,
and to support the people unto the
saving of the soul. Make them to
govern with a good conscience, and
finally, to render account to Thee,

their God and Supreme Lord, in the day when Thou shalt call them. Touch the hearts of those in authority over us, O God and Father, with the mighty and keen sword of Thy Word, that they may realize what great power they have received, to be faithful shepherds and guardians of Thy people. Make them to feel that Thou wilt finally require the blood of Thy sheep at their hands, that they may seek not their own, but the glory of Thy Name, and with all zeal promote the welfare of Thy people. Grant that they may exercise justice and execute judgment without partiality or favor to any one; that they be swayed neither by gift nor emolument; that they follow Thy law day and night, seeking to do Thy will; and not be swerved either to the right or the left hand

from following the same. Assure
them, O God, our Father, of Thy
support, even as Thou didst unto the
leaders in Thine ancient Israel, to
Moses and to Joshua. Make them
to feel Thy presence in all their do-
ings, or in whatsoever they leave undone, a righteous Judge of all the
world. Lead them unto true, whole-
some fear of God, that they may ever
promote Thy people in all obedience
and holiness of life by their godly
lives and government; through Jesus
Christ, our Redeemer. Amen.

(From the Reverent, Christian Prayers
of Frederick William, Duke of Saxony.
New Edition, 1671.)

335.

For Those Who Are in Trouble.

O LORD God, Creator of heaven
and earth, all things obey Thy
command, and none may oppose Thy

majesty. Therefore I humble my
heart before Thy divine and mighty
majesty, and pray Thee, by Thy Son,
Jesus Christ, look upon Thy servant
—N. N.—with mercy, for he is sorely
tempted, stricken, and afflicted of
Satan, the enemy of Thy holy Word.
The evil one purposes not only to
destroy him, but reviles Thy Word
for weakness. O Lord God, defeat
and put to naught the enemy's
machinations and presumptions, that
the enemies of Thy Word may not
feel moved to rejoice and say:
"Where is now thy God?" O Lord,
confuse and scatter all who rise up
against Thy Word, and let them come
to shame. In Thee alone is our comfort and our help. Quickly hear our
prayer and turn sorrow into joy.
Let Thy hand rest mercifully upon
this—N. N.—who is a faithful ser-

vant of Thy Word. Guide and keep him in Thy truth. Strengthen him in all knowledge of Thee; and, abide with him mightily in every temptation and sickness of body and soul. By Thy mercy, defend him from the spirit of evil, and graciously complete the work which Thou hast begun in him, unto the honor and glory of Thy holy Name. This, grant us, Most Merciful Father, through Jesus Christ, our Lord, our Savior, our Mediator. Amen.

336.
Prayer for Innocent Prisoners.

ALMIGHTY Lord God, Who didst help the Apostle Peter free from prison: mercifully regard the estate of Thy imprisoned servants, and loose their bonds, that we may rejoice in their release, and give

praise and thanks unto Thee;
through Jesus Christ, Thy Son, our
Lord. Amen.

337.

Prayer for Those Who Have Asked Our Prayers.

O MERCIFUL and Ever Faithful
High Priest, Who hast power
to save all who come and deal with
the Father by Thee, our Lord Jesus
Christ, since a seeking brother (sis-
ter), whose name, whose need and
desire Thou knowest best, commended himself (herself), to my prayers;
and, I myself am nothing, nor avail
anything, scarce fit to lift up mine
eyes and my lips for mine own sins,
and know not what I should pray:
therefore, in full assurance of Thy
exceeding grace I come to Thee, Who
art offered unto us for a seat of

grace, that we poor sinners might of
Thy fullness receive grace for grace.
Besides myself, I commend unto
Thee the person who requests my
prayers. O Lord, accept my prayer
and sustain it before Thy heavenly
Father, that all these trials may be
turned for good. Comfort him (her)
in every time of trial and distress.
Strengthen him (her) in every hour
of temptation. Depart not from him
(her) in the hour of need. Enlighten
him (her) in ignorance. Cast him
(her) not away when he (she)
erreth. Let him (her) not fall. For
his (her) sin grant him (her) the
healing remedies from the fountain
of reconciliation. Sanctify him (her)
totally, and make him (her) to live
through Thy death, Who art the life.
Grant all this unto the glory and
praise of Thy Father, unto Whom,

in unity with Thee and the Holy
Ghost, be and remain all glory,
power, and majesty, henceforth,
forevermore. Amen.

Prayers for our Enemies.

338.

O LORD, Almighty, Everlasting,.
God, Gracious Father, Thou
hast commanded us to pray for all
our enemies. Grant me, then, the
spirit of meekness, that I may
patiently bear the enmity, injustice,
and injuries which mine enemies inflict, even as I know Thou Thyself
hast borne in the past, and dost bear
even unto this day. Grant that I
commit no injustice in deeds, seek
no revenge in words, desire no vengeance in my heart, and so absolutely
depart from all vindictiveness that I
may serve mine enemies with all my

powers, praying for them, and desiring every good thing for them.
Thus let me live, that I may remain
a child of Thine, Who causest the
rain to fall upon the just and the
unjust alike; and to be the servant of
Thy dear Son, Who, even on the
cross, did intercede for His enemies.
O Lord, do not destroy my enemies
for my sake; but rather, preserve
them as I pray; for I desire their
amendment and not their confusion
and destruction. Grant also, dear
Father, that they with me, and I with
them may be re-united in constant
love; to walk together in the way that
leadeth to the heavenly home. There,
let us finally rejoice, jointly and
severally, in Thy love, unto all
eternity. Amen..

339.

LORD Jesus Christ, my Redeemer and my Savior, Thou art inclined and ready to pardon all men. Toward Thy most bitter enemies, who rejected, despised, and finally crucified, slew, and murdered Thee, Thou wast so resigned, friendly, and gracious, that Thou didst heartily pray for them unto Thy Heavenly Father. O be gracious and merciful unto me in my sins, and in all I do against Thee. Grant me also to follow in Thy footsteps and to love my enemies; to bless them that curse me; to do good unto them that hate me; to pray for them that despitefully use and persecute me: yea, let me always overcome evil with good, and rejoice that, unworthy servant though I be, I may become like unto my Lord and Master here in suffering, but also hereafter in eternal joy. Amen.

Prayers for all Classes of Men.

340.

O LORD God, Who lovest Thy Church, I pray Thee for her servants; that, by Thy word and a pure life, they may lead and draw the congregations which Thou hast entrusted to them unto the eternal fatherland.

For the President of the United States, the Governor of this Commonwealth, and all who occupy stations of honor and power, I pray; that they may ever show themselves fathers and judges unto all widows and orphans; to be merciful unto the poor and the suffering; and justly to deal in judgment, so that they use not their power of government in such a way as to lose their eternal inheritance.

For all married people, I pray, cause them thus faithfully to perform their duties toward one another, that they may not lose their earnest desire for the heavenly fatherland.

For all widows and for all who live out of the bonds of wedlock, I pray; let them not desire the passing pleasures of this world as though these could satisfy the soul; but, cause them to seek the things of the world to come, and to serve Thee alone.

For all men, I pray: but, O Lord God, what is this, that I forget mine own sins and undertake to pray for others? O Lord, not in mine own righteousness, but by Thy great mercy I cast myself before Thee in prayer, doubting nothing, but Thou wilt hear me; for I remember the Publican who went down to his own house justified, and how Thou cleansedst a Magdalene of her sin, and even hadst regard to the petition of the malefactor on the cross. Therefore, of Thy mercy, hear also my prayer for myself and for all conditions of men. Amen.

341.

O LORD, increase our faith, love, and trust in Thee. Cleanse and purge us from all sin and evil, all enmity, all unbelief, error, and heresy. Rebuke the erring, convert the unbelieving, and lead back again the backsliders into the unity of the Christian Church; and show them the light of Thy truth.

Save all pastors and elders of

Thy holy Christian Church, and all sorts and conditions of men in the Church, together with all in authority, from every danger and harm to body and soul.

O Lord, grant true repentance to all sinners. Support the righteous and increase every good purpose and desire in their lives. Have mercy upon all Christian people. Defend and preserve in Thy service all who have consecrated themselves unto Thee. Strengthen all faithful laborers. Comfort the sorrowing and those who mourn. Unto the sick grant restoration of health in body and soul. Give unto the poor and needy whatsoever of bodily and spiritual comforts they need. To all that journey, and to those in misery, being banished or in prison, grant a joyful return to their country. Them that are in danger upon the seas lead into safe havens according to their desires.

Unto all women with child, grant a joyful prospect of deliverance in mercy. Undo the bonds of all prisoners. All with whom I have committed sin, or whom I have in any wise led or caused to sin, and me also, forgive, O merciful Father. All whom I have in any wise harmed, distressed, angered, deceived, or injured do Thou, in my stead, reward and restore. Unto all my relatives, my wife (or husband), my children, my brothers and sisters, all friends, kindred, neighbors, servants, and benefactors, whose benefits I daily enjoy, and all, who in their prayers remember me, and for whom I pray, or ought to pray, even as Thou knowest all their circumstances and desires, and whose names are never unknown to Thee; O Lord, unto all these grant every good thing; shield them from all evil; cause them to abide in Thy service unto Thy glory even unto the end; and after this life let them all come unto Thee, Who art the true home and joy, and their eternal reward. When they cry to Thee in fear, hear them, O Lord; and, when comes the last hour of this life, be Thou their helper, and save their souls from destruction by the enemy. Grant these things also unto our enemies. And, unto us all, friends and foes, grant that we have true love, peace, and joy in mind and body.

For the fruits of the earth grant us good and seasonable weather; and whatsoever else we may need, whether in body or soul, physical or spiritual, grant us from Thy gentle and gracious hand.

Toward all men, grant me to have a patient, lowly, gracious, peaceful, merciful, and, in all cases, sweet and loving heart; to bear all without malice, envy, hatred, or jealousy.

I would remember before Thee also my parents, pastors, teachers, children, kindred, and benefactors, who have gone before me in blessed faith and are now at home with Thee. If, through Jesus Christ, my prayer find favor in Thy sight, do Thou, in my stead, repay unto them my thanks and love, in whatever manner it be possible.

Unto all whom I have ever pained, deceived, or caused to sin, or whom I have robbed of honor, health, or possessions, whom I can no longer ask for pardon, nor restore unto

them, because they already are gone
into joy and pardon of every sin,—
gone home to Thee,—to all these, O
Lord, grant good for all my evil,
both now and in the day of the
resurrection of the just; even as
Thou knowest how, and in how far
all this which I ask can be granted.

As for myself, let me spend my
remaining days in prayer, and in
adoration of the Most Holy Name of.
Jesus, and in praise and thanksgiving for the hearing of my prayers
and those of all Christian people
which have ever been offered up unto
Thee through Jesus Christ. Amen.

342.

Prayer of Commendation Unto God.

LORD God, Heavenly Father, have
mercy upon us poor sinners.
Save and defend us, and never leave

us. Thou, God of Abraham, God of
Isaac, God of Jacob, have mercy
upon me and send me Thy holy angel
to help me, that he may at all times
be with me, to save and defend me
from the evil one, from all enemies,
visible and invisible; from all pestilence and from an evil death; from
every evil to body and soul: so that
no evil befall me in forest or field,
whether I ride, walk, or stand;
wherever I may be, sleeping or
waking. Let Thy holy angel ever
be between me and all mine enemies.

O Savior of the world, come to
the rescue of a poor sinner like me.
Be gracious unto me, and save me
from every evil to body and soul.
O Lord God most holy, O Lord most
mighty, O everlasting and most
merciful Savior, Immortal God, have
mercy upon me, a poor sinner. By

Thy holy passion and death support
me. By Thine innocence shield me.
By Thy bitter pangs of suffering and
dying, and by Thy glorious resurrection from the dead, save me! In the
name of the Father, the Son, and the
Holy Ghost. Amen.

343.

For Good Purposes in Life.

ALMIGHTY Lord Jesus, for Thy
perfect love's sake, by which
Thou hast so faithfully sought our
salvation, I pray Thee, grant unto
all Christian people in all their undertakings and acts, thoughts and
purposes, to be pure and simple;
that, in all their lives, they seek,
plan, or desire nothing but what will
serve their soul for good unto their
salvation, being fruitful unto the
welfare of our fellowmen, and ac-

ceptable unto Thy divine majesty:
who livest and reignest with God
the Father and the Holy Ghost, the
only true God, world without end.
Amen.

344.

L ORD God Almighty, Everlasting,
and Gracious: grant me and all
Christians a heart that will daily
understand Thy word through the
Holy Spirit; submissive under the
yoke of Jesus Christ, and obedient
to His holy law. Amen.

345.

Prayer for a Godly Life.

A LMIGHTY God and Father,
since man has not in himself
power to do good and live in accordance with Thy holy will, though he
has the ability to sin even more than
he will; and in the flesh and blood

there is no good thing; I pray Thee,
for Christ's sake, grant unto Thy
people the gift of the Holy Ghost,
that, by Thy power and might, Thy
rule and governance, they may dur-
ing· all their lives be honoring and
praising Thee, Father eternal, as Thy
dearly purchased and redeemed
children. Teach them to do Thy
will. Lead and direct them in Thy
paths. Cause them to rejoice and
love Thy commandments. Grant
Thy grace unto me and unto all
people, that whenever we stray, or
even fall, overcome by the devil or
by our own flesh and blood, we may,
by a true recognition of our sins, by
true repentance and sorrow, soon
rise again, heartily to confess and
lament our transgressions before
Thee, and seek grace before Thee
unto pardon; and, though we be

impotent children, who being washed
and cleansed, soon again begrime
and soil themselves, yet, we will evermore continue to offer our feet to
Thy dear Son, and be washed and
cleansed in His blood; until, at last,
we may arise from our graves,
totally cleansed, to live with Thee
eternally, without weakness and
without sin. Amen.

The Litany.

346.

L ORD, have mercy upon us.
    Lord, have mercy upon us.
  Christ, have mercy upon us.
    Christ, have mercy upon us.
  Lord, have mercy upon us.
    Lord, have mercy upon us.
  O Christ, hear us.
    O Christ, hear us.

O God, the Father in Heaven,
> Have mercy upon us.

O God the Son, Redeemer of the World;
> Have mercy upon us.

O God, the Holy Ghost;
> Have mercy upon us.

Be gracious unto us.
> Spare us, good Lord.

Be gracious unto us.
> Help us, good Lord.

From all sin;

From all error;

From all evil:
> Good Lord, deliver us.

From the crafts and assaults of the devil;
> From sudden and evil death;
> From pestilence and famine;
> From war and bloodshed;
> From sedition and rebellion;
> From lightning and tempest;

From all calamity by fire and water;

And from everlasting death:

Good Lord, deliver us.

By the mystery of Thy holy Incarnation;

By Thy holy Nativity;

By Thy Baptism, Fasting, and Temptation;

By Thine Agony and Bloodv Sweat;

By Thy Cross and Passion;

By Thy precious Death and Burial;

By Thy glorious Resurrection and Ascension;

And by the coming of the Holy Ghost, the Comforter:

Help us, good Lord.

In all time of our tribulation;

In all time of our prosperity;

In the hour of death;

And in the day of judgment:
Help us, good Lord.
We poor sinners do beseech Thee;
To hear us, O Lord God.
And to lead and govern Thy holy
Christian Church in the right way;
To preserve all pastors and ministers of Thy Church in the true
knowledge and understanding of
Thy Word, and in holiness of life;
To put an end to all schisms and
causes of offence;
To bring into the way of truth all
such as have erred, and are deceived;
To beat down Satan under our
feet;
To send faithful laborers into
Thy harvest;
To accompany Thy Word with
Thy Spirit and grace;
To raise up them that fall, and to
strengthen such as do stand;

And to comfort and help the weak-hearted and the distressed:

We beseech Thee to hear us, good Lord.

To give all nations peace and concord;

To preserve our country from discord and contention;

To give to our nation perpetual victory over all its enemies;

To direct and defend our President, and all in authority;

And to bless and keep our magistrates, and all our people:

We beseech Thee to hear us, good Lord.

To behold and succor all who are in danger, necessity, and tribulation;

To protect all who travel by land or water;

To preserve all women in the perils of childbirth;

To strengthen and keep all sick persons and young children;

To set free all who are innocently imprisoned;

To defend and provide for all fatherless children and widows;

And to have mercy upon all men:

> We beseech Thee to hear us, good Lord.

To forgive our enemies, persecutors, and slanderers, and to turn their hearts;

To give and preserve to our use the fruits of the earth;

And graciously to hear our prayers:

> We beseech Thee to hear us, good Lord.

O Lord Jesus Christ, Son of God;

> We beseech Thee to hear us.

O Lamb of God, that takest away
the sin of the world;
Have mercy upon us.
O Lamb of God, that takest away
the sin of the world;
Have mercy upon us.
O Lamb of God, that takest away
the sin of the world;
Grant us Thy peace.
O Christ, hear us.
O Christ, hear us.
Lord, have mercy upon us.
Lord, have mercy upon us.
Christ, have mercy upon us.
Christ, have mercy upon us.
Lord, have mercy upon us.
Lord, have mercy upon us.
Amen.

The Lord's Prayer.

347.

The Litany for the Dying.

L ORD, have mercy.
     Lord, have mercy.
   Christ, have mercy.
      Christ, have mercy.
  Lord, have mercy.
     Lord, have mercy.
  O God, the Father in heaven;
     Have mercy upon him.
  O God the Son, Redeemer of the world;
     Have mercy upon him.
  O God, the Holy Ghost;
     Have mercy upon him.
   Be gracious unto him.
     Spare him, good Lord.
   Be gracious unto him.
     Help him, good Lord.
   From Thy wrath;
   From an evil death;
   From the pains of hell;

From the power of the devil;
From all evil:
    Good Lord, deliver him.
By Thy holy Nativity;
By Thine Agony of Bloody Sweat;
By Thy Cross and Passion;
By Thy Death and Burial;
By Thy glorious Resurrection
and Ascension;
By the Grac of the Holy Ghost,
the Comforter:
    Help him, good Lord.
In the hour of death;
And in the day of judgment:
    Help him, good Lord.
We poor sinners do beseech Thee
    To hear us, O Lord God.
That Thou wouldst spare him;
    We beseech Thee to hear us,
    good Lord.
Lord, have mercy.
    Lord, have mercy.

Christ, have mercy.
    Christ, have mercy.
Lord, have mercy.
    Lord, have mercy.
      Amen.

———

PART VI.

CONCLUSION.

ADDENDA.

348.

Luther's Daily Prayers.

O HEAVENLY Father, I acknowledge, and Thou knowest and seest that in all things, wherever I go or stay, both inwardly and outwardly, in body and in soul, I have entirely merited the torments of hell. Thou knowest also, O Father, that in me there is no good thing; nay, not a hair upon my head is good: all, and in all, I rightly deserve to be in the depths of hell where is the very devil. Why should I multiply words? Yet. dear Father, I beseech Thee; though I be what I may, I pray Thee and

will have Thee importuned every
day, that Thou wilt not have Thy
supervision and regard for me, nor
turn Thine eyes unto me, as upon a
sinner, such as I even am. Nay,
though I had a thousand worlds to
support me; yet, if Thou wilt so regard me, then am I lost and perished.
But, this I pray Thee, turn Thine
eyes, and look upon and behold the
face of Thine Anointed, even Jesus
Christ Thy dear Son, my Mediator,
High Priest, and Intercessor, my
Redeemer and Savior; and, for His
sake, I pray Thee, O Father beloved,
have mercy and be gracious unto me;
and, for the sake of the same, Thy
Son Jesus Christ, grant me a blessed
end, a joyful resurrection from the
dead, and help me, now and evermore, in body and in soul. For the
sake of His precious blood, which

He so graciously shed upon the cross
unto the pardon and blotting out of
my sins, I beseech Thee, O heavenly
Father, do not in Thy righteousness
regard the blood of the same, Thy
beloved Son, as lost upon me, a miserable creature, on account of my
sins which can not be told or numbered; but, of Thine unfathomable
mercy, cause it to bestow the benefit
and bring such fruit as it was
ordained by Thee from all eternity
to bring and bestow, and for which
it was shed by Thy Son, upon the
cross; namely, That Thou mightest
regard it sufficient unto the pardon
of my sin; so that, when Thou comest,
whether by day or by night, to take
away again my spirit, which Thou
didst breathe upon me in the first
place, I will ever pray Thee, O Father, let the same, my spirit and my

soul, be committed into Thy hands.
Amen.

349.

Prayer for the Present Needs of the Church.

(To be used at vesper service.)

O LORD God, Gracious Father of
our Lord Jesus Christ, Who, in
times past hast been gracious unto
Thy people, to forgive all their sins,
have mercy upon Thine own who
now feel the burden of their sins and
the weight of Thine avenging hand
driving them to pray unto Thee.
Thou Who didst banish Israel unto
Babylon for their sin's sake, but
didst hear their cries and lead them
back again into their beloved
country, and unto Thy holy Mount
Zion, behold how we dwell in misery
and long for Thy Zion. Yea, Thy
poor Church, indeed, is dwelling in

Babylon now; and the children of Babylon reside among her children. We who heretofore, in spite of our manifold sins, were united in the word and confession of faith, hear no more the sound of the trumpet-cry of Thy word and the confessions which kept our fathers steadfast in Thy truth. We have tarried long, but there returneth not unto us the ancient glory. Schisms and false doctrines have entered in among us, and the disagreements of pastors and teachers have scattered the people. Thus have thousands again become as erring sheep, each looking to his own ways, and all are turned from the true Shepherd and Bishop of their souls, knowing no more to find the way of peace. How shall they have one faith when they hear the one doctrine no more; for faith cometh by the hearing of the word; and now, by false preaching has come false faith, and by manifold teachings must come manifold confessions, schisms, and divisions. How shall they be one in love, one flock and one fold, if they be not one in spirit and in faith? O Lord, how great misery has befallen us, that men scarce recognize Thy Bride; and therefore do the children of death no more gather about her. Where is she? How shall she be found, since Thy signs, Thy light and counsel, Thy pure word, the unity of confession and concord of doctrine have departed from her? O Lord, hear us and all who in these days bring one plaint and one petition to Thine ear, in Jesus' Name; and since the day is far spent, let there be light even at eventide. Send forth Thy Holy

Spirit from high heaven, that He may
banish from the hearts of all that
love Thee this multiplicity of doctrines and conceptions. Take away
from the souls of all who with us
eat one bread and drink of the one
cup, everything which hinders them
from being one in Thy truth.
Cleanse, purify, and revive also the
hearts of all of us who desire the only
true peace of Thy word. Grant us
moderation, discretion, and patience
that we withstand not Thy Spirit
with impious souls, and so tear down
instead of building up what Thy
hand has even yet maintained among
us of concord and peace. Especially
strengthen all who have yielded
themselves unto Thee, to overcome
divisions and to seek true concord.
Unto all such, grant wisdom, understanding, zeal, and constancy, alert

senses, and incorruptible hearts,
that they be not ensnared in the
world's seeming keenness and glittering temptations. Help, Lord, and
grant us success. Cause us to acknowledge Thy ways in the earth,
and lead us in Thy paths. Reveal
Thy work unto Thy servants, and
Thy glory unto their children. The
more the world departs from Thee
and follows its own ways and modes
of thought, so much the more powerfully cause Thy servants to speak
Thy word, to defend Thy confessions,
Thy doctrine; and, in ever growing
circles, cause unity in the Word, and
unity of doctrine and faith and confession to increase. As time passes,
so increase Thou the assembly of
Thy people in one spirit, and one
body, unto one desire and one work,
to one prayer and one petition, to

one battle for Thy peace, which cometh alone through Christ Jesus,
Thine only begotten Son. The oftener and the more frequently we pray,
so much the more oftener do Thou
hear us and help us who seek and
desire naught but that Thy Name be
hallowed, Thy kingdom come, and
Thy will be done on earth as it is in
heaven.

The Lord's Prayer.
Amen.

350.

L ORD Jesus Christ, with us abide,
   Far it is now toward eventide;
And let Thy Word, that light divine,
Continue in our midst to shine.

In these last days of sore distress
Grant to us all true steadfastness,
That we may cleave, till life be spent,
To Thy pure Word and Sacrament.

Lord Jesus, help, Thy Church uphold,
For we are listless, slothful, cold;
Endow Thy Word with pow'r and
       grace
And prosper it in ev'ry place.

O let Thy Word e'er with us stay;
Curb Satan's guile and rage, we pray,
And withal let Thy Church increase
In grace, in concord, and in peace.

O God, we are by evil prest,
Here on this earth there is no rest.
Both sects and schisms manifold
In one great legion we behold.

Those haughty spirits, Lord, restrain
Who fain would o'er Thy people reign
And always offer something new,
Devised to change Thy doctrine true.

The cause and honor, Lord, are Thine,
Not ours; wherefore to us incline
And come, the mighty help to be
Of those who put their trust in Thee.

Our heart's true comfort is Thy
      Word,
And well it shields Thy Church, dear
      Lord;
So let us in Thy Word abide,
That we may seek no other guide.

Thus keep us in Thy Word, we pray,
While we continue on our way,
And help us, when this life is o'er,
To be with Thee forevermore.

351.

Psalm 20.

THE Lord hear thee in the day of
   trouble; the name of the God
of Jacob defend thee;

2. Send thee help **from the** sanctuary, and strengthen thee out of Zion;

3. Remember all thy offerings, and accept thy burnt sacrifice; Selah.

4. Grant thee according to thine own heart, and fulfil all thy counsel.

5. We will rejoice in thy salvation, and in the name of our God we will set up our banners: the Lord fulfil all thy petitions.

6. Now know I that the Lord saveth His anointed; He will hear him from His holy heaven with the saving strength of His right hand.

7. Some trust in chariots, and some in horses: but we will remember the name of the Lord our God.

8. They are brought down and fallen: but we are risen, and stand upright.

9. Save, Lord: let the king hear us when we call.

352.

Psalm 67.

GOD be merciful unto us, and bless us; and cause His face to shine upon us; Selah.

2. That Thy way may be known upon earth, Thy saving health among all nations.

3. Let the people praise Thee, O God; let all the people praise Thee.

4. O let the nations be glad and sing for joy: for Thou shalt judge the people righteously, and govern the nations upon earth. Selah.

5. Let the people praise Thee, O God; let all the people praise Thee.

6. Then shall the earth yield her

increase; and God, even our own God, shall bless us.

7. God shall bless us; and all the ends of the earth shall fear Him.

APPENDIX.

PRAYERS FOR CHILDREN.

A Word to Parents.

"Many are ashamed to be seen pious and worshipful—a shame that cometh from no good spirit. But thou, be not thou ashamed to appear in every good place and at all times, as a Christian ought and shall be."

(Loehe.)

"Educate children without devout religion, and you make a race of clever devils."

(Wellington.)

Parents of the Coming Generation:

In God's stead you are placed in your relation to them. Whither would the Heavenly Father have them led? Whither are you leading them?

Lead your children to Jesus Christ!

Give your child the best model.—The Galileean mothers brought their children not to Peter, or James, or John; they did not seek to kindle their hearts by leading them to Andrew, or Philip, or to Nathanael, they went to the highest—to Jesus.

Mothers of Our Land:

Will you be less shrewd than were the mothers in Galilee? Your children may now seem to you a "little life," but, in your heart, you are already planning for your babe's education to make it a "great life." You are looking forward to the day of the schools, when paid teachers shall teach your child in routine fashion about great men, and to emulate their virtues. Seek not to kindle your child's heart at mere wax tapers or candles. Little lives need the great sunshine of mother's love, and the great heat of Christ's benediction. Suffer me to speak a word of experience from the schools where they will learn of great men; Caesar will not teach them such courage; Washington will not inspire them with such patriotism;

Socrates will not show them such calmness;
David will not impress them with such chiv-
alry; Moses will not move them with such
meekness; Elijah will not imbue them with
such earnestness; Daniel will not touch them
with such manliness; Job will not nerve
them with such patience; Paul will not fire
them with such love, as will their daily little
devout intercourse with Jesus Christ, in the
prayers they learn to lisp while yet in your
arms, or to repeat while yet kneeling at your
knee. Lead them there, and their future man-
hood and womanhood will rise up to call you
blessed.

Precious in the sight of our Lord are the
prayers of our children. It was T. E. Brown
who wrote:

"I was in Heaven one day when all the prayers
Came in, and angels bore them up the stairs
  Unto a place where he
  Who was ordained such ministry
Should sort them, so that in that palace bright
The presence-chamber might be duly light;
For they were like to flowers of various bloom;
And a divinest fragrance filled the room.

Then did I see how the great sorter chose
One flower that seemed to me a hedgling rose,
    And from the tangled press
    Of that irregular loveliness
Set it apart! and—"This," I heard him say,
"Is for the master;" so upon his way
He would have passed; then I to him:
"Whence is the rose, O thou of cherubim
The chiefest?" "Knowest thou not?" he said
            and smiled:
"This is the first prayer of a little child." '

For our children, therefore, the translator
of Loehe's Seed-Grains of Prayer, has select-
ed and added this appendix of prayers.

A.

GENERAL PRAYERS.

1.

OUR Father, Who art in Heaven;
    Hallowed be Thy name; Thy
kingdom come; Thy will be done on
earth, as it is in Heaven; Give us this

day our daily bread; And forgive us
our trespasses, as we forgive those
who trespass against us; And lead us
not into temptation; But deliver us
from evil; For Thine is the kingdom,
and the power, and the glory, for ever
and ever. Amen.

2.

FATHER, I am weak and small,
      Thou the mighty Lord of all;
Yet with tender love and care,
Thou wilt listen to my prayer;
Let me not a stranger be,
But a loving child to Thee. Amen.

3.

SAVE me, Lord, from sinning,
      Watch me day by day;
Help me now to love Thee,
Take my sins away. Amen.

4.

I AM Jesus' little friend;
On His mercy I depend;
Jesus will forsake me never;
He will keep me safe for ever;
How I wish my heart could be,
Loving Savior, more like Thee.
Amen. (Fanny Crosby.)

5.

THERE'S not a child so small or
weak
But has his little cross to take,
His little work of love and praise
That he may do for Jesus' sake.
Amen.
(C. F. Alexander.)

6.

LORD, Thy comfort may I share;
Take soul and body to Thy care.
Fold me, dear Savior, in Thine arm;
In grace defend me from all harm.
Amen.

7.

LORD, I know Thou livest,
　　And dost plead for me;
Make me very thankful
　　In my prayer to Thee.
Soon I hope in glory
　　At Thy side to stand;
Make me fit to meet Thee
　　In that happy land.　Amen.

8.

I WAIT for Thee with joyful heart;
　Come Lord, Thy gifts to me impart.
Still to the end abide with me,
And take me then to Heaven with
　　　Thee.　Amen.

9.

MAY the grace of Christ our Savior,
　　And the Father's boundless love,
With the Holy Spirit's favor,
Rest upon us from above.　Amen.

SCHOOL PRAYERS.

B.

Opening.

O GOD, we pray Thee, be with us now to bless us as we learn, that as Thy dear children we may remember and profit all the days of our lives, to the glory of Thy Holy Name; through Jesus Christ our Lord. Amen.

O LORD Jesus Christ, Who didst call little children unto Thyself, and didst take them up in Thine arms and bless them: give to us Thy blessing also, this day, and all the days of our lives. Grant that we may ever love Thee with our whole heart, and may earnestly seek the things Thou givest us from above. Bless our dear parents and friends, our

pastor and our teachers; make us to
honor, serve, obey, love, and esteem
them as those whom Thou hast set in
Thy place over us; and in the end,
grant us all a place in Thy Kingdom
of Glory, O Thou, Who with the Father
and the Holy Ghost, livest and
reignest, ever one God, world without
end. Amen.

Closing.

O LORD, we thank Thee for what
we have now learned. Help us
to keep it, and with our whole heart
use it always in serving Thee, in true
obedience to our life's end; through
Jesus Christ our Lord. Amen.

O LORD, dismiss us with Thy
blessing; go with us to our
homes; let Thy mercy be upon our
parents, teachers, brothers, and
sisters; bless our pastor and all our

friends, and all Thy Church, and help us to be faithful here until we shall come to Thy glory above, through Jesus Christ, our Lord. Amen.

ALMIGHTY Father, Who hast promised that they who seek Thee early shall find Thee, and find Thy wisdom more precious than all the wisdom and treasures of the world: send down upon us Thy grace, that we, being trained in the nurture and admonition of the Lord, may choose and love Thy way, and not depart from it for ever more; all which we ask for the sake and in the name of Jesus Christ, our only Savior, Who liveth and reigneth with Thee and the Holy Ghost, ever one God, world without end. Amen.

C.

CHURCH PRAYERS.

Entering Church.

DEAR Father, we come to thank Thee here, that by faithful hands and labors Thou hast preserved Thy Church until our day, to proclaim to us Thy Holy Word, and to give us Thy Sacraments. We have all been baptized into Thy Holy Name, and are Thine. Speak to us here at Thy Holy Altar. Bless our pastor, and all who hear him, and grant him all grace to inform, instruct, and admonish us in Thy Word. Bless all members of our congregation, and help us all to be faithful to Thy Church here below, until we shall be brought into the Glory of Thy Church above; through Jesus Christ, our Lord. Amen.

Upon Entering the Pew.

L OWLY bending at Thy feet,
On this Thy Holy Day:
O come, dear Lord, while here we
meet
To hear, and praise, and pray.

Our many sins forgive;
Thy Holy Spirit send;
And teach us to begin to live
The life that knows no end. Amen.

At the Close of the Services.

B LESSED Lord God, I thank Thee
with my whole heart for the
privilege I enjoyed here today. Holy
Savior, Blessed Jesus, Thou hast
loved me ever: let Thy love go with
me, and let the Holy Spirit dwell in
my heart to guide and direct all my
ways. Most Holy Father, Son, and
Spirit, go home with us all, and bless

all who have this day worshipped at Thy Holy Altars. Amen.

D EAR Heavenly Father, in Thy Name let me bless my parents, my brothers, and sisters, my pastor and teachers, and all my friends. Hear the blessing I pronounce upon them, and even at Thy Heavenly Throne confirm it. Send them all help out of Thy Holy Temple and give them strength out of Zion. Blessed be they who bless them; and turn away evil from them, in the Name of the Father, and of the Son, and of the Holy Ghost. Amen.

A DAY in Thy courts is better than a thousand. O Lord, seal unto me now, all I have heard, give me an understanding heart, and bless all Thy Church; through Jesus Christ our Lord. Amen.

CREATE in me a clean heart, O God, and renew a right spirit within me. Cast me not away from Thy presence, and take not Thy Holy Spirit from me. Amen.

D.
MORNING PRAYERS.

1.

NOW I awake to see the light;
Lord, Thou hast kept me through the night.
To Thee I lift my voice and pray,
That Thou wilt keep me through the day.
If I should die before 'tis done,
O God, accept me through Thy Son.
Amen.

2.

DEAR Father in Heaven, for Thy care which kept all danger from me while I slept, I thank Thee, and pray help me this day to show my thankfulness by being good and obedient, for Jesus' sake. Amen.

3.

O HELP me, Lord, this day to be
Thy own dear child, and follow
Thee;
And lead me, Savior, by Thy hand,
Until I reach the Heavenly land.
Amen.

4.

A LL through this day,
I humbly pray:
Be Thou my guard and guide;
My sins forgive,
And let me live,
Blest Jesus, near Thy side. Amen.

5.

GENTLE Jesus, hear me pray,
Thy child accept and bless;
And lead me by Thy grace this day
In paths of righteousness. Amen.

6.

IN the Name of the Father, and of
the Son, and of the Holy Ghost.

I give thanks unto Thee, Heavenly
Father, through Jesus Christ, Thy
dear Son, for having preserved me
through the night from all harm and
danger. And I beseech Thee to preserve me, this day also, from all sin
and evil, so that my whole conduct
and life may be well-pleasing in Thy
sight. For into Thy hands I commend my body and soul, and all
things. Give Thy holy angels charge
concerning me, that the adversary
have no power over me. Amen.

(Luther.)

E.
EVENING PRAYERS.

1.

A T the close of every day
Lord, to Thee I kneel and pray.
Look upon Thy little child,
Look in love and mercy mild.
O forgive and wash away
All my naughtiness this day;
And both when I sleep and wake,
Bless me for my Savior's sake.
            Amen.

2.

W ATCH o'er a little child tonight,
Blest Savior from above,
And keep me till the morning light
In Thy sweet arms of love.   Amen.

3.

J ESUS, by Thy mercy blest,
Now I give myself to rest;
Shouldst Thou come before I rise,
Savior, take me to the skies.   Amen.

4.

L OOK now upon me, Lord,
Ere I lie down to rest;
It is Thy own dear child
That cometh to be blest. Amen.

5.

G OD'S loving ear
Is ever near
His children's prayers to hear,
So happily
And peacefully
I lay me down to rest in Him. Amen.

6.

T IRED now, I go to rest,
Jesus, Savior, ever blest,
In Thy name I close mine eyes;
Watch Thou by me till I rise.
Thou my best and kindest friend
Thou wilt love me till the end!
Let me love Thee more and more,
Always better than before. Amen.

7.

NOW I lay me down to sleep,
   I pray Thee, Lord, my soul to
      keep;
If I should die before I wake,
   I pray Thee, Lord, my soul to take;
   And this I ask for Jesus' sake.
      Amen.

8.

I GIVE thanks unto Thee, Heavenly
Father, through Jesus Christ,
Thy dear Son, for having graciously
protected me through the day. And
I beseech Thee to forgive all my
transgressions, whereby I have
sinned against Thee, and to protect
me graciously this night. For into
Thy hands I commend my body and
soul, and all things. Give Thy holy
angels charge concerning me, that
the adversary may have no power
over me. Amen.   (Luther.)

F.
GRACE BEFORE MEAT.

1.

THE eyes of all wait upon Thee,
O Lord; and Thou givest them
their meat in due season; Thou openest Thine hand and satisfiest the
desire of every living thing. Amen.

(Ps. 145:15, 16.)

2.

COME Lord Jesus, be our guest,
And let Thy gifts to us be blest.
Amen.

3.

HEAVENLY Father, bless this
food
To Thy glory and our good. Amen.

4.

GREAT God Thou giver of all good,
Accept our praise and bless this
food.

Grace, health, and strength to us
    afford,
Through Jesus Christ, our risen Lord.
    Amen.

5.

JESUS, bless what Thou hast given,
    Feed our souls with bread from
       Heaven;
Guide and lead us all the way,
In all that we may do and say.
    Amen.

6.

BLESS the Lord, O my soul; and
all that is within me, bless His
Holy Name. Bless the Lord, O my
soul; and forget not all His benefits.
Who satisfieth thy mouth with good
things, so that thy youth is renewed
like the eagle's.   (Ps. 103:1, 2, 5.)

G.
GRACE AFTER MEAT.
1.

WE thank Thee, O Lord, for Thou art good, and Thy mercy endureth for ever. Amen.

2.

WE give Thee thanks, O Almighty Father, for these and all Thy benefits; through Jesus Christ our Lord. Amen.

3.

AS Thou hast nourished our bodies to strengthen and refresh them, even so, Lord, nourish our souls with Thy grace; through Jesus Christ our Lord. Amen.

4.

THE Lord is my Shepherd; I shall not want.

He maketh me to lie down in green pastures:

He leadeth me beside the still waters.

He restoreth my soul: He leadeth me in the paths of righteousness for His name's sake.

Yea, though I walk through the valley of the shadow of death, I will fear no evil: for Thou art with me; Thy rod and Thy staff they comfort me.

Thou preparest a table before me in the presence of mine enemies: Thou anointest my head with oil, my cup runneth over.

Surely goodness and mercy shall follow me all the days of my life: and I will dwell in the house of the Lord for ever.

(Ps. 23.)

TABLE OF CONTENTS.

624 Table of Contents.

2. Monday.

APPENDIX.

The Four Seasons.

V.
INTERCESSORY PRAYERS.

Alphabetical Table of Contents.

INDEX.

I

am Alpha and Omega,
the beginning and the ending,
saith the Lord,
Which is, and Which was,
and Which is to come,

the Almighty.
(Revelation 1 : 8.)